Breakthrough Business Negotiation

Breakthrough Business Negotiation

A Toolbox for Managers

Michael Watkins

JOSSEY-BASS
A Wiley Company
www.josseybass.com

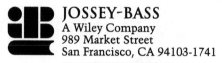

JOSSEY-BASS
A Wiley Company
989 Market Street
San Francisco, CA 94103-1741

www.josseybass.com

Jossey-Bass books and products are available through most bookstores. To contact Jossey-Bass directly, call (888) 378–2537, fax to (800) 605–2665, or visit our website at www.josseybass.com.

Substantial discounts on bulk quantities of Jossey-Bass books are available to corporations, professional associations, and other organizations. For details and discount information, contact the special sales department at Jossey-Bass.

We at Jossey-Bass strive to use the most environmentally sensitive paper stocks available to us. Our publications are printed on acid-free recycled stock whenever possible, and our paper always meets or exceeds minimum GPO and EPA requirements.

Library of Congress Cataloging-in-Publication Data

Watkins, Michael, date.
    Breakthrough business negotiation: a toolbox for managers/Michael Watkins.—1st ed.
      p. cm.
    Includes bibliographical references (p. 241) and index.
    ISBN 0-7879-6012-8
    1. Negotiation in business—Handbooks, manuals, etc.   I. Title.
    HD58.6 .W37 2002
    658.4'052—dc21
                                                    2002001382

FIRST EDITION
HB Printing 10 9 8 7 6 5 4 3 2

Contents

To Shawna, Aidan, and Maeve

Preface

Although there are many how-to books on negotiating, they provide little useful guidance on how to conduct complex real-world negotiations. Advice on conducting two-party negotiations about a modest number of issues isn't hard to come by, but few negotiations are that simple. While dealing with the other side, negotiators typically also have to manage difficult internal negotiations, work to prevent disputes from escalating, and build supportive coalitions. The models of the negotiation process presented in how-to books are therefore misleadingly oversimplified. To treat negotiations as interactions involving a couple of parties and sharply delineated issues is inevitably simplistic, because few actual negotiations conform to that tidy scenario. It's equally unrealistic (and potentially dangerous) to expect, as many authors on negotiation assume, that negotiators' interests and alternatives will remain static as the process unfolds. As we will see, golden opportunities flow from the ability to shape others' perceptions of their interests and alternatives in a dynamic negotiating game.

To illustrate the deficiencies of simplistic models of negotiation, consider what happens when you negotiate to buy a house. This commonplace situation is typically treated as a one-time negotiation involving two parties and a few issues (price, repairs, timing for closing). You choose the house you want to buy, do the necessary prenegotiation preparation, pinpoint your goals and bottom line, and speculate about those of the seller. You make an offer and the seller responds. The process advances through the dance of offer and counteroffer until you seal the deal or abandon your efforts. Viewed in this way, the key is to prepare well and then formulate a strategy for making and responding to offers.

But is it really that simple? In practice, things tend to get a lot more complicated. You may be considering several houses, and the seller may be dealing with multiple potential buyers. You may be uncertain at the outset about what kind of house you need, and different houses usually represent very different trade-offs. Your perceptions of your interests and alternatives, far from being static, may change sharply as the process unfolds. You may be exploring several financing options. If you need to sell your current home and move by a certain date, deadlines may shape the process. You may have to negotiate with your spouse about what will satisfy you both. Finally, you will probably have to negotiate with a real estate agent who represents the seller but also has independent interests, such as pursuing other business and maintaining a good reputation. In sum, even something as apparently routine and self-contained as a house purchase turns out under scrutiny to be a multiparty, multi-issue negotiation characterized by trade-offs, deadlines, representatives with mixed motives, and linkages among sets of negotiations. It may also be full of perplexing ambiguities: partial information, hidden agendas, competing priorities, impasses and dead ends, and conflicts that could escalate.

Most negotiations exhibit these sorts of complexities. In fact, if you go searching for simple negotiations, you'll have trouble finding any. Complexity is the rule in negotiation, not the exception. It is this built-in complexity and the uniqueness of each situation that make a repertoire composed of generic tactics and a talent for persuasiveness inadequate. Readers hoping for a few easy-to-grasp maxims and techniques that apply to all types of negotiations might as well revise their expectations now. Negotiation strategy can't be summed up in three or four rules of thumb because you need to be able to play many different games. In fact, much of the process of negotiation is devoted to defining the game—or, to put it another way, to shaping the context in which the at-the-table deliberations will proceed.

Because strategy is contingent on situation, there is no single best way to negotiate. But strategies need not be worked out from scratch each time. Experienced negotiators, like experienced chess players, don't waste time exhaustively evaluating every single possibility. They develop an intuitive sense of the state of play and combinations of moves that will and won't work. They draw on their own mental libraries of openings, gambits, and counters—combinations of moves that have worked well in similar situations, and they construct customized strategies out of familiar materials. They also continue working to reshape the structure of the negotiating game as it proceeds. Even as you engage in discussions at the table, you can advance your interests by altering who participates, reframing the issues to be negotiated, linking and delinking sets of negotiations, and influencing deadlines and rules for decision making. As we will discuss in detail, expert negotiators pay as much attention to shaping the structure of their negotiations as they do to planning for and participating in at-the-table interactions.

The breakthrough approach to analyzing complex negotiations as dynamic systems grew directly out of my early training as an electrical engineer. It is a basic principle of engineering that complex systems can be understood by identifying their fundamental components and characterizing the interactions among the components. As I delved more deeply into the negotiation process, I became convinced that systems engineering provides a powerful framework for managing the fluid and intricate situations that characterize most negotiations. Individual negotiations can be analyzed in terms of their basic components: parties and issues. More complex negotiating situations are made up of linked sets of individual negotiations (modules, if you will) that interact in predictable ways. Key dynamics, both within and among negotiations, can be described in terms of feedback loops: virtuous cycles that build momentum toward agreement and vicious cycles that contribute to impasse and breakdown. A negotiator who grasps the underlying structure of a situation possesses a strong antidote to confusion and manipulation, and is in a powerful position to shape the structure of that situation in a consistently clear-eyed and productive way. The ultimate goal of learning to negotiate is therefore to be an architect of structure and processes, not a passive participant in situations defined by others.

HOW TO BECOME A BREAKTHROUGH NEGOTIATOR

So how do you learn to be a breakthrough negotiator? The right training helps. It is not surprising that more and more business schools and law schools teach negotiating skills. Negotiation is a first-year requirement at the Harvard Business School, and more than half our students take advanced negotiation electives. But how can you acquire and hone your negotiating abilities if you're already out in the trenches? Experience can be a superb teacher, but only if it produces a systematic set of effective mental models for the wide array of situations you can expect to face. Because negotiations come in so many shapes, learning by experience alone can be time-consuming and haphazard, and the mistakes you make along the line can hurt.

This book is designed to equip you with the tools you need to become a breakthrough negotiator. Because ample practice sizing up a broad spectrum of situations is crucial, negotiation analysis and strategy development skills are best learned using cases. A case allows you to stop the action for purposes of analysis, and exposure to a well-chosen array of cases helps to build your intuition. Fortunately, cases lend themselves well to presentation in book form. You can count on your profession and your personal life to offer you a wealth of opportunities for direct negotiating experience. This book offers you, in an accessible and actionable format, a set of tools for sizing up these situations and making the most of them.

February 2002

Michael Watkins
Cambridge, Massachusetts

Acknowledgments

Many people's contributions are reflected in this book. The intellectual foundations on which I constructed the breakthrough negotiation framework were built by Max Bazerman, Roger Fisher, David Lax, Bob Mnookin, Howard Raiffa, Robert McKersie, Robert Robinson, Jim Sebenius, William Ury, and Richard Walton. I am grateful for their insight.

My thinking about negotiation has also been strongly influenced by my work with Robert Aiello, Joel Cutcher-Gershenfeld, John Eckert, Dwight Golann, Steven Holtzman, Eric Mersch, Sam Passow, John Richardson, Sydney Rosen, Bruce Stephenson, and Kim Winters. Thanks too to colleagues at the Kennedy School of Government and Harvard Business School for their support, especially Geri Augusto, Nancy Beaulieu, David Garvin, Brian Mandell, Guhan Subramanian, and Michael Wheeler. Special thanks to Ann Goodsell for her efforts to make this book more accessible.

The research for this book was supported by the Program on Negotiation (PON) at Harvard Law School and the Division of Research (DOR) at the Harvard Business School. I very much appreciate the support of PON executive directors Marjorie Aaron and Sarah Cobb and DOR research directors Teresa Amabile, Dwight Crane, and Mike Yoshino.

Finally, I want to express my heartfelt appreciation to Jim Sebenius for his insight and support. He has been deeply influential in my thinking about negotiation and has provided indispensable guidance for my work. Jim is a rare combination of gifted negotiator, committed teacher of negotiators, and deep thinker about the negotiation process.

M.W.

Introduction

Whatever business you are in, whether you are an entrepreneur or a manager in a large company, you are negotiating all the time. Think about your daily responsibilities: How much of what really matters involves negotiating? If you are like most other businesspeople, you are constantly negotiating for support and resources internally even as you deal with external constituencies such as customers, suppliers, investors, banks, and government agencies. Negotiation skills are vital to your success.

Most businesspeople are embedded in networks of negotiations like the one illustrated in the figure on page xviii. This book could have been organized around that reality, with chapters devoted to negotiating with suppliers, negotiating with investors, negotiating with unions, and so on. That approach would have been plausible because negotiations in different contexts are shaped by different rules of the game, such as securities law or contract law or labor law.

But proceeding in that way would have obscured a powerful underlying truth: that there is a set of foundational concepts that can be applied to all negotiations. It's essential to learn these first, before delving into the nuances of negotiations in different contexts.

This book will give you the tools you need to achieve breakthrough results in all types of business negotiations. You will learn to negotiate more skillfully by tracing the thinking processes of

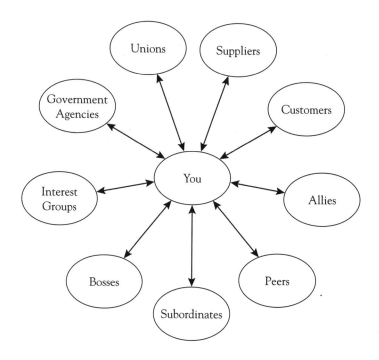

negotiators who face classic business challenges, and you will gain insight into the principles and lessons that flow from these examples. In the process, you will acquire a practical, actionable framework for approaching any future negotiation.

We will begin with a handful of overarching principles of breakthrough negotiation. Keep them in mind as you make your way through the chapters that follow. Spelling out some of the important take-home lessons up front will help you zero in on essential commonalities in the situations you will encounter in this book and in your professional life.

PRINCIPLE 1: NEGOTIATIONS HAVE STRUCTURE

However complex a negotiation is, it can be mastered by breaking it down into its key components and interactions. Every negotiation has a structure: it involves certain parties and certain sets of issues, which result in predictable dynamics.[1] More complex negotiation systems can be analyzed as interlinked sets of negotiations. Consider, for example, a manager advocating for a change initiative, a legislator seeking support for a crucial vote, and a family member promoting a favorite vacation destination. On the face of it, these negotiations have nothing in common. But closer examination reveals that they share an underlying structure: all three are negotiations involving more than two parties in which no one wields veto power. As a result, negotiators must build coalitions to advance their interests. Breakthrough negotiation is founded on this kind of structural analysis. Without it, you will end up thrashing about and being swamped by complexity, or being blindsided when a threat emerges from an unexpected direction. Thorough diagnosis of the situation and its structure is a core negotiating skill and a hallmark of breakthrough negotiators.

PRINCIPLE 2: STRUCTURE SHAPES STRATEGY

There are no one-size-fits-all approaches to negotiation, because strategy has to be matched to the situation and its structure. Breakthrough negotiators carefully assess their situations and develop strategies and tactics accordingly. They don't adopt a single style and apply it to all situations; they understand that context matters—that deal making demands different approaches than dispute resolution does and that multiparty negotiations pose fundamentally different challenges than two-party ones do. Think about the difference between a two-party negotiation over the sale of a new car and a merger negotiation between two large multinational companies. To be successful, the company leaders have to build support internally and win approval from many external parties: regulators, Wall Street analysts, and shareholders. This means that they have to be good at coalition building. The number of parties (a key characteristic of structure) shapes negotiators' strategies. As one experienced negotiator put it, "When you have a multilateral negotiation, you need to be able to build coalitions. You need to find ways of getting different people on board." It is thus crucial to figure out early on whose support is necessary and who wields influence with other important players. Effectiveness at coalition building is not a requirement in straightforward two-party negotiations. The bottom line is that good negotiators develop strategies based on a clear diagnosis of the structure of their situation.

PRINCIPLE 3: THE STRUCTURE OF NEGOTIATIONS CAN BE SHAPED

Breakthrough negotiators never treat the structure of a negotiation as preordained or fixed. In other words, the game can be played as it's dealt, but it can also be changed. Structure shapes strategy—but strategy can also shape the structure, often by means of actions taken to influence who will be at the table and what the agenda will be. Skilled negotiators act as architects of structure by, for example, transforming two-party negotiations into multiparty negotiations by inviting in additional parties. Much of what is decisive in shaping the structure, such as decisions about whom one negotiates with and what the issue agenda is, takes place *before* the parties sit down across the table from each other.[2] Similarly, actions taken away from the table can be as important as what goes on at the table. Even after the negotiation has begun, adroit negotiators continue shaping the structure by altering the agenda, introducing action-forcing events, and linking or delinking negotiations. When negotiating is based on clear-eyed analysis, adept efforts to shape the structure have a powerful impact on outcomes.

PRINCIPLE 4: PROCESS CONTROL IS A SOURCE OF POWER

It's easy to become overly caught up in the substance of negotiations—assessing interests, developing positions, making offers—at the expense of opportunities to influence the process. But control of process design is a potent source of power, one that enables you to steer the proceedings toward desired outcomes. This calls for early attention to designing negotiation processes, such as influencing the agenda, possibly well before others even realize that the game has begun. It also means acting to take control of the flow of information, managing who interacts with whom and who gets access to what information when. Skilled negotiators understand the importance of framing arguments and approaching people in the right order to win their support. They appreciate that one-on-one negotiations are suited to some situations and group negotiations to others. They are cognizant of the potential benefits and costs of setting up a secret channel. Above all, they are reflective about the process-design choices they make, acutely aware that a bad process—one perceived as unfair, illegitimate, or confusing—creates unnecessary barriers to agreement and that good process design can help to create momentum.

PRINCIPLE 5: THE FLOW OF NEGOTIATION CAN BE CHANNELED

Negotiations rarely proceed smoothly from initiation to agreement. Instead, they ebb and flow, with periods of deadlock or inaction punctuated by bursts of progress until agreement is reached or breakdown occurs. Lawsuits, for example, may grind along for months or even years and then suddenly be settled on the courthouse steps. Breakthrough negotiators recognize these patterns and work to channel the flow of the process productively. Successfully identifying shared interests and developing an attractive vision of a desirable future pulls the other side forward toward desirable agreements. The flow of the process can also be facilitated by proposing a new formula for agreement or a face-saving compromise that breaks a logjam. But irreversible movement can also be created by setting up barriers to backsliding that propel the process forward. By getting early agreement on basic principles or a framework for detailed bargaining, for example, a negotiator can make reversal more costly. Action-forcing events such as deadlines are another tool for spurring others to make hard choices. By channeling the flow in these ways, skilled negotiators are able to create and claim substantial value.

PRINCIPLE 6: EFFECTIVE NEGOTIATORS ORGANIZE TO LEARN

Those who organize to learn most effectively have a big advantage in negotiation. Effective learning means much more than figuring out what your counterparts and constituents need and want (although this is very important). Breakthrough negotiators immerse themselves in information about their environments, searching for emerging threats and opportunities; they systematically identify and tap into good sources of information and build networks of relationships to support intelligence gathering. They also reflect on their past experiences in order to learn from them.

Good negotiating *organizations* also organize to learn. If a company is depending on acquisitions or strategic alliances to drive its growth, it had better be good at negotiating these deals, or work to get better fast. More generally, organizations often employ many negotiators who pursue similar negotiations with different counterparts. Consider, for example, a manufacturing company with many purchasing managers and salespeople. What happens if these negotiators don't learn from their past negotiations, capture the resulting insights, and, crucially, share these insights among themselves? The answer is that precious opportunities to improve organizational performance are lost. Knowledge about how to negotiate effectively is a precious resource. It is therefore important to focus on management of organizational learning, not just development of individual competence.

PRINCIPLE 7: GREAT NEGOTIATORS ARE LEADERS

Great leaders are often great negotiators, and the reverse is also true: the actions of individual negotiators can make all the difference in the outcomes of complex negotiations. This is certainly true when a chief executive officer decides to acquire another company, or national leaders decide to negotiate a new international trade regime. But it's also true when less senior negotiators represent their organizations; they too have to lead. When skilled negotiators are asked, "Which is harder, dealing with the other side or your own side?" they overwhelmingly respond that managing internal differences poses the biggest challenge. At the same time, breakthrough negotiators constantly look within the other side for opportunities to build cross-cutting coalitions. In a merger negotiation, for example, there may be serious internal rifts within each side about the desirability of doing a deal. On both sides, some managers stand to lose and others to gain. Those in favor on both sides represent a potential coalition in favor of a deal, while the losers share the goal (in which they may tacitly collude) of trying to kill it. The negotiator thus has to manage external negotiations, internal deliberations, and the interactions between the two. The best negotiators are never passive go-betweens. They lead from the middle, shaping the perceptions of those they represent as well as those of their counterparts across the table.

PART ONE

Foundations of the Breakthrough Approach

It is both tempting and foolhardy to focus narrowly on what happens at the negotiating table. Such a focus can lead you to ignore the work you should be doing before meeting with your counterparts for the first time and between negotiating sessions as well. This is a matter of far more than just gathering information; it also involves thinking through how you can improve your bargaining position. Can you alter your counterparts' perceptions of their alternatives to an agreement with you? These are the objectives of four tasks you undertake at and away from the table:[1]

Diagnosing the situation: Systematically assessing the components of the negotiation to identify potential barriers to agreement

Shaping the structure: Influencing who participates, what the issues are, and what your alternatives are, so you don't find yourself playing someone else's game

Managing the process: Preparing for and conducting face-to-face interactions in order to build momentum

Assessing the results: Setting goals and periodically evaluating how you are doing in order to refine your diagnosis and rethink how to shape the structure and manage the process

	Away from the Table	*At the Table*
Diagnosing the situation	Analyze the structure of the negotiation and develop hypotheses about counterparts' interests and alternatives.	Learn in order to test and hone your hypotheses.
Shaping the structure	Shape who participates and how current negotiations are linked to others.	Work to set the agenda and frame what is at stake.
Managing the process	Plan how to learn and influence counterparts' perceptions of the bargaining range.	Influence counterparts' perceptions of what is acceptable.
Assessing the results	Establish goals before going to the table. Between sessions, evaluate how you are doing.	Periodically assess what is happening so you can make midcourse corrections.

These four core tasks are not undertaken in lock-step sequence; breakthrough negotiators shift back and forth among them as their negotiations evolve. We will discuss them one by one, but the cases will also illustrate how analysis and interaction, strategizing and bargaining, and actions at and away from the table intersect in the course of actual negotiations.

Chapter One will demonstrate how to diagnose a negotiation by pinpointing unexplored opportunities in a recruiting situation at a start-up. Chapter Two uses an impasse in a commercial lease deal to explore the process of shaping the structure of a negotiation. Chapter Three examines how to orchestrate face-to-face interactions by looking closely at negotiations between an airline and its pilots' union. And Chapter Four follows up on all three cases to illustrate how to judge the success of ongoing negotiations and make midcourse corrections. These four chapters constitute the fundamental tools for managing complex negotiations. In Part Two, we will explore how the breakthrough approach can be applied in challenging situations that managers routinely face: dealing with power imbalances, building coalitions, leading teams, representing others, and negotiating crises.

1

Diagnosing the Situation

In late 1997, Daniel Riley, the thirty-seven-year-old director of Alpha Microsystems' Technology Center in Austin, Texas, received a call from a headhunter. She told Daniel that a Colorado-based entrepreneur wanted to talk to him and members of his team about joining a new software venture.

Barely a month earlier, Alpha Micro had announced its decision to close the Austin facility and transfer its personnel elsewhere. The move was intended to consolidate Alpha's programming staff. Daniel, recruited by Alpha five years earlier to build the Austin center, had successfully assembled and led a respected forty-member team of skilled programmers. Nevertheless, he had learned of Alpha's decision only one day before the formal announcement. Because the Austin center had a very low attrition rate, Alpha management expected most of its engineers to agree to move. But Daniel knew otherwise:

> The executive team at Alpha mistook the low attrition rate for an indication of pure love of Alpha. And that was certainly a factor, because we had a lot of dedicated Alpha employees. But I think a very significant reason was that people were very rooted in the community. They were motivated to stay here if they could. I conveyed this to management.

I said that there are lots of high-tech opportunities here in Austin, and I think people will elect to stay.

Daniel himself had long toyed with launching his own business in Austin, and now he began to think seriously about doing so. He had been with a start-up before joining Alpha and had found it exhilarating to build an enterprise from the ground up. His top people all expressed interest in joining him. By year's end, Daniel's warning to Alpha had been borne out: few of his colleagues were planning to leave Austin.

When the headhunter heard that a team of experienced software engineers was scouting opportunities, she had told Ken Gourlay, an accomplished forty-five-year-old Colorado entrepreneur with a Stanford M.B.A. and solid experience in the software industry. Ken envisioned Omega Systems, his new start-up, as a provider of turnkey systems solutions to managed care organizations. Ken immediately flew from Colorado to Austin to meet with Daniel and four of his top engineers.

Daniel and the other engineers knew little about managed care, but Ken's vision and the strength of his business plan excited them all. They were confident they could deliver the core technology rapidly and reliably. For all five, the main issue was that the company be located in Austin. For his part, Ken was delighted to come across the core of an experienced engineering team whose proven ability to work together was likely to have a positive impact on time to market. Potential competitors were sure to be eyeing the same opportunity, and it was essential to get there first.

Ken made simultaneous written offers to Daniel and the four other engineers. His offers were all well in line with what they thought they could get elsewhere. Daniel was offered the position of vice president of engineering, a competitive salary, and 2 percent of the equity in the company. The other four engineers would be team leaders; each would get 0.5 percent of equity. The options would vest at 25 percent per year for four years. Ken expressed reluctance to move the company to Austin but left the question open. The key to making the move, he said, was that the five engineers would have to take the lead in recruiting the rest of a thirty- to forty-member engineering team from among their group at Alpha. Ken also said that he was negotiating with venture capitalists for early financing and wanted to tell them that he had engineers on board. He needed their decisions within a week.

What would you advise Daniel to do?

In reality, Daniel and the four other engineers accepted Ken's offers. Ken's willingness to move the company was easily implemented, because he was its sole employee at the time. To Daniel's delight, all but three members of his forty-person Alpha team decided to follow him to Omega Systems, giving the company a running start in developing its core systems. Three years later, Omega Systems went public, with a market capitalization of over $350 million. The company's ultimate success was still uncertain, but Omega Systems had a dozen major accounts. Daniel was worth several million dollars on paper, but he had been replaced as vice president of engineering once development of the system was complete; he was languishing in a special-projects assignment waiting for his options to vest. His four team leaders remained in their positions, but many other team members had departed once the bulk of the software development was complete. This was far from a disastrous outcome, of course—but suppose Daniel had it to do over. What could he have done differently?

The first step in preparing to negotiate from a position of strength is to diagnose the particulars of the situation thoroughly. For Daniel, this would have meant taking a hard-headed look at each of the seven key structural elements of his negotiation with Ken:[1]

> *Parties:* Who will participate, or could participate, in the negotiation?
>
> *Rules:* What are the rules of the game?
>
> *Issues:* What agenda of issues will be, or could be, negotiated?

Interests: What goals are you and others pursuing?

Alternatives: What will you do if you don't reach agreement?

Agreements: Are there potential agreements that would be acceptable to all sides?

Linkages: Are your current negotiations linked to other negotiations?

The purpose of exploring these questions is to identify barriers to achieving your goals and ways to overcome them.[2] Naturally, there are constraints on your ability to gather all the information you might like to have. But as Louis Pasteur so aptly put it, "Chance favors the prepared mind." It's essential to do this kind of analysis in order to gain the informational high ground. Daniel should undertake an information-gathering blitz: he should talk to colleagues in the industry, recruiters, and venture capitalists, and he should do some background research on the managed care industry and on Ken. And because diagnosis is never a one-time event, he should continue to invest in learning and update his assessments as the negotiation proceeds.

PARTIES: WHO WILL PARTICIPATE, OR COULD PARTICIPATE, IN THE NEGOTIATION?

The key parties to a negotiation may appear self-evident, and sometimes they are exactly as they appear to be. Often, however, particularly in a nominally two-party negotiation, other less conspicuous players are already involved. Sometimes other parties unexpectedly enter the negotiation and change it in unforeseen ways. And sometimes you would gain by pulling in other parties yourself. It is essential to take the time to identify the active and potential parties to the negotiation and ask yourself whether you would benefit from the participation of others.

Identify All the Players (and Potential Players)

First, Daniel should try to find out who else Ken is negotiating with. What venture capitalists is he talking to, and what are they offering? Has Ken interviewed other candidates for the vice president of engineering position? Are there key technologies that are not yet under Ken's control? Is he talking to anyone about situating the company somewhere other than Austin? These are questions that Daniel can legitimately put to Ken and expect to get accurate information. By asking such questions, gauging Ken's responses, and cross-checking his answers, Daniel could also gain insight into the character of his negotiating partner. Other information (such as what terms Ken is being offered by the venture capitalists) he will have to pursue by more indirect methods, such as consulting another venture capitalist or friends who have launched companies.

Daniel should then ask himself whether it would be advantageous to try to shape the game by pulling in other parties.[3] Should he try to cultivate offers from other potential employers? Negotiate jointly with the other engineers? Talk to venture capitalists about other companies in need of engineering talent? If so, how should he go about it? In what order should he undertake such discussions?

Analyze Coalitions

In negotiations involving more than two parties, outcomes are almost always strongly shaped by coalitions.[4] So one of the first orders of business is to look for existing and potential alliances, both supportive and antagonistic.

The other engineers on Daniel's team are potential allies. Ken is clearly trying to deal with Daniel and his colleagues separately rather than as a group, perhaps as an intentional divide-and-conquer strategy to prevent them from coalescing. But if Daniel and his team negotiated collectively, they could substantially increase their bargaining power. Their value as an intact team is far greater than their value as a collection of individuals.

Alone or with his colleagues, Daniel should explore questions about other coalitions. What alliances might Ken try to create? Whose support is necessary to achieve his objectives? Who wields influence over other key players? If they learn that Ken is talking to another group of engineers, that changes the equation. And if they conclude that Ken needs a team in place before the venture capitalists will fund the company, the venture capitalists are de facto allies.

Look into the Other Side

It's always a mistake to treat the other side as a monolithic block. You don't negotiate with an organization; you negotiate with the people who make the decisions, only some of whom are typically at the table. Daniel should probe how decisions are made within Omega Systems. Has Ken recruited a board of directors? Have "angel" investors already committed funding to the company, and, if so, what say do they have in deals with Daniel and the other engineers? What about other key management positions? Who is in place, and who isn't?

Daniel should clarify Ken's authority to commit to a deal. If he has full authority, fine. If not, Daniel should expect him to use the need for others' approval to veto deals particularly favorable to Daniel and his team—a *ratification tactic* that car salesmen and their managers often use.

In negotiations with large organizations, the crucial questions about decision-making authority within the other side are:

- Who has the authority to make which decisions? Does the other side's representative have the authority to make a deal, or do others have to ratify it?

- How is the performance of the people at the table measured and rewarded?

- Are there any differences between the interests of the ultimate decision makers and those of their representatives at the table?

These questions often arise in commercial negotiations in which the authority of the salesperson or purchasing agent is restricted. Business development representatives in alliance negotiations often need sign-offs from higher-ups. Salespeople are typically rewarded for meeting quotas and hence may become more flexible as their deadlines draw near.

Draw Up a Party Map

Sketching a party map can help clarify who the participants and potential players are. Daniel's party map for his negotiation with Ken, shown on page 12, includes possible participants whom he hasn't even contacted yet, such as other venture capitalists and other potential employers. He could consider extending the analysis even further by including parties whom Ken might involve, such as other job candidates.

PRACTICAL APPLICATION: DIAGNOSING THE PARTIES

This is the first of a series of boxes that will help you to apply key concepts to your own negotiations. Choose a negotiation you know well—past, ongoing, or upcoming—and want to understand better. Apply these questions to that negotiation, making an effort to think inventively and broadly.

- Are the right parties at the table?
- Are there too many parties? Too few?
- Could other parties get involved and change the game?
- Could opposing coalitions form?
- Could you build supportive coalitions?

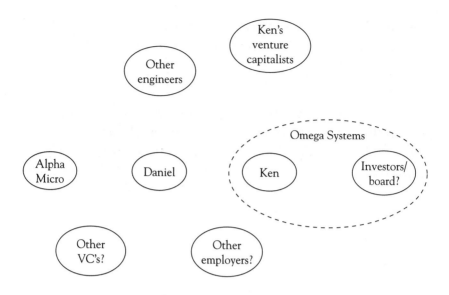

RULES: WHAT ARE THE RULES OF THE GAME?

At this point, Daniel and Ken are feeling their way into a negotiation, inventing it as they go along, but they aren't making up
all the rules from scratch. Their interactions are unavoidably subject to certain established codes of conduct, or rules of the game.
The nature of these rules and conventions varies with the circumstances, making it particularly important for Daniel to ask
himself which set of rules governs his negotiation with Ken. The
rules of business negotiations, for example, are quite different from
those of personal injury lawsuit settlement talks or international
trade negotiations. And even within business, the logic of merger
negotiations is very different from that of union-management bargaining. What we are calling rules here can consist of laws and regulations, social conventions, and professional codes of conduct.

For Daniel, the rules that matter most flow from intellectual
property law and employment law. Omega Systems is not a direct
competitor to Alpha Micro, Daniel's current employer, but if Alpha
considers the tools and techniques that Daniel developed under
its aegis as trade secrets, he may not be allowed to take them with

him to a new employer. Failure to understand these constraints could trigger litigation that would cripple Omega.

Soliciting other Alpha employees to work for Omega could also pose problems. Fortunately, Daniel isn't explicitly prohibited from doing so by his employment contract, but Alpha may sue him and Omega anyway in order to delay or deter a hemorrhaging of talent. Daniel should discuss these issues with an employment lawyer before he makes any decisions about Ken's employment offer.

A thorough understanding of the rules of the game can be a source of advantage because other players may not fully understand their implications. If Daniel doesn't hire a good lawyer and doesn't understand the employment law issues, he may inadvertently make serious errors. For example, suppose Ken asks him to sign a restrictive noncompete agreement, and Daniel does so without fully understanding the consequences. Or suppose he fails to realize that Ken can unilaterally change his job responsibilities later.

PRACTICAL APPLICATION: DIAGNOSING THE RULES

Return to the negotiation you have begun analyzing and answer the following questions:

- What laws and regulations apply here?
- What social conventions shape the parties' behavior?
- Are there professional codes of conduct that apply here?
- What other rules of the game will influence other parties' behavior?

ISSUES: WHAT AGENDA OF ISSUES WILL BE, OR COULD BE, NEGOTIATED?

It's easy but dangerous to treat the agenda as fixed. To do so is to fail to take actions to shape it in favorable ways. The agenda—the set of issues the parties decide to negotiate—is itself subject to negotiation. Ken will have his preferred agenda, but Daniel may want to add or subtract issues. If Daniel wants to get his issues considered, he will have to introduce them early on and perhaps even press for a prenegotiation session with Ken about the agenda. As we will see in Chapter Two, efforts to mold the agenda are an important piece of shaping the structure of negotiations.

Identify the Full Set of Issues

However obvious the issues in a negotiation appear to be, it is worthwhile to probe beneath the surface. How has the agenda of issues been defined, and who defined it? Is the agenda too narrow, or overly broad? What existing or potential sources of conflict could become blocking issues?

It's particularly useful to think through contingencies that might occur, such as a sale of the company before it goes public; doing so will point you to issues you might otherwise miss. It's impossible to foresee all potential contingencies, but failure to lay out all the relevant issues often flows from imprecise shorthand thinking. In a situation where both sides are jockeying for advantage, the side that fails to identify the full set of issues can be exploited.

Unbundle the Issues

As David Lax and Jim Sebenius have noted, issues often get intertwined, so it's crucial to unbundle them.[5] In Daniel's negotiation, the issues are typical of a hiring negotiation: location, compensation, and job title. Compensation bundles salary and equity (in the form of stock options); equity in turn is a question not just of how many options but also of how quickly they vest. And what about protecting them against dilution? Should Daniel try to add that to the agenda?

Job title and responsibilities can also be unbundled. Daniel should ask himself whether he cares about being a founder of the company. Should he press to be chief technology officer (CTO), or is the vice president of engineering title okay? Should he ask for a seat on the board? How will his job responsibilities be defined, and—crucially—under what conditions can they be changed? What will happen once the technical work on the system is done? Should he seek some protection (such as immediate vesting) in the event that another firm acquires Omega? The table below sets out what a fully unbundled list of Daniel's issues might look like.

Assess Whether Relationships Are an Issue

What is the nature of Daniel's relationship with Ken, and how does it influence their negotiation? There is a world of difference between negotiating a *deal* and resolving a *dispute*. In a deal, pre-existing antagonism is not an issue; the parties tend to approach the negotiation coolly and rationally, at least at the start. In disputes, feelings of grievance or victimization often provoke urges to harm the other side, even at a cost to oneself.[6] Conflict also tends to distort perception, leading to breakdowns in communication and tendencies to dismiss conciliatory gestures by the other side. As a result, the relationship between the contending parties often

Daniel's Issues

Location	Compensation	Job Responsibilities	Status
Location of engineering group	Salary Options Number Vesting schedule Antidilution protection	Title Protection against changes in job responsibilities Protection in the event of sale or change in control	Founder Board seat

becomes the central issue in a dispute, and it is wise to address the relationship early on.

We can differentiate similarly between a negotiation whose context is a long-term *relationship* (established or anticipated) and a one-time *transaction*. You are likely, for instance, to negotiate differently with a neighbor over the joint purchase of a fence than with a stranger whose car you're buying. With your neighbor, the desire to maintain a good relationship promotes equity and consensus rather than back-and-forth bargaining over price.

The intersection of deal versus dispute and transaction versus relationship yields four distinct types of negotiations: deal making, relationship building, dispute resolution, and conflict management (see the table below). The type of negotiation says a great deal about its internal logic and has implications for the behavior of the participants. The most difficult of all negotiations are those that arise in a long-term bitter dispute between parties who must continue to interact on an ongoing basis. Such conflicts can rarely

Four Types of Negotiations

	Transaction	*Relationship*
Deal	*Deal making* • Selling a business unit Parties will not interact in the future, but there are no preexisting animosities.	*Relationship building* • Creating a corporate alliance Parties anticipate a long-term relationship, but its basis has not yet been determined.
Dispute	*Dispute resolution* • Resolution of a personal injury lawsuit Relationship is likely to be characterized by animosity, but parties will not interact after resolution.	*Conflict management* • Settling a strike The current dispute is likely to be part of a longer-term pattern of contention, which may create barriers to agreement.

be definitively resolved; negotiations focus instead on managing tensions and ensuring the continuation of uneasy coexistence. Fortunately, this is not Daniel and Ken's situation—at least not yet.

What Daniel and Ken are engaged in is relationship-building negotiations. We can thus predict that in the name of building the relationship, both will abstain from highly aggressive value-claiming behavior (trying to claim the biggest piece of the pie at the other party's expense). The need to cooperate and engage in an ongoing relationship may lead both sides to moderate their demands and refrain from doing anything to poison the relationship early on.

The type of negotiation they are pursuing, however, can easily shift over time: every effort at deal making is a dispute waiting to happen. If Daniel and Ken fail to address important contingencies in their initial agreement, they could easily end up negotiating to manage damaging conflicts later on. And efforts to negotiate a merger or work out a restructuring of a company's debt can easily escalate into a dispute and break down in acrimony.

Identify and Deal with Toxic Issues

Certain issues can be toxic in the sense that they are exceedingly difficult to agree on. Their inclusion thus poisons the potential for agreement on less contentious issues. A classic example of a toxic issue in merger negotiations is the question of who will lead the combined entity, an issue fraught with dueling egos and other pitfalls. In cross-border mergers, the question of where the headquarters will be located can also prove highly contentious.

It may be prudent to defer a toxic issue until most of the rest of the deal is worked out. Alternatively, it could be best to resolve it early so that it doesn't cast a shadow over the entire process. Which way to go will depend on whether you consider the tough issue to be resolvable early. If so, success in doing so can create momentum. If not, it's best to wait until your counterparts have more invested in the process and, ideally, until you have developed more confidence in each other. For Daniel, the question of location has the potential to be toxic. There is no point in continuing to negotiate if Ken isn't willing to consider locating the company in Austin. Should Daniel make that a precondition? Should he propose a package deal? Should he postpone it until the end?

PRACTICAL APPLICATION: DIAGNOSING THE ISSUES

- Are you negotiating the right agenda of substantive issues?

- Are relationships an issue in this negotiation, or is it a transaction? What are the implications for how people will behave?

- Is past conflict part of the picture? Does the prospect of a long-term relationship create opportunities?

- Would deferring toxic issues or dealing with them up-front help move things forward?

INTERESTS: WHAT GOALS ARE YOU AND OTHERS PURSUING?

Early on, often in parallel with efforts to nail down the agenda, negotiators typically begin to stake out positions. *Positions* are essentially demands, often backed up by some combination of rationales, principles, commitments, and threats. When Ken made Daniel and his colleagues industry-standard employment offers, he was simultaneously framing the agenda—defining the issues he wanted to negotiate—and taking a position. Daniel could respond with a counteroffer on Ken's agenda items, perhaps asking for more equity or accelerated vesting of his options. Or he could try to broaden the agenda by indicating that he wants to discuss a seat on the board, an antidilution clause, and a different job title.

As a rule, though, taking a hard position early is rarely a good idea. As Roger Fisher and William Ury stress in *Getting to Yes,*

Daniel is likely to benefit more in the long run by concentrating first on assessing *interests*—the underlying goals and desires he and Ken are pursuing.[7] By analyzing interests, you can often discover ways to *create value*—to enlarge the pie—and avoid focusing only on claiming value, or getting the biggest possible slice of a small pie.[8]

Suppose Ken says he wants to keep Omega Systems in Colorado. The question of where to situate the company could easily become a battle of incompatible positions. Now suppose Daniel probes further and learns that Ken wants to be near key investors and customers and that Ken's family is rooted in Colorado. By exploring interests in this way and then generating creative options, Daniel and Ken could decide to situate the engineering group in Austin and the headquarters and marketing arm in Colorado—a value-creating outcome.

When exploring interests, keep in mind the three basic principles for creating value in negotiations:

> *Seek out shared interests.* Look for things that you and your counterpart both care about and can achieve better by combining your resources.
>
> *Propose mutually beneficial trades.* Identify things that are more valuable (costly) to your counterpart than to you, and trade them for things that are more valuable to you than your counterpart. For example, Daniel is willing to give up some compensation if Ken will agree to locate the engineering group in Austin.
>
> *Secure insecure contracts.* If you don't fully trust each other, find ways to minimize your vulnerability and thus avoid the defensiveness that constrains value creation. By getting clear guarantees about what happens if the business is sold, for example, Daniel might feel more secure about entering into an employment agreement.

Seek Out Shared Interests

Even negotiators with many conflicting interests may be able to cooperate to advance the interests they share. This can be true even when the parties are engaged in a bitter dispute. "Two elements must normally be present for negotiation to take place: there must be both common interests and issues of conflict," a shrewd commentator on negotiation has observed. "Without common interests there is nothing to negotiate for; without conflicting interests there is nothing to negotiate about."[9] If the parties to a lawsuit want to see it resolved expeditiously, for example, they may implicitly cooperate to speed things up. But to do so, they have to be willing to acknowledge their shared interests and not let spite govern their decisions.

Achieving shared goals is sometimes as simple as combining forces to accomplish something you can't do alone. In a merger, for example, rationalizing purchasing systems can generate economies of scale and reduce costs. If the companies have complementary technologies or operate in different markets, they can also realize economies of scope in serving diverse markets. The key is to do a thorough analysis of interests, and then to identify and explore promising opportunities to advance shared goals.

Both Daniel and Ken want Omega to have a strong engineering team, so they share an interest in recruiting Daniel's team members from Alpha. Daniel and Ken bring complementary resources to this endeavor, and the potential for joint economic gain is the core rationale for entering into an agreement. At the same time, Daniel may be able to use Ken's need to get a good team on board quickly to claim some value, such as by proposing that the size of his own equity stake be tied to his success at recruiting.

Propose Mutually Beneficial Trades

If you and your counterpart weigh the importance of specific issues differently, your differences could create opportunities for cross-issue trades. Start by thinking hard about your own interests and the kinds of trades you would be willing to make; you are unlikely to care equally strongly about achieving gains on all the issues. Suppose you and a friend are negotiating to trade some wine. You are willing to trade two bottles of chardonnay to get one bottle of cabernet. Now suppose it emerges that your counterpart prefers chardonnay to cabernet. You have the basis for a mutually beneficial trade.

This process of assessing *trade-offs*—concessions you are willing to make in exchange for gains—can be made more rigorous by explicitly ranking the relative importance of achieving gains on each issue. For Daniel, location is of prime importance. But what about job title, a board seat, protection against dilution, and changes in responsibilities, salary, and options? What trade-offs would he be willing to make across these issues? How much compensation would he forgo to get the company to move to Austin? What is founder status or a board seat worth to him?

Once you have a clear grasp of your own interests, analyze the other parties' as best you can, asking yourself how much weight they are likely to assign to each issue and what trade-offs they might be willing to make. If this analysis reveals complementary differences in interests, it may be possible to realize gains through trade.

The trade-off matrix shown on page 22 summarizes Daniel's appraisal of his own trade-offs and his provisional assessments of Ken's.[10] The direction of the arrows in the matrix signifies the nature of a preference, and the number of arrows indicates its relative strength (on a scale of 1 to 5). What opportunities for trades show up here? We have already discussed possible shared interests on job title and Daniel and Ken's differences on location (as well as a possible creative resolution). Equity seems likely to be a sticking point, because both care a lot about it. But trades appear possible on other issues: Daniel probably cares less than Ken does about a seat on the board, antidilution protection, and accelerated vesting; he cares more about protection against changes in his job responsibilities. If Daniel succeeds in broadening the agenda, he may be able to

A Trade-Off Matrix

Issue	Daniel	Ken
Location in Austin	↑↑↑↑↑	↓↓↓
Higher salary	↑↑	↓
More equity	↑↑↑	↓↓↓↓
Quicker vesting	↑	↓↓
Antidilution protection	↑	↓↓↓
Seat on the board	↑	↓↓↓
Chief technology officer title	↑↑↑	↑
Restrictions on changes in responsibilities	↑↑↑↑	↓↓↓

fashion a package deal by ceding on issues he cares less about in exchange for concessions on those he cares more about.

It may also be possible to create value by trading on other differences in interests:

Are there differences in sensitivities to time? Ken appears to be in far more of a hurry than Daniel is. Daniel will get a decent severance package from Alpha, and he has some savings, so he should be in no rush. Because Ken wants to capitalize on first-mover advantage in carving out a new market, he may be willing to give on other issues in return for getting a deal done quickly.

Are there differences in attitudes toward risk? If there are, it might be possible to craft agreements that shift risk (and return) to the less risk-averse party. Daniel is more risk-averse than Ken, so he might accept more compensation in the form of salary and less in equity.

Are there differences in expectations of the future? Suppose Daniel is more optimistic than Ken that he will be able to recruit a full thirty-person team quickly. A contingent agreement would reward Daniel with more equity if he meets certain recruiting goals.

Secure Insecure Agreements

Worry about the sustainability of an agreement effectively shrinks the pie, because hedging against risk makes negotiators conservative and even defensive. Right now, Daniel's value to Ken's enterprise is very high. But he would be wise to think about what will happen once he and his team have finished building the system. If he trusted Ken, it might be possible to rely on goodwill to resolve ambiguities and deal with future contingencies. But because they barely know each other, he should recall the admonition against leaving the fox in charge of the henhouse even if you have an agreement that he will care for the chickens.

What can you do if you don't fully trust your counterparts, or if you simply don't know whether they might ignore or try to renegotiate your agreement if things change? To find ways to secure agreements in the absence of trust or if future contingencies could threaten the integrity of your agreements, ask yourself the following questions:

Would it help to set standards or establish guiding principles? Daniel could press for additional stock options tied to specific performance goals.

Would it help to embed decision-making and dispute-resolution mechanisms in the agreement? Daniel and Ken can't possibly anticipate every circumstance that will arise in the next four or five years. But Daniel can insist on a decision-making and dispute-resolution mechanism that gives him adequate control over how he is treated in the future. For example, he could press for a clause specifying that his job responsibilities cannot change without mutual agreement and a provision for mediation if no agreement can be reached.

Would it help to set up monitoring regimes? Daniel could press for a seat on the board, which would involve him in regular reviews of company strategy and direction.

Would it help to create guarantees? Daniel might negotiate a golden parachute if his job responsibilities change substantially or the company is sold.

Would it help to proceed incrementally? It is sometimes wise to implement agreements in small, mutually verifiable steps. This approach makes future gains contingent on meeting current obligations so as to avoid *end-game effects*—the tendency to claim as much value as you can when you know a relationship is about to end. This is why venture capitalists and entrepreneurs like Ken require stock options for key personnel to vest over time and not right away.

Advancing shared goals, trading on differences, and securing insecure agreements jointly constitute a toolbox for crafting attractive package deals. But it is important to guard against focusing too narrowly on the substance of the deal and ignoring the people across the table.

Factor in Personal Interests

Along with forging a good deal, virtually all negotiators care about their self-images, reputations, and future effectiveness. Your counterparts may even be willing to give up something of substance to protect these intangible assets. Conversely, threats to their sense of competence or reputations can hobble a good substantive agreement. The questions in the box will help you think about how your counterparts experience (or want to experience) the process.[11]

ASSESSING YOUR COUNTERPARTS' PERSONAL INTERESTS

Every negotiator seeks to protect and advance personal interests in every negotiation. Sometimes your counterparts' reputations and tactics are well known. Sometimes others who have negotiated with them in the past can offer insight into their styles and personalities. And sometimes you just have to reach your own conclusions by carefully observing them at the table. As a starting point, ask yourself how much the following values matter to your counterparts:

- *Preserving reputation.* Do they care a lot about maintaining or enhancing their reputations as effective (firm or tough) negotiators?

- *Demonstrating competence.* How urgently do your counterparts want to feel competent and skillful at negotiation? Are they seasoned experts or novices insecure about their skills?

- *Remaining consistent.* Do your counterparts care about consistency with their prior commitments or statements of principle, and about avoiding undesirable precedents?[12]

- *Minimizing transaction costs.* Do your counterparts care about minimizing the direct costs (time and resources) of negotiation and about the opportunity costs of forgoing other initiatives?

- *Achieving side effects.* Are your counterparts using the negotiation with you to pursue objectives external to it, such as improving relationships with other influential parties or tapping into new resources?[13]

PRACTICAL APPLICATION: DIAGNOSING INTERESTS

- What do the other parties care most about? What trade-offs might they be willing to make across the issues?

- Do you and they share any goals that could be achieved by combining resources? Are there ways to realize economies of scale or scope?

- Could you create value by making trades across issues or

by trading on your differences with regard to time, risk, or expectations of the future?

- Is sustainability a potential problem? Would it help to incorporate standards or dispute-resolution provisions into the agreement?

If Daniel is going to organize the engineers and press Ken for more equity and more decision making in the running of Omega, he should think hard about how to manage the process so that Ken doesn't react defensively. Roger Fisher and William Ury counsel negotiators to "separate the people from the problem." By collecting data on what others have received in similar situations, Daniel can ground his position in facts and head off emotional reactions. A demand without a supporting rationale risks poisoning the relationship and the deal. To take the sting out of his demands, he could also link them to successful recruitment of a full engineering team, ensuring the creation of more value for Ken. As William Ury puts it, Daniel should build Ken a "golden bridge" and not push him to the edge of a cliff.[14]

ALTERNATIVES: WHAT WILL YOU DO IF YOU DON'T REACH AGREEMENT?

It sounds self-evident that you should enter into an agreement only if that will yield more value than not doing so. But negotiators contemplating a potential agreement often fail to ask themselves the obvious question: As compared to what? Unless you have worked out what you will do if you can't reach agreement, you won't know how to answer this question. Roger Fisher and William Ury have called this option your best alternative to a negotiated agreement, and its acronym, *BATNA*, has entered the standard vocabulary of negotiation.[15] The diagram on page 27 illustrates the decisions that Daniel and Ken face between agreement and their respective BATNAs.

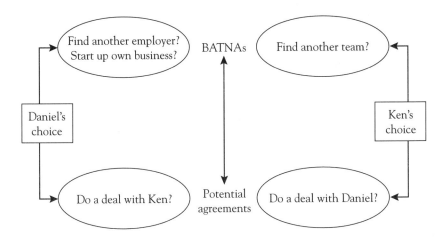

Work Out Your BATNA

A BATNA is a course of action; it is what you will do if there is no agreement. Depending on what's at issue, it could be to go to court, strike, or seek a divorce. Taking time to think through your BATNA rigorously will solidify your alternatives and clarify your situation. The better your BATNA is, the better your agreement is likely to be. A strong BATNA has to be built; it isn't just handed to you. What are Daniel's alternatives to a deal with Ken? He hasn't cultivated other offers or developed a compelling idea for starting his own business. At this point, his BATNA is vague and weak.

Daniel should also make a careful assessment of Ken's BATNA. It's easy to forget that the other side also has to be convinced that a deal is beneficial—that it yields more value than their BATNA. Daniel can't hope to craft an advantageous deal if he doesn't understand how Ken perceives and values his alternatives (as distinct from how Daniel thinks Ken *should* perceive his alternatives, a common mistake). Can Ken quickly recruit another skilled and cohesive team? If so, Ken probably would have mentioned it, so his silence conveys information about his BATNA. Does he need to move quickly before someone else makes a move into the same market? If so, Ken's BATNA is weak and Daniel is in a strong position. Discussions with venture capitalists who specialize in this area might help Daniel gain some insight.

Define Your Walk-Away Position

The next step is to define your *walk-away* position: What minimum value do you need to get to enter into an agreement? Establishing this value as a benchmark and keeping it in the forefront of your mind helps protect against the pitfalls of getting so committed to your demands that you refuse deals that are better than your walk-away and allowing yourself to be pushed below your walk-away in the heat of the process.

Translating a BATNA (a course of action) into walk-away positions (the minimum values you would accept in an agreement) isn't always straightforward.[16] Suppose you're buying a new car and debating whether to sell your old one or trade it in. Is your walk-away in a private sale identical to your walk-away in a trade-in at a dealership? It may be higher, because you don't want the hassle of advertising and selling your car.

Suppose Daniel's BATNA is to find another employer. How should he go about pinpointing his walk-away in negotiations with Ken? Thorough analysis of the market for engineering talent is a good starting point. He thinks Ken's offer is approximately what he could get elsewhere, but he needs to make sure, perhaps by talking with recruiters and colleagues who have recently taken new jobs. Another way to establish value is to generate competing offers.

Assessing walk-aways is harder when you are negotiating multiple issues. The key is to identify possible trade-offs across the issues (how many bottles of chardonnay is one bottle of cabernet worth to me?) and then to develop an approach—even a spreadsheet model—that enables you to compare the value of different package deals. If Daniel can't assess the value of the packages Ken offers, he will have trouble either creating or claiming value. Suppose Daniel is offered 3 percent of the equity in the company and the title of vice president of engineering. How should he compare that offer to 2 percent of the equity, the title of chief technology officer, and founder status?

Explore the Effect of a Coalition on Your BATNA

When there are more than two parties to a negotiation, it is more complicated to establish BATNAs and walk-aways. Parties who find their alternatives to submitting to others' demands unappealing can often dramatically improve their BATNAs by joining a coalition. And changes in coalitional alignments can dramatically change BATNAs or even cause coalitional BATNAs to vanish.

Suppose Daniel and his engineers negotiate as a team. Collectively, they are worth much more than they are individually, but what is an intact engineering team worth to an early-stage start-up in the current market? Suppose they contacted venture capitalists and offered to auction the team to the highest bidder: What could they hope to get under such circumstances? Certainly much more than the 2 percent of the company that Ken is currently offering them, as well as representation on the board. So building a solid coalition can substantially improve your BATNA.

At the same time, Daniel must be careful not to become too dependent on a coalition. It is often better to "hang together rather than hang separately," but it's essential to think through what will happen if the coalition breaks down. For Daniel, this means developing his own personal BATNA as well as collective options.

Consider the Impact of Time

Never forget that one option in negotiation is always to do nothing, and that patient negotiators often have an advantage over their less patient counterparts. Ask yourself whether there is a good reason to act now. Will your alternatives improve or worsen as time passes? What about those of your counterparts? Will options that are currently unavailable open up?

Now suppose Daniel can convince Ken that delay costs him practically nothing. If Ken will incur substantial costs as time passes (including opportunity costs if he risks falling behind his competitors), we can expect him to make concessions to close the deal.[17] No specific event triggers this action; instead, the pressures of cumulating costs eventually provoke activity.

Action-forcing events like deadlines, by contrast, are break points that compel action. They are intended to change the game by eliminating doing nothing as an option and compelling your counterparts (and perhaps others on your own side) to make hard choices in order to avoid large and irreversible costs. Ken has imposed a deadline on Daniel and the others by linking his negotiations with them to his negotiations with venture capitalists, and by making them *exploding offers*—offers that will expire after a deadline, backed by an assertion that they will not be renewed. He has also pumped up a sense of urgency by suggesting that the opportunity will be lost if they don't move quickly. But it isn't clear what time constraints Ken really faces. Does he need to conclude this deal quickly to get funding, or is this simply a negotiating ploy? Is he really worried that allowing more time to pass will allow Daniel to explore other offers or to organize the engineers to negotiate as a group? It is probably in Daniel's interest to slow things down. "I understand that you want to move quickly," Daniel can say, "but we need more time to consider our options. In the meantime, I would be pleased to talk with the venture capitalists about the opportunity."

It's essential for Daniel to understand that his bargaining leverage is greatest *before* he makes a commitment to join Omega Systems. He can use the power of coalitions and competition to build his BATNA (and, by extension, to weaken Ken's). Once he has signed an employment agreement and joined the company, his ability to renegotiate terms is extremely limited. This is why it's crucial for him to secure the time to improve his BATNA so he can negotiate the best possible deal.

Guard Against Overconfidence and Overcommitment

It's sometimes difficult to nail down your BATNA because of uncertainty about what will happen in the event of no agreement. If I turn down this job, will another good one come along? If I refuse the union's terms, will they strike? If I go to court, will I win? By and large, people are notoriously poor at evaluating their no-agreement options in the face of uncertainty. Overconfidence about winning in court, for example, is a well-recognized barrier to settlement of legal disputes.[18] So it's essential to be rigorous and realistic about assessing potential outcomes and their probabilities in order to clarify your BATNA when there is uncertainty. Is the company's likelihood of success 10 percent, or is it 25 percent? Consulting a venture capitalist with experience in this area might help to sharpen Daniel's estimates.

PRACTICAL APPLICATION: DIAGNOSING BATNAS

- What will you do if you are unable to reach agreement? What will your counterpart do?

- Can you think of ways to strengthen your BATNA or weaken your counterpart's?

- Are you or your counterpart overconfident about what you will get if you don't reach agreement? How do you know you aren't overconfident?

- Can you alter others' perceptions of their BATNAs by building coalitions? By promoting competing offers?

- Are cumulating costs forcing you to make concessions? If so, can you reduce your costs or raise your counterparts'?

- Are action-forcing events pressuring you to make unattractive choices? If so, can you find ways to neutralize deadlines or impose your own?

AGREEMENTS: ARE THERE POTENTIAL AGREEMENTS THAT WOULD BE ACCEPTABLE TO ALL SIDES?

If potential agreements exist that would leave both you and your counterpart better off than your respective walk-away values, we say that there is a bargaining range.[19] Ordinarily, negotiators won't know whether such a range exists until they begin to explore interests and options at the table. Even so, Daniel should try to discern the rough outlines of the bargaining range before meeting with Ken.

Try to Find the Bargaining Range

Using his assessment of Ken's interests and BATNA, Daniel can try to estimate Ken's walk-away. He will be dealing in uncertainty, of course, but so will Ken. And the exercise of trying to locate the bargaining range is likely to stand Daniel in good stead when negotiations begin, because he will be in a position to probe more effectively. He will probably have to revise his assessment, but at least he'll have an assessment to revise.

Bargaining Range in Distributive Negotiations

The nature of the bargaining range depends on whether a negotiation is, or its participants believe it to be, purely about *claiming value* (dividing the pie) or whether there are opportunities to create value and enlarge the pie.[20] Sometimes negotiations are *distributive:* there is a fixed pie to be divided among the parties, and anything one side gains, the other loses. The objective of both sides is therefore to claim value—to get as big a wedge of the pie as possible.

If the negotiation between Daniel and Ken were solely about the size of Daniel's equity stake in Omega, Ken would have to lose for Daniel to gain and vice versa. A hypothetical bargaining range for this negotiation could look like the one in the following diagram.

Bargaining Range for a Pure Value-Claiming Negotiation

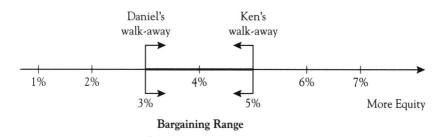

Bargaining Range

Ken won't give Daniel more than 5 percent, and Daniel is willing to accept a minimum of 3 percent, so the bargaining range occupies the region between 3 percent and 5 percent. The range defines the universe of potential agreements, but it doesn't specify where within it (or even whether) they will reach an agreement. The exact outcome will emerge from the process and will depend on the tactics that Ken and Daniel employ.

It is also possible that Daniel and Ken have incompatible walkaways. If this is the case and nothing can be done to enlarge the pie, no agreement is possible and there is no bargaining range. Suppose, as illustrated in the diagram on page 34 showing no bargaining range, Ken is unwilling to give Daniel more than 3 percent, but Daniel won't accept less than 5 percent. Unless something happens to transform one or both of their walk-aways, no agreement is possible. Such lack of agreement isn't necessarily a bad thing: it's essential to keep in mind that no agreement is better than a bad one.

As David Lax and Jim Sebenius recognized, if you are negotiating over a fixed pie and there is no way to enlarge it, you need to be adept at claiming value.[21] Common approaches to doing this, which we will discuss further in Chapter Three, are anchoring and commitment tactics. *Anchoring* means using offers and concessions to anchor the negotiations at the favorable end of the bargaining range by shaping your counterpart's perceptions of your walk-away. For instance, Daniel could ask for 6 percent and gradually concede

No Bargaining Range

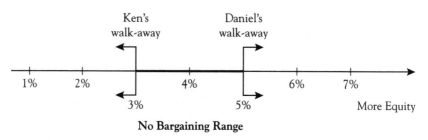

No Bargaining Range

to 5.5 percent, then 5.15 percent, and finally 5 percent. Of course, Ken could counter with 2 percent, then 2.5 percent, and so on. The risk of anchoring, obviously, is that both participants will conclude there is no bargaining range.

Negotiators employ *commitment tactics* when they assert a position so unequivocally that it will be costly, even humiliating, to make additional concessions.[22] If Daniel says, for example, "Five percent is the very least I could possibly take," his reputation will suffer if he makes further concessions. Constraints imposed by others—such as "I promised my wife I wouldn't move the kids out of Austin"—can also operate as commitments.

Commitments have to be used with caution; they can lock you into untenable positions, undermining the potential for beneficial agreements. On the other hand, if you can credibly commit to a position that is within the bargaining range but favorable to you, you may be able to create value.

Bargaining Range in Integrative Negotiations

Few real-world negotiations are purely a matter of claiming as much value as possible. Most situations offer opportunities for *creating value*—enlarging the pie through cooperation and mutually beneficial trades. Eventually, of course, the value that gets created still has to be divided or claimed. Negotiations of this kind are therefore *integrative*: they combine efforts to integrate interests and create value (to enlarge the pie) with efforts to claim value (to divide the pie). Typically, value creation is accomplished by negotiating several issues simultaneously and creating package deals.

Suppose you are negotiating to buy a house that needs extensive repair. You have tentatively agreed on a price, with the proviso that the seller will make certain repairs. The seller plans to hire a contractor, which will take time and cost several thousand dollars. Now suppose you want to occupy the house quickly, enjoy home repair, and think the materials would cost no more than five hundred dollars. This is an opportunity to create value: the seller can take a lower price, and you can perform the repairs. How much lower the price will be remains to be negotiated: value has been created, but it must also be claimed.

Let's look at this point another way. If Daniel and Ken expand their negotiation to include other issues besides the amount of Daniel's equity, the possibility of creating value by means of package deals transforms the bargaining range for their negotiation from a line to a region. In the figure on page 36, the x-axis represents the total value of potential package deals to Daniel, and the y-axis represents the value of the same package deals to Ken.

To make this more concrete, suppose Daniel and Ken negotiate the issues sequentially and agree first that Daniel's equity stake will be 4 percent. The resulting partial deal, shown as point A in the diagram, is acceptable to both, but just barely. It's better for both Daniel and Ken than their respective walk-aways, but opportunities to create joint gains have gone unrealized.

Now let's hypothesize a package deal B that gives Daniel a guaranteed 2.5 percent equity stake and another 2.5 percent contingent on successful recruitment of a complete team by a certain date. Value gets created here, but Ken captures most of it because Daniel gets only a bit more equity than in deal A if he succeeds, but ends up substantially worse off if he fails.

Bargaining Range for an Integrative Negotiation

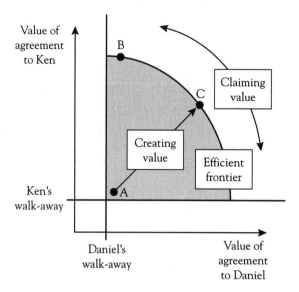

Let's also hypothesize a deal C that gives Daniel the same equity stake contingent on successful recruitment but with contractual protections against changes in job responsibilities, including provisions in case the company is sold. Here, value has been created, and both sides have claimed balanced portions of it.

There are limits to the amount of joint value the parties can create through trades. Negotiation theorists call the outer limits of joint value the *efficient frontier*,[23] represented in the bargaining range diagram as a line. Agreements situated on this frontier are termed efficient because neither party can be made better off without making the other worse off. Agreements inside the frontier (such as the one at point A) are inefficient because other feasible agreements would benefit at least one party without harming the other's interests.

The take-away lesson from this short detour into theory is that value gets simultaneously created and claimed in most negotiations. The implication for action is that you need to think both about whether you can create more value and about how you will claim value. In real-world negotiations, of course, it is often very difficult to tell whether more value can be created. Daniel and Ken may never know how near they have gotten to the efficient frontier. And appraisals of who has claimed how much value are inevitably murky and subjective, mainly because of uncertainty about the other party's interests and alternatives.

Harness the Power of Good Information

If you and your counterpart know a lot about each other's interests and bottom lines, you can work together openly to create value with little risk. Usually, though, you know far more about your own interests, BATNA, and walk-away than about your counterpart's. Daniel understands his own side of the equation but is much less certain about what Ken will accept. This means that he must be very cautious about sharing information. Otherwise he could succeed in creating value, only to end up letting Ken claim the lion's share.

Suppose that Ken has learned a lot more about Daniel's interests and BATNA than Daniel has about Ken's, perhaps simply by asking the right questions. Ken could exploit this informational imbalance by concealing information, or even by being actively misleading, in order to shape Daniel's perceptions of the bargaining range. Daniel, because of his informational disadvantage, can't do the same. Because there is no alternative to acting on the basis of your own understanding, however partial it is, having better information is a clear advantage. That's why prenegotiation information gathering and effective learning at the table are so important.

Now suppose that both sides are highly uncertain about each other's interests and BATNAs: both will work to shape each other's perceptions of the bargaining range, and their efforts to claim value may prevent them from finding a bargaining range even when it exists.

Probe Shared Uncertainties

Both Daniel and Ken are uncertain how Omega Systems will do: Will it attract customers and achieve critical mass, or will it encounter unexpected competition and crash and burn? In the face of shared uncertainties about the future, negotiators tend to make self-serving predictions about their BATNAs. Ken may be overconfident that Omega will succeed, and he may believe that he can easily find another engineering team. Daniel may be comparably overconfident about finding a more attractive offer of employment. As a result, both could mistakenly conclude that no agreement is preferable to agreement. (However, as we saw when discussing trade-offs, these differing beliefs about the future can also be grist for mutually beneficial trades through contingent agreements.)

The key to situations characterized by extreme uncertainties and high stakes is good scenario planning. This doesn't mean evaluating the full range of potential outcomes; it means developing a set of plausible scenarios: best guess, optimistic, and pessimistic. Daniel would imagine that Omega does okay and gets acquired, that it is a huge success and goes public, and that it fails. Then he would use these scenarios to probe potential contingencies and structure deals that take them into account. Without such scenarios, he could end up blindsided by an unexpected outcome.

PRACTICAL APPLICATION: DIAGNOSING POTENTIAL AGREEMENTS

- Have your negotiations been taken over by value claiming at the expense of opportunities to create value? If so, how could the negotiation be reframed?

- Are you being unrealistic about your BATNA? Is your counterpart? Can you create a bargaining range by altering your perceptions of your own alternatives or theirs?

- Do you and your counterpart have more or less equivalent

knowledge, or are asymmetries generating uncertainty and feelings of vulnerability?

- Are there important unknowns? Could differing beliefs about the future make it possible to fashion contingent agreements?

LINKAGES: ARE YOUR CURRENT NEGOTIATIONS LINKED TO OTHER NEGOTIATIONS?

Stand-alone negotiations are surprisingly rare.[24] Even as simple a negotiation as buying a house typically involves competition with other purchasers, dealings with mortgage lenders, and sometimes interactions with several sellers. Negotiators' BATNAs tend to be strongly influenced by such linkages. If the prospective seller gets another offer or the prospective buyer finds another attractive house, the dynamics of the negotiation can shift dramatically.

Mapping Linked Negotiations

As it happens, Daniel's negotiations with Ken interact with at least seven other sets of negotiations. The party map Daniel constructed earlier can help him get a handle on these links:

- Daniel's negotiations with Ken
- Daniel's negotiations with the other engineers
- The other engineers' negotiations with Ken
- Ken's negotiations with venture capitalists
- Daniel's (possible) negotiations with other employers
- Daniel's (possible) negotiations with venture capitalists about a start-up of his own
- Daniel's (possible) negotiations with Alpha Microsystems to keep the Austin facility open

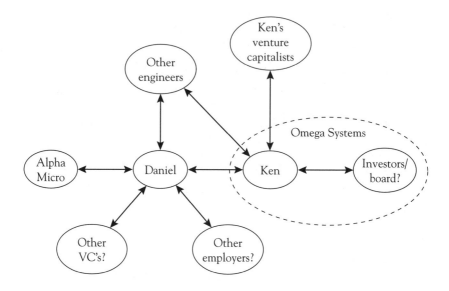

- Negotiations within Omega if other key players (investors or a board) are already involved

If Daniel were talking to another potential employer, those negotiations would be *competitively linked* to his negotiations with Ken. Only one deal could reach fruition, and Daniel might be able to play off the two potential "buyers" of his talent against each other. If the other offer gave him a larger equity stake, he could use that fact to persuade Ken to sweeten his offer—possibly giving him still more leverage with the other potential employer.

By contrast, Ken's negotiations with venture capitalists and his negotiations with Daniel are *reciprocally linked*: both must reach fruition if the overall enterprise is to go forward. Ken is clearly trying to bootstrap by getting the talent lined up first and then going to the venture capitalists. But if Daniel hesitates to commit himself before Ken has funding, Ken has a chicken-and-egg problem. One solution is for Ken to negotiate *conditional commitments* with Daniel and the venture capitalists whereby each agrees to a deal if the other also agrees.

Types of Linked Negotiations

Linkages between separable issues

Synergistic linkages combine issues that could be negotiated separately in ways that potentially create value.

Antagonistic linkages poison the potential for agreement. Some toxic issues not only can't be settled but also hinder settlement of other issues.

Linkages in time

Sequential linkages arise when earlier negotiations affect later ones, or future negotiations cast a shadow over current talks.

Concurrent linkages arise when linked negotiations coincide in time or overlap.

Competitive linkages occur when one party negotiates with two or more others, but only one of these negotiations can reach fruition.

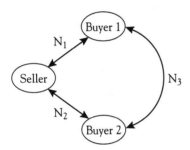

Competitive Linkage
- Negotiations N_1 and N_2 are competitively linked
- Seller cycles between buyers
- Buyers may attempt to collude in negotiation N_3

In *reciprocal linkages*, one party negotiates with two or more others, and all of the negotiations must reach fruition for an overall deal to occur. In *conditional agreements*, each deal is made conditional on reaching agreement in the others.

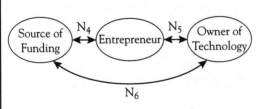

Reciprocal Linkage
- Negotiations N_4 and N_5 are reciprocally linked
- Entrepreneur must secure conditional commitments in both negotiations
- Entrepreneur risks being cut out of the loop in negotiation N_6

Restructuring the Linked System

Mapping the links sets the stage for the next step: restructuring the linked system in favorable ways. We will look at this process in more detail in Chapter Two, but it is worth noting here that Daniel could do a number of things to shape the structure in favorable ways. He could agree with the other engineers that they will negotiate collectively and that Daniel will be their representative. This move would prevent Ken from playing them off against each other. On his own, Daniel could seek out offers from other employers or investors.

Daniel should also think about the sequence of his moves in the linked negotiations. Whom should he talk to first, and what should he try to achieve? Daniel's first priority should be to talk to the other engineers and solidify his coalition. Then he should probably talk to local venture capitalists about opportunities.

PRACTICAL APPLICATION: DIAGNOSING LINKAGES

- Can you combine separate issues to create new opportunities for trades?

- Can you build momentum by undertaking negotiations in a particular sequence?

- Can you use competitive linkage to enhance your bargaining power?

- Have reciprocal linkages created any constraints that hinder agreement? If so, can you delink negotiations or relax the constraints?

IDENTIFYING BARRIERS AND OPPORTUNITIES

Having undertaken this thorough diagnosis, Daniel is in a much stronger position to proceed. He now has some ideas about ways to create value by broadening the agenda and seeking mutually beneficial trades. He also recognizes that he has opportunities to improve his BATNA by building a coalition with the other engineers, creating competitive linkages, and buying himself time to explore his options.

As Jim Sebenius has noted, the point of all this analysis is to pinpoint potential barriers to agreement and opportunities to shape the negotiation favorably.[25] The accompanying table lists typical barriers and opportunities associated with each element in a negotiation. You may want to use it to help diagnose the situation in your next negotiation.

Identifying Barriers and Opportunities

	Barriers	Opportunities
Parties	The wrong parties are at the table.	Invite in allies, and try to exclude adversaries.
	Too many parties are at the table.	Reduce the number of parties by convincing some to be represented by others.
Rules	Legal, historical, social, or cultural factors constrain strategy.	Understand the rules better than your counterparts do. Try to change the rules by influencing rule makers and referees.
Issues	The agenda is too narrow or too broad.	Broaden or narrow the issue agenda.
	The sequence in which issues are being negotiated is disadvantageous.	Establish control of the sequence in which issues get negotiated.
	Bad relationships have become an issue in their own right.	Build productive working relationships with counterparts.
Interests	Parties are locked into incompatible positions.	Focus on interests, and find opportunities to enlarge the pie.

Identifying Barriers and Opportunities (*continued*)

	Barriers	Opportunities
Alternatives	The alternatives to agreement are unattractive.	Take away-from-the-table actions that transform alternatives.
	You are overconfident about prevailing if there is no agreement.	Try to establish a common basis of facts with your counterpart to temper overconfidence.
	The cost of delay is high.	Shape your counterparts' perceptions to create a sense of urgency.
	Action-forcing events limit your flexibility.	Relax or set up other action-forcing events.
Agreements	Negotiations are framed purely in value-claiming terms.	Reframe the negotiations to enhance opportunities to create value.
	No bargaining range seems to exist.	Alter perceptions of walk-aways to create a bargaining range.
Linkages	Linkages cause binding constraints.	Try to decouple negotiations to create more flexibility.
	Your counterparts use competition to your disadvantage.	Create new linkages of your own.

2

Shaping the Structure

Claire Prescott, the young founder and CEO of a year-old commercial real estate company, was close to abandoning her negotiations with BargainMart's newly hired regional director for development, Eric Mersch. Claire had been negotiating to sign BargainMart, a respected nationwide discount retailer, as the anchor tenant in a shopping mall she was developing in Fairfield, a midsized city north of Boston. Three days earlier, her discussions with Mersch had broken down acrimoniously. Claire was nearly ready to call it quits when he requested another meeting. His call raised her hopes of getting the negotiations back on track, but she was uncertain how to move in a more productive direction.

Claire was under a great deal of pressure to get a deal done. Eleven months earlier, after leaving an established development company to start her own firm, she had negotiated a one-year option on an attractive parcel of land in Fairfield. The resulting mall project was her new company's first major deal, and she was counting on it to put her on the map. Failure to reach an agreement with BargainMart or another retailer of equivalent stature would be a severe setback.

Claire's development plan for the mall called for one large anchor store and many smaller satellite stores. She had planned to close a fifteen-year deal (with options to extend) with a good anchor tenant and then to negotiate seven-year leases with satellite tenants. Once these leases were signed, she would conclude a financing deal with a local commercial bank and exercise her option on the land. The bank had provisionally agreed to a ten-year repayment schedule if the credit officer was satisfied that Claire had put together a viable mall.

Progress was smooth until Claire hit a snag over zoning. Although ultimately resolved satisfactorily, the permitting process ate up nine months of precious time. Claire then quickly initiated discussions with the best anchor-tenant candidate, BargainMart. She had considered approaching BargainMart's arch-rival, Value-Shops, too, but her early conversations with Eric had been very encouraging. He had seemed to want to close a deal promptly, so Claire had focused on coming to terms with him.

Initial discussions over the size and configuration of the space went smoothly, but then the tone changed. Eric expressed misgivings about Fairfield's economy—vibrant but highly dependent on the defense industry—and pressed for very low rent and broad flexibility to transfer the lease to another firm if BargainMart didn't prosper. He also insisted on carte blanche about use of the space. It was BargainMart's policy, he said, not to enter into agreements that restricted its use of space or its freedom to sublet portions of the space to others. Eric invoked BargainMart's standard clause about use, transfer of the lease, and subletting, and asserted that he could not deviate from it: "The premises may be used for any lawful purpose. Tenant may transfer this lease or sublet the whole or any part of the premises, but if it does so, it shall remain liable and responsible under this lease."

This clause was a deal breaker for Claire. Her bank would not finance the project under such conditions, and satellite tenants would not be likely to find the mall attractive without some constraints on BargainMart's ability to enter new lines of business, sublet to potential competitors, or close up shop without warning. Claire's suspicion that Eric was playing hardball with her led to an angry exchange. With only weeks left before expiration of her option on the land, she felt up against the wall. For BargainMart, this project was only one of many potential opportunities, but for her company it was make-or-break. Claire was facing up to the prospect that the entire project would collapse when she received Eric's call.

Take a few minutes to decide what advice you would give Claire about what to do now. And if she had it to do over, what should she have done differently?

THE DIAGNOSIS

Before meeting with Eric for the first time, Claire should have carefully diagnosed her situation using the tools developed in Chapter One: a party map, an assessment of barriers and opportunities, and a trade-off matrix. Let's review the diagnosis she could have made and then look at where she stands now and how she can repair her disadvantages.

Mapping the Linked System

Claire should have begun by identifying all the parties, actual and potential, and mapping the linked system of negotiations as shown in the figure below.

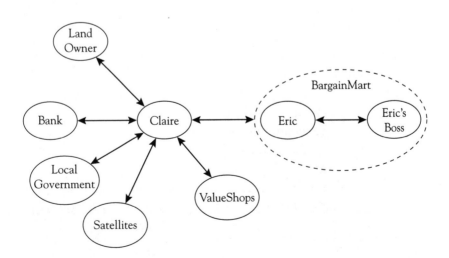

What might Claire have learned from this map? First of all, her negotiation with Eric is only one strand in a web of linked negotiations. Second, existing and potential linkages create some formidable barriers and opportunities. Her negotiations with Eric are sequentially linked to her previous negotiations with the landowner over the option, which is the time bomb she hears ticking. Her negotiations with the bank, on the other hand, are reciprocally linked to her negotiations with Eric; she can't do a deal with the bank without doing a deal with Eric, and vice versa. The time and funding constraints that flow from these two linkages are complicating her discussions with Eric. But Claire also has opportunities to create competitive linkages that could strengthen her bargaining position, such as by initiating discussions with BargainMart's competitor ValueShops.

Diagnosing Barriers and Opportunities

A thorough analysis of the structure of the negotiation as it stands now, using the seven-element structural framework presented in Chapter One—parties, rules, issues, interests, alternatives, agreements, and linkages—will help Claire identify barriers and opportunities in her negotiations with Eric.

	Barrier	*Opportunity*
Parties	The negotiation was defined as a two-party interaction, though there are other influential parties.	Make an overture to ValueShops.
	Eric may try to use ratification tactics.	Negotiate to build a coalition of attractive satellite shops.

	Barrier	*Opportunity*
Rules	Zoning problems delayed the project.	Find out if local government would offer tax breaks to improve the economics of the project.
	The bank's credit standards impose constraints.	See if the bank is willing to be more flexible or explore whether BargainMart can help with financing.
Issues	Multiple issues are bundled into BargainMart's standard uses clause.	Unbundle the issues of use, lease transfer, and subletting, and analyze their relative importance.
	Acrimonious interactions with Eric may have poisoned the relationship.	Work to defuse bad feelings.
Interests	Both Claire and Eric are locked into positions.	Look for shared goals and mutually beneficial trades.
Alternatives	Claire has no alternative to dealing with BargainMart, but Eric is under no pressure to close a deal.	Make an overture to ValueShops.
Agreements	The negotiations have been framed as purely value claiming in nature.	Try to reframe the negotiations to emphasize potential joint gains.
	Eric may feel pressure to produce a big win in his first deal for BargainMart.	Look for ways to help Eric back away from his position gracefully.
Linkages	The deadline on the land option is forcing action.	Negotiate to extend the option, if possible.
	The bank is imposing restrictive conditions.	Talk to other potential sources of financing.
	BargainMart is the only option.	Set up competitively linked negotiations with ValueShops.

By doing this analysis, what does Claire learn? First, she discovers that her BATNA is weak and Eric's is probably strong. Her BATNA is to abandon this project and invest her time and resources elsewhere. She hasn't developed alternatives and is therefore in a vulnerable position; she urgently needs to strengthen her BATNA. As for Eric, Claire doesn't know for certain whether he has alternatives locally or elsewhere, but it is reasonable to assume that he is exploring options, including the option to focus on a different market altogether. She may be able to pick up clues by querying others in the industry and by studying publicly available information about BargainMart's strategy and plans.

Second, the negotiation has clearly become focused on claiming value, although there appear to be significant opportunities to create value. Claire should try to reframe the proceedings to emphasize opportunities for joint gain. Because the focus on BargainMart's standard clause about use, transfer, and subletting is obscuring the fact that these are separable issues, she should try to unbundle them in order to identify opportunities to enlarge the pie.

Third, Claire needs to figure out whether BargainMart's standard clause is a hard constraint or—as is more likely—a bargaining position. If Claire can persuade developers who have previously dealt with BargainMart to describe the provisions of their deals on use, lease transfer, and subletting, she can probably figure out how much substance there is in Eric's invocations of company policy.

In hindsight, Claire could have negotiated more effectively to influence how local government applied its regulations to her project. The problems with zoning were probably foreseeable and avoidable, and early discussions might have led to tax breaks and agreements on infrastructure that would have helped make the project more attractive.

Creating Value

Claire should analyze her own and Eric's interests and trade-offs. Suppose this analysis resulted in the accompanying trade-off matrix. (Obviously, this initial assessment of Eric's interests must still

Approaches to Creating Value

Issues	Parties	
	Claire	Eric
Lease price	↑↑↑	↓↓
Use	↓↓↓↓	↑↑
Transfer of the lease	↓↓	↑↑↑↑
Subletting	↓	↑↑

be validated through learning at the table.) What does it suggest about potential opportunities to make mutually beneficial trades?

The issues of use and transfer of the lease appear to present a promising opportunity: if Claire's analysis is correct, Eric might be willing to accept some constraints on use in return for more attractive terms on transfer. There could also be room for a trade on the issues of lease price and subletting.

As the final step in her diagnosis, Claire could brainstorm ways to advance shared goals, make beneficial trades, and create mechanisms to secure agreements. The resulting analysis is summarized in the table on pages 52–53. Be sure to note how the standard value-creating tools described in Chapter One, such as trades across time and risk-shifting agreements, potentially help Claire to expand the pie.

FROM DIAGNOSIS TO SHAPING THE STRUCTURE

Now Claire is ready to address the second major element of the breakthrough framework: shaping the structure of the negotiation. This calls for a shift of focus from diagnosis to thinking like an architect about how to fashion the components of a negotiation into favorable configurations.

It's possible to shape the structure of negotiations because they are, to a degree, socially constructed. This means that (1) the parties and the issue agenda are not fixed in advance but influenced

Source of Joint Gains	General Approach	Specific Example
Advancing shared goals	Economies of scale	BargainMart and the satellite stores pursue joint marketing stategies facilitated by Claire's firm.
	Economies of scope	BargainMart is permitted to sublet to providers of complementary services (such as a children's play area) in exchange for revenue sharing of the incremental rents with Claire's firm.
Making beneficial trades	Cross-issue trades	BargainMart gets more flexibility on lease transfer and subletting in exchange for somewhat higher rent and more stringent use provisions.
	Trades across time	BargainMart gets more flexibility on use and lease transfer in the future (such as after five years) and Claire gets more stability up front so she can secure funding.
	Risk-shifting agreements	BargainMart's rental payments are linked to its in-store sale revenues.
	Contingent agreements	Transfer of the lease is tied to an index of local economic activity: the healthier the local economy, the less flexibility for BargainMart.
Securing insecure agreements	Standards and principles	BargainMart can transfer the lease, but only to an agreed-on list of reputable companies. Changes in use may not directly compete with major satellite stores. Subletting is permitted up to a specific percentage of the space.

Dispute-resolution provisions	Provisions for how disagreements will be handled, possibly including mediation and arbitration clauses, are included in the contract.
Monitoring regimes	Regular independent inspections are made of the space and its condition.
Incremental implementation	The lease is structured for a ten-year initial term with an option to renew.
Guarantees	Performance bonds are posted for timely completion of the project.

by the negotiators, and (2) perceptions of interests, BATNAs, and bargaining ranges are inescapably subjective, often unclear to the negotiators themselves at the outset, and subject to change as the process unfolds. Although markets, organizations, laws, and customs establish boundaries for the bargaining range and shape the rules of the game, you almost always have scope to influence the basic structure of your situation and the perceptions of your counterparts. And perceptions are often more important than realities. What is your bottom line? It's what you think it is, or what your counterpart believes it to be.

It's essential to begin this design work before going to the table. As Abraham Lincoln astutely remarked, "If I had eight hours to chop down a tree, I'd spend six sharpening my ax."

SELF-ASSESSMENT: SHAPING THE STRUCTURE

- Have you tended in the past to take negotiating situations more or less as they are presented to you?

- Have you focused too much on what happens at the negotiating table, and not enough on actions you can take away from the table?

- Can you recall a negotiation that other parties shaped in ways that were disadvantageous to you? How were they able to do so?
- What might you have done differently?

So far, Claire has played Eric's game. She hasn't tried to influence who participates or to set the agenda. She is also at the mercy of a deadline she negotiated, and she hasn't cultivated attractive alternatives. Fortunately, she has recognized this dilemma in time, and she is eager to repair it using all of the structure-shaping tools at her disposal:

- *Changing the players:* Influencing who participates by adding and eliminating parties
- *BATNA building:* Improving your own alternatives or weakening your counterparts' (or both)
- *Setting the agenda:* Adding issues, deferring or eliminating others, and influencing the order in which issues get negotiated
- *Framing and reframing:* Influencing your counterparts' understanding of what is at stake and what is possible
- *Controlling information:* Influencing who gets access to which information and when
- *Forcing and delaying action:* Imposing deadlines and other kinds of time pressure that force your counterparts to make hard choices
- *Developing a sequencing plan:* Deciding on the order in which you will deal with other parties and make moves in linked negotiations

These strategies are implemented through a mutually reinforcing mix of actions at and away from the negotiating table. Away from the table, you can influence who participates and improve your BATNA. Controlling the agenda and framing (or reframing) the basic problem calls for face-to-face interaction. Will Claire be able to use these tools to level the playing field and correct her previous missteps? We'll look at some of the moves available to her and then work out a sequencing plan.

Changing the Players

A particularly potent way to shape the game is to influence who plays.[1] One method of doing this is to invite other players into the negotiation. Claire could consider inviting the bank into her negotiations with Eric. She can't do a deal with Eric unless she gets approval from the bank; her credit officer could bolster her case by saying to Eric, "We can't provide funding for this project if you [BargainMart] insist on these conditions." This maneuver could in turn help generate some creative agreements. For example, Eric might agree to help Claire find an alternative source of funding or provide some sort of guarantee.

At the same time, Eric might be able to convince the bank to relax its constraints. Note that Claire has positioned herself here as a kind of intermediary in negotiations between BargainMart and the bank; by changing the players, she has changed the game. She can support the bank on some points and Eric on others, all the while working to advance her substantive agenda. Of course, there are potential costs: by inviting in other players, Claire gives up some control over the process.

Inviting in parties is one way to change the players; working to exclude parties is another. Sometimes, though not in Claire's situation, it is advantageous to try to prevent parties from participating or to remove them from the game. In coalition-building situations, for example, it may be possible to marginalize implacable opponents in order to withhold from them the standing and opportunity to wield veto power. In some complex multiparty negotiations, there are simply too many participating parties to make expeditious progress. It may be possible to convince some to allow themselves to be represented by others as a way of reducing the core of negotiators.

PRACTICAL APPLICATION: CHANGING THE PLAYERS

Return to the negotiation you began to analyze in Chapter One, and answer the following questions:

- Could it be advantageous to invite other parties into the negotiation?
- Would it make sense to bring in a mediator?
- Are there parties involved that you might be able to exclude?
- If there are too many parties, can you convince some to allow themselves to be represented by others?

BATNA Building

Good alternatives to agreement are rarely lying around in plain sight, ripe for the picking. A more typical scenario is that your BATNA must be painstakingly built, maintained, and improved. But what if, like Claire, you are on the wrong side of a power imbalance? She runs a small, untested company, and this deal is crucial for her. Eric represents a large and respected retailer for whom this is one deal among many. Claire has no obvious way to influence Eric's BATNA unilaterally or to improve her own. What can she do?

Actually, Claire can do a lot to strengthen her alternatives (and weaken Eric's) before she resumes negotiations. But she has to think carefully and take some actions before returning to the table. Specifically, she should consider activating the latent power of competition, coalitions, and constraints.

Promote Competition. To harness the power of competition, Claire could have cultivated alternative negotiating partners and conducted competitively linked negotiations with them. Even now, it may not be too late to do so. How would Eric's perception of his alternatives shift if Claire opens negotiations with BargainMart's arch-rival, ValueShops? It depends on the threat posed by Value-Shops' interest, which in turn depends on the uniqueness of what Claire has to offer. Suppose that (1) ValueShops and BargainMart are locked in a fierce battle for market share, (2) Claire controls a very attractive site in an untapped market, and (3) the presence of one would effectively shut out the other. This combination of factors would substantially strengthen Claire's potential bargaining power: it would simultaneously worsen Eric's BATNA and improve Claire's.

Build Coalitions. In a situation like Claire's that involves more than two parties, coalitions can profoundly alter all the parties' BATNAs. A supportive coalition consisting of an attractive set of satellite stores would enhance Claire's ability to influence Eric. She might begin by negotiating with a few high-quality satellites, eventually making them conditional commitments along the lines of "Assuming that I'm successful in getting BargainMart, would you be interested in coming on board?" With a critical mass of conditional commitments, she can then go back to BargainMart to say, "If you are willing to sign on, I can deliver this very attractive set of satellites." At the same time, Claire can use the existence of the coalition of satellites to persuade Eric to be more flexible on use, assignment, and subletting by arguing, "They won't be willing to sign on unless they get assurances concerning non-competition in the event that you decide to alter your strategy, or to sublet portions of the space." Once Claire has BargainMart's commitment, she can return to negotiating over terms with the satellites.

Relax Constraints. When two negotiations must both reach fruition for an overall deal to go forward (reciprocal linkage), constraints in one negotiation can paralyze the overall deal. The key is to look for ways to loosen the most binding constraints. What are the most pressing constraints that Claire has to contend with?

The time pressure she is under because the option will run out and the restrictions imposed by her bank. To relax these constraints, Claire could negotiate with the landowner to extend her option on the land. She could also explore whether other sources of financing might offer more flexible conditions. She might even talk to several financing sources in parallel, once again drawing on the power of competition to improve her position. Successfully relaxing the constraints on timing and financing will simplify her dealings with Eric.

At other times, constraints in one negotiation can actually help you claim value in others. If the bank is unwilling to be more flexible, Claire can try to invoke the bank's requirements to convince Eric that he must be more flexible. Eric, in turn, can use constraints imposed by his boss (real or feigned) to convince Claire that he can't make concessions. Both would thus be using the constraints they face in a linked negotiation to bolster the credibility of their commitments to their positions.

PRACTICAL APPLICATION: BUILDING ONE'S BATNA

- How can you build your BATNA and (possibly) weaken the BATNA of your counterpart?
- Can you use the power of competition to strengthen your position?
- Can you build supportive coalitions?
- Can you relax binding constraints in linked negotiations or use them to bolster your commitments?

Setting the Agenda

It is crucial to have an impact early when the agenda is being set—when what will and won't be negotiated is being defined—before momentum builds in the wrong direction, or irreversible commitments are made, or too much time passes. Breakthrough negotiators treat the agenda not as fixed but as something that can be shaped. "Pay great attention to the agenda of the debate," cautions one experienced commentator on negotiation: "He who defines the issues and determines their priority is already well on the way to winning. . . . It is just as important, and on the same grounds, to deny your opponent the right to impose his language and concepts on the debate, and to make sure you always use terms that reflect your own values, traditions, and interests."[2]

Skilled negotiators typically negotiate over the agenda early on, seeking to define certain issues as nonnegotiable and to set preconditions before negotiating the substance. The Israelis declare that Jerusalem will remain their undivided capital; a union leader states that she will not consider pay-for-performance systems; Eric asserts that use, assignment, and subletting are effectively nonnegotiable. Negotiations over process details, such as where the negotiations will take place and who will represent the sides, also take place early on. Agenda setting often takes place during a prenegotiation session and sometimes continues at the negotiating table.

As we have seen, it is sometimes possible to create value by broadening the agenda to allow for mutually beneficial trades. Claire's diagnosis suggested the possibility of getting BargainMart to help with financing for the project. Claire could therefore try to add financing to the agenda by inquiring whether BargainMart would help her secure financing from a more flexible source. Success in doing this could allow her to give BargainMart more latitude on use, assignment, and subletting—and to create joint gains.

Agenda setting sometimes involves (though not in this case) postponing toxic issues or eliminating them from consideration. Inclusion of toxic issues can stymie progress on the rest of the agenda. If they can be deferred, agreement may be possible on the other issues. In a negotiation over a merger, for example, the question of who fills which positions in the combined entity is often left to the end. That way, both sides can more fully appreciate the benefits of the combination before grappling with the very difficult issue of control. Here again, early negotiations over the agenda can help to build momentum and prevent barriers from sabotaging the entire process.

PRACTICAL APPLICATION: SETTING THE AGENDA

- How did the agenda get defined?
- Who had the most influence in defining the agenda, and how did they influence it?
- Could you have added issues in order to expand opportunities for mutually beneficial trades?
- Could issues have been deferred or excluded to eliminate barriers to agreement?

Framing and Reframing

Framing is defining the problem to be solved and the set of potential solutions in a favorable way, by means of argument, analogy, and metaphor.[3] Skillful framing resonates with the target audience, evoking images and emotional reactions that influence the behavior of your counterparts, constituents, and other influential parties. Efforts to frame (or reframe) often consist of coordinated actions both at the negotiating table (by means of argument) and away from the table (such as through use of the media).

Negotiators often compete in a *frame game*—attempting to define the dominant frame for the negotiation, not only to persuade each other but also to influence the perceptions of other influential parties. Consider, for example, the efforts of a coalition of U.S. pharmaceutical, software, and entertainment companies in the early 1990s to win stronger protection for their intellectual property.[4] These companies were losing billions of dollars annually because of copying of drugs, computer programs, videos, and CDs in China, India, and other countries. Although copying was legal in those countries, the coalition undertook a campaign to label it as intellectual piracy, thus invoking powerful images of plunder and illegitimacy. The developing countries tried to frame the situation in terms of fairness, arguing that control of technology was a new form of colonialism. But the piracy framing stuck because it resonated with such key audiences as the U.S. Congress, the administration, and the press, and it strengthened efforts to build a supportive coalition in the United States, Japan, and Europe. The net result was agreement at the 1994 Uruguay Round of the General Agreement on Tariffs and Trade negotiations on a sweeping new set of global rules protecting intellectual property.

Framing is a particularly potent tool when your counterparts haven't yet decided what is at stake or fully developed their positions. By providing a compelling frame of reference that defines the problem (such as piracy) and a set of criteria for distinguishing good outcomes from bad, skilled negotiators can gain advantage at the start. Framing tactics work because (1) people's assessments of what is at stake tend to crystallize only when they confront the need to make choices, and (2) the conceptual frameworks, or mental models, that people employ to make sense of a situation depend on how that situation is presented to them.[5] As the intellectual piracy example illustrates, the art of framing is a matter of defining the problem and the options in ways that tap into particular preconceived beliefs and attitudes, elevating the importance of some interests and leaving others dormant.

Reframing is necessary when the existing frame has become a barrier to agreement.[6] Claire's diagnosis of the situation suggests that Eric has framed their negotiation in purely value-claiming, win-lose terms. He is not open to creative solutions or joint problem solving. He probably thinks he holds all the cards, which is why he is taking such a hard line. But she has pinpointed several promising opportunities for joint value creation. What can Claire do to reframe Eric's view of the problem and the options? As a start, she can try to convince him that no agreement is possible if he continues to approach the negotiation in this way.

Persuasive arguments are sometimes enough to accomplish this. What is the best argument Claire can make to convince Eric that BargainMart's standard clause can't be the basis for agreement? It would probably be most effective to point out the external constraints she faces. She could say to Eric, "If you insist on this clause, it won't be possible to go forward with the project. I won't be able to get financing, and I won't be able to convince satellite stores to sign on. I personally don't care that much about the provisions on use, transfer, and subletting. But we have to address the concerns of the bank and other potential tenants in order to move things forward."

If argument alone is not enough, Claire can leverage her BATNA-altering efforts to reframe the proceedings. Claire might tell Eric straightforwardly that she has extended her option on the land and begun discussions with ValueShops, putting him on notice that she has an alternative to dealing with him.

Once Eric is "unfrozen," she can work to plant a new conceptual structure in his head. For instance, she could prompt him with a suggestive model for joint gains that illustrates how differences in interests can create value: "I understand that you need some flexibility to alter your business to respond to changing conditions, but I can't give you unlimited flexibility. Also, I'm concerned about the short term, while you seem to want long-term flexibility. Perhaps we can reach a compromise that gives you more flexibility later on."

Finally, successful reframing often calls for helping your counterparts find face-saving ways to back away from their positions gracefully. Claire could say to Eric, "I understand BargainMart has a policy on these issues, and you're obligated to uphold it. But surely there have been other special situations in which you've made exceptions. We're a young company and don't have the same bargaining power with banks and satellites that larger developers do. Perhaps you could confer internally on this."

PRACTICAL APPLICATION: FRAMING AND REFRAMING

- How did the problem and the options get framed?
- Who was most influential in establishing the dominant frame, and how did they go about it?

- Did you overlook opportunities to reframe the game? What might you have done differently?

Controlling Information

Power flows to those who control other parties' access to information.[7] Information control techniques are especially potent when you have private access to valuable information (which makes sharing versus withholding it a key decision) and when negotiations involve multiple parties and interlocking levels of decision making (which makes who to share it with, and when, highly significant). Consider, for example, Claire's linked negotiations with ValueShops and BargainMart. Neither knows that she plans to conduct these negotiations in parallel, so Claire has an informational advantage: she knows something important that the other players don't. When and how should she reveal this information, given that it is clearly in her interest to do so at some point?

Suppose she could start over and decided to negotiate first with ValueShops. Should she reveal that she planned to negotiate with BargainMart too? Not right away, because she would want ValueShops to feel invested in these negotiations and hence to make an attractive offer (which she can then shop to BargainMart). If ValueShops asked, she could have truthfully answered that she approached them first and that her next steps would depend on how things go in their discussions; the specter of BargainMart need not have been raised explicitly at this point.

Now suppose that her initial discussions with ValueShops went well. Should she proceed to negotiate a detailed agreement with ValueShops? Probably not. Instead, she might say she that had some thinking to do and open up dialogue with BargainMart. Should she then reveal to BargainMart that she had been talking to ValueShops? Yes—but she should frame her message with care. She could say, truthfully, that she had had some initial discussions with ValueShops, but that they had not reached the point of serious negotiation. She could also reveal her preference for a deal with BargainMart and work at launching serious negotiations with them, while making clear that she planned to continue her discussions with ValueShops. If things went well with Bargain-Mart, she might solicit a detailed offer. But if progress bogged down, she could return to ValueShops and let BargainMart know that she was doing so. Once she had an offer from BargainMart, she could communicate it to ValueShops to see if she could get substantially better terms, and so on. In this way, Claire could use her position as a bridge between linked negotiations to shape the perceptions of other players.

Broadly speaking, information control relies on several types of techniques:

- *Sharing information selectively.* As Claire has demonstrated, privately held information and analysis can be employed as a tool to shape the beliefs and attitudes of other parties. This type of information control is a matter of "withholding information, releasing information at pre-determined times, releasing information in juxtaposition with other information that may influence perceptions, . . . [and] communicating information to selected audiences."[8]

- *Influencing patterns of communication.* Another form of information control consists of encouraging or discouraging communication among other parties to the negotiation. Convening potential allies—such as, in Claire's case, a group of prospective satellite tenants—can have a potent effect on coalition building. Although not the case in Claire's situation, it is sometimes also possible to disrupt potential opponents' efforts to communicate and organize.

- *Drafting agreements.* The question of who will draft agreements provides another opportunity for information control. If Claire can convince Eric to let her draft the first comprehensive written proposal, she will gain some control over how key provisions are phrased. As one experienced corporate deal maker put it, "We always do the drafting, partly because we think we are better at it. These are very complex deals, and your ability to do the drafting gives you an advantage."

Efforts to control who gets access to what information often go hand in glove with decisions about issue sequencing, or the order in which issues get negotiated. Issue sequencing can have a powerful impact on your ability to create and claim value. In multiparty situations, furthermore, the sequence in which issues get negotiated can influence the formation of coalitions. By focusing on an issue that divides potential opponents early on, you can sometimes forestall formation of a blocking coalition; and opening with an issue on which you and potential allies agree may help to seal a winning coalition and build momentum.[9]

Consider Claire's linked negotiations with BargainMart and with potential satellite tenants. It would probably make sense for her to try to get some good satellites on board before talking to BargainMart. She could then reveal to Eric that she has provisional agreements, thus influencing his perceptions of the attractiveness of the deal. But should she negotiate a full set of terms with the satellites before negotiating with BargainMart? Probably not, because the satellites would press for more attractive terms if they knew she had not yet signed BargainMart. Instead, she might negotiate over the basic outlines of an agreement with key satellites, then do a deal with BargainMart, and finally return to negotiate the details with the satellites—an example of *bootstrapping*.

PRACTICAL APPLICATION: CONTROLLING INFORMATION

- Did you have (or could you have had) access to important information that other parties lacked?
- Would it have been more advantageous to share that information or to withhold it?
- When was the best time to reveal what pieces of information?

- Could you have advantageously promoted or impeded communication among other parties?

- Could you have exerted more control over the drafting of agreements?

- How might information control have been synchronized with issue sequencing?

Forcing Action or Buying Time

Deadlines and other forms of time pressure can effectively build momentum toward agreement.[10] Claire is facing a serious *action-forcing event:* she has to do the deal before her option on the land runs out. Meanwhile, though, she may be able to engineer her own action-forcing events to induce Eric to make hard choices.

Linkages among negotiations offer one way for Claire to create time pressure. Suppose she gets ValueShops to make an attractive offer and then communicates it to Eric. Claire may then be able to propose an exploding offer: a take-it-or-leave-it package linked to a deadline for acceptance or rejection. In response, Eric could feel compelled to make a concession. Action-forcing events play a role in internal decision-making processes as well. If Eric is facing internal resistance to relaxing company policy, Claire's efforts to force action by negotiating with ValueShops may actually help Eric to move things forward. In this and other ways, negotiators explicitly or implicitly collude to build momentum.

Similarly, the need to complete one set of negotiations before undertaking another (sequential linkage) can be used either to stimulate action or to excuse delay. Success in driving the first set of negotiations to completion may stimulate action in the follow-on set. Similarly, delaying completion of one set of negotiations may effectively delay the second set of negotiations.

Negotiators frequently use delay to buy time for their alternatives to improve, or for others' interests to shift. When an action-forcing event is disadvantageous, you should look for ways to relax its hold over you. If Claire can extend her option on the land, for instance, she will gain time to make other structure-shaping moves. Of course, your counterpart may try to prevent such moves. Eric could try to wriggle out of Claire's exploding offer, for example, by accepting it "provisionally" and asserting that he has concerns he has to raise with higher-ups, attempting to use a ratification tactic.

Action-forcing events need not be deadlines. Simply calling a meeting or scheduling the right telephone call can sometimes serve to force action.

PRACTICAL APPLICATION: FORCING OR DELAYING ACTION

- What forced action to occur? How were the parties (including you) induced to make the hard choices necessary to reach agreement?

- Who was more effective at shaping the pace of the process, you or your counterparts?

- Could you have used action-forcing events to build momentum?

- If you were subject to time pressure, could you have relaxed its impact on you?

Developing a Sequencing Plan

Claire has already begun to develop a *sequencing plan* that moves the process in desired directions, as we saw in our discussion of her dealings with ValueShops and BargainMart.[11] Now she is ready to flesh out her sequencing plan in more detail, working out the series of moves she will make to create momentum in the linked system of negotiations.

Her first move (M_1—that is, Move 1—in the figure on page 68) should clearly be to buy more time by negotiating to extend the option on the land. Making this a top priority is in keeping with a basic rule of thumb for sequencing: *seek to relax your most binding*

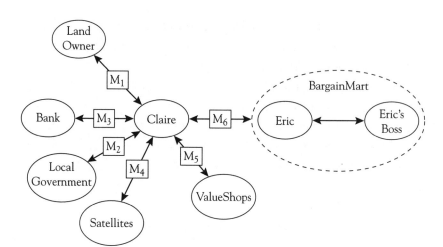

constraints early on. If you can't do that, you may not have the time or resources to work through the rest of your plan. If Claire can get an additional six months, life gets a lot easier.

Her next move should be to talk to local government about building the infrastructure to support the mall, such as roads and utilities. She might also explore whether she can get a tax break. It's important for Claire to talk to the municipality before she goes too far down the road with the project. Key officials must believe that the community has something at stake in making the project work and not be presented with a fait accompli. If Claire already had all the details wrapped up and agreements signed with BargainMart and the satellites, the town would know she was irreversibly committed and would have no incentive to make concessions. This is an example of another sequencing principle: *nail down agreements with parties who have a strong stake in the outcome early, before you are committed to going forward regardless.*

Her third move is to talk to the bank and other possible sources of financing. The agenda here is not just to see if the bank will loosen its requirements, but also to clarify precisely what those requirements are. This move embodies another general sequencing rule: *seek to solidify advantageous external constraints, and then lever-*

age those constraints in linked negotiations. If Claire can go to Eric with an iron-clad set of conditions from the bank, she will be well situated to get him to back away from his position or to help her come up with a creative option.

Her fourth move is to begin to build a coalition of satellites by launching exploratory negotiations with them. Here too, sequencing matters. Claire should think carefully about the order in which to approach potential allies, keeping in mind another principle of sequencing: *once you have the right initial ally or allies, it is easier to recruit others.* She should begin by thinking through who defers to whom on a given set of issues—or, to put it another way, who is likely to be swayed by whose endorsement?

This kind of sequencing transforms uncommitted parties' perceptions of their BATNAs. Initially, their options are twofold: to join your coalition or not. Once you have assembled a critical mass of support, they face quite a different choice: to join the coalition or be left behind. This is the critical mass principle at work: as your likelihood of prevailing grows, recruiting becomes increasingly easy. Claire might decide to approach a highly respected satellite first and then leverage its support. Alternatively, she might choose to recruit a few very good satellites first, to create a *bandwagon effect*, and only then approach the tougher-to-recruit ones.

Then, with a better grasp of her constraints and resources, she will be in a stronger position to open up dialogue with ValueShops (M_5). And not until this point would she go to the table to negotiate with Eric (M_6). As we have seen, Claire can potentially gain leverage by sequencing back and forth between these competitively linked negotiations. This strategy illustrates yet another sequencing principle: *preserve your options in competitively linked negotiations as long as possible.* Eventually, Claire will have to do a deal with BargainMart or ValueShops, so at some point she will have to break off one of these negotiations. But if she does so too early, she leaves herself in a more vulnerable position, like the one she got into by negotiating only with BargainMart in the first place.

This is not the only feasible sequence of moves open to Claire, but it's a good initial plan. Naturally, Claire should keep in mind that other players will also try to shape the game, and she should be prepared to respond to events flexibly. The first mover has an important advantage, so it's well worth the effort to try to anticipate others' moves and get there first. At the same time, you should try to forestall *reactive coalition building*. If other parties are alarmed by your coalition-building moves, you may provoke formation of a blocking coalition.

You should also be prepared to respond to your counterparts' efforts to use sequencing to undermine your position in linked negotiations. For example, Eric may be negotiating over another site, elsewhere in the area, without Claire's knowledge. He could even be dragging out his negotiations with her to prevent her from doing a deal with someone else until he completes the other negotiations.

PRACTICAL APPLICATION: DEVELOPING A SEQUENCING PLAN

- How effective were you at planning a sequence of moves that advanced the process in favorable directions?
- Could you have exploited patterns of deference?
- Were there opportunities to sequence in building coalitions?
- What might you do differently the next time?

CHANGING THE GAME

At the beginning of the chapter, Claire appeared to be disadvantaged by her own initial missteps. But if she implements the corrective plan she has developed, she will be in a much stronger position. Claire will have leveled the playing field by purposefully shaping the structure—by changing the players, altering BATNAs, setting the agenda, reframing Eric's view of the process, controlling the flow of information, forcing and deferring action, and developing a promising sequencing plan.

Now that you are familiar with shaping the structure of a negotiation, we will take a close look at the next core task: managing the process of interacting with your counterparts across the table.

3

Managing the Process

Van Bolton, Global Corporation's new CEO, had expected things to go quite differently. Bolton had recently announced Global Airways' intent to acquire Regional Air, a small East Coast carrier, for $100 million in cash. To his surprise, the resulting bitter dispute with Global's pilots' union had already cost Global over $70 million in lost revenues and saddled the union with a $10 million fine that threatened to bankrupt it.

Bolton had expected a more favorable reaction from the pilots' union, in that the takeover would boost traffic on Global's East Coast routes, thus preserving jobs. It would also expand the union's membership base. The company's eighty-five hundred pilots were represented by the Airline Pilots' Union (APU), an in-house union. Regional Air's three hundred pilots belonged to the rival International Pilots' Society (IPS), the far larger union that represented pilots at most other U.S. airlines. Now they would become members of the APU.

Even before the acquisition, Global's relations with its pilots had been badly strained. Throughout the 1980s and 1990s, Bolton's predecessor had sought to reduce labor costs sharply. During a downturn, the former CEO had successfully imposed a two-tier wage system that sharply lowered the pay of newly hired pilots and provoked rifts within the union. Later, he had furloughed over six hundred pilots for two years, costing them both lost wages and service time for calculating pensions and other benefits. This history of conflict had radicalized Global's pilots, and the union leaders who came to power in the mid-1990s had campaigned on a platform of "no more givebacks." Bolton had been CEO for less than a year, but he had been with Global for close to twenty years. He had a reputation for toughness and attention to detail. The pilots understandably viewed him and his management team with distrust.

When Bolton announced the Regional Air acquisition, union president Stuart Adams, a former air force fighter pilot and aggressive defender of union rights, fired off a letter of protest, demanding a meeting to discuss how the smaller airline would be integrated into Global. The APU leader feared that Global would operate Regional as a separate low-cost carrier, using lower-paid pilots. But Bolton pushed the deal through without reaching agreement with Adams over how to merge Regional into the larger company. Adams's second letter of protest, distributed to the union's membership, asserted that management's handling of the acquisition was in violation of the collective bargaining agreement's stipulation that "all flying done for Global must be done by Global pilots" and demanded full and immediate integration of Regional. Bolton shot back, "During our last round of negotiations, APU never proposed that we abandon the established practice of maintaining an acquired carrier as a separate entity while a transition agreement is negotiated, a practice that has taken place at Global and is common in the industry."

Adams pointed out that "a senior Regional captain flying a 150-seat MD-80 earns less than a Global captain flying a 55-seat regional jet. That would be a terrible precedent, to allow that to continue." Global captains earned $150,000, Regional pilots roughly half of that. Invoking the earlier negotiations that had produced the two-tier wage structure, Adams expressed alarm "that the Regional Air acquisition could well represent another effort by management to establish a two-tier wage scale at Global Airlines."

Adams demanded that Regional pilots start at the bottom of the APU seniority list but receive immediate raises to match

Global's wage scales. The additional cost to Global was estimated at $50 million. A spokesman for the Regional pilots protested, "We should not have all our years of service ripped away from us. Many of us are in the last years of our career here, and we should-n't be treated as new hires."

Knowledgeable observers pointed out that the dispute actually had little to do with Global's acquisition of Regional. The real is-sues appeared to be the integrity of the APU contract and Global's strategy in a consolidating industry. One senior Global executive was on record as having said, "It's about control. The pilots want to be right there in the decision of whether we buy another com-pany or not."

Global's pilots were prohibited by federal labor law from strik-ing over the Regional Air dispute. But soon after the acquisition was announced, the pilots refused to work overtime and began call-ing in sick. At the peak of the ensuing ten-day sick-out, Global cancelled over 50 percent of its flights. The cost to the airline was estimated at over $70 million. Global's management immediately sought an injunction in U.S. district court. The judge issued a tem-porary restraining order to end the sick-out, comparing the pilots' response to "killing a gnat with a sledgehammer." But the union refused to back down.

On the eighth day of the sick-out, the court found the union in contempt and imposed a $5 million fine. The sick-out ended, but the dispute remained unresolved. The judge then ordered the APU to pay Global $10 million in damages, more than the union's total assets. Adams and other union officers were also found per-sonally liable. The union appealed unsuccessfully.

If the APU was forced to pay, Bolton knew, it would bankrupt the union. Destruction of the in-house union could, in turn, trig-ger a move by Global's pilots to the industry-wide International Pilots' Society (IPS), increasing the larger union's clout. This was not a desirable outcome. Meanwhile, Bolton understood, dissatis-faction with APU leadership was growing within the union, es-pecially among more radical pilots who saw no reason to end the sick-out. Adams could be difficult, but Bolton preferred dealing with him to the probable alternatives.

Further complicating matters, Global was facing other issues in its negotiations with the APU. The pilots' contract was due to expire in a year, and the union was pressing management for a stipulation that its members fly all jets with more than fifty seats, including those increasingly being flown by Global Focus, the company's lower-cost commuter subsidiary, which was not unionized. (Both Global Airways and Global Focus were wholly owned subsidiaries of Global Corporation.)

How should Global's CEO Bolton approach negotiations with the APU's President Adams over the integration of Regional Air?

DIAGNOSING THE SITUATION

First, take a few minutes to apply some of the principles you have already encountered to this negotiation. Examine the situation with Global's interests in mind, but devote equal attention to analyzing the union's point of view, interests, and circumstances.

Begin by sketching out the parties and linked system of negotiations, answering the following questions:

1. Have past negotiations between the company and the union created important precedents? Are the current negotiations being carried out in the shadow of future ones? Are concurrent sets of negotiations linked?

2. Give some thought to negotiations *within* the company and the union. What are the key dynamics there? What barriers and opportunities do they present?

3. Think about the rules of the game. What sets of rules influence these negotiations? How might Bolton use the rules to his advantage?

4. Define the issues. What are the existing and potential issues in the dispute between Global and the APU? How might issues be linked or delinked?

5. Assess each party's interests and BATNA. What do the managers and union leaders really care about, and what are their alternatives in the event of no agreement?

6. Think about potential bases for agreement. How might Bolton and Adams bridge key differences? What might a potential deal look like?

7. Based on this assessment, what are the *key barriers and opportunities facing Bolton?*

SHAPING THE STRUCTURE

Think about how Bolton could shape the structure of the negotiation. Should he try to bring in other parties, such as a federal mediator? If so, who, how, and when? Should he try to broaden the originally agreed agenda, perhaps by proposing to Adams that they link the Regional acquisition to the issue of who will fly Regional jets? Or should he try to narrow the agenda? How should he try to frame the situation? With whom should he meet, and in what sequence? Take a few minutes to fill out the following table.

Shaping the Structure	Possible Approaches
Changing the players	
BATNA building	
Setting the agenda	
Framing	
Controlling the flow of information	
Sequencing	
Setting up action-forcing events	

MANAGING THE PROCESS

The next task before going to the negotiating table is to think through how Bolton should manage the face-to-face negotiations. Managing the process is the third major element of the breakthrough negotiation framework. Whoever controls the process powerfully influences the substance and outcomes of negotiations. This is especially true in complex situations that allow one to take advantage of the fog of negotiation—that is, the atmosphere of complexity, ambiguity, and uncertainty that characterizes most real-world negotiations.

Managing the at-the-table process requires, first and foremost, understanding the core dynamics of the negotiation process. To fully understand a process as complex as the negotiation that Taylor and Adams are engaged in, we have to examine it from several complementary points of view. First, it helps to recognize the sequence of stages through which this negotiation proceeds. It is also productive to deepen this macro-look with a more micro-examination of the turbulent minute-by-minute interactions among the participants. At the same time, we can benefit from an attentive look at the evolution of the negotiators' internal mental states as the process proceeds. These perspectives represent progressive levels of resolution. We have chosen to call them the macro-flow lens, the micro-interaction lens, and the mental process lens. Each lens provides a distinct perspective on an important dimension of negotiation. Together, they provide negotiators with the complete view of negotiation dynamics necessary to effectively manage the process.

The Macro-Flow Lens

As William Zartman and Maureen Berman pointed out, virtually any negotiation—whether it involves dispute resolution or deal making—passes through distinct phases as it progresses from initiation to agreement or impasse.[1] During the diagnostic phase, negotiators evaluate the circumstances and opportunity and decide whether to go to the table. This is the juncture that Bolton and Adams are at right now. If they decide to negotiate, they will move on to the formula stage and begin to grope for the basic framework, or formula, for a deal. If they find a promising formula, they will move on to the detailed-bargaining stage and shift to hard bargaining over details. If agreement eludes them, they may cycle back and search for a better formula. Or they may break off negotiations, triggering a new round of escalation in their dispute. The characteristic features of each phase are summarized in the table at the bottom of the page.

Tailoring Your Posture to the Phase. Different phases call for different negotiating postures. The diagnostic phase is the time to establish (or repair) relationships. Van Bolton would be well advised to work on Global's relationship with the union by involving third parties or carefully crafting his negotiating team or by reaching out personally to the union's leaders.

The formula phase is the time to cast a wide net in pursuit of ways to create value and bridge differences. If he gets to the table with Adams, Bolton should use his analysis of potential agreements to put forward a promising formula, perhaps broadening the agenda to permit more trades to be made.

The detailed-bargaining phase is the time to hammer out the minutiae—calling for persistence, a steady eye on the goal, and a strong stomach. Whatever relationship capital you can amass in the diagnostic and formula phases will be spent when the going gets tough in the detailed-bargaining phase.

Matching People to the Phase. Different phases of negotiation often involve different people. When should Van Bolton get personally involved, and when should he put the negotiations in the

Phases in the Flow of Negotiation

Diagnostic phase	The parties weigh the merits of negotiation and its alternatives, gather information (learn) in support of this objective, and engage in exploratory prenegotiation dialogue.
Formula phase	The parties seek the basic formula: the core set of principles and trades that will serve as an overarching framework for agreement.
Detailed-bargaining phase	The parties bargain over specific terms.

hands of subordinates? In merger and acquisition negotiations, the CEOs of the buyer and seller organizations typically meet at the start to agree that a deal makes sense and again at the end to make final concessions and bless the deal. In between their bookend appearances, subordinates and investment bankers work out the basic formula while lawyers hammer out tax and warranty considerations and draft the agreement. Similarly, diplomats hammer out the details of agreements initiated and concluded by national leaders. Bolton should probably plan to meet with Stuart Adams to launch the process, set the agenda, and agree on goals and ground rules. Most of the hard bargaining will be delegated to knowledgeable subordinates, and Bolton and Adams can reconvene at the end to seal the deal.

PRACTICAL APPLICATION: IDENTIFYING THE STAGES

Think about the various types of negotiations you engage in:

- What stages do they usually go through?
- What are the characteristic challenges of each stage?
- How do you alter your approach from one stage to the next?
- Who is usually involved at each stage, and what roles do they play?

The Micro-Interaction Lens

Viewed through the macro-flow lens, negotiations can seem to flow smoothly from phase to phase. We may occasionally wish this were the whole story, but if it were, negotiation would be a less compelling pursuit. Viewed at a higher level of resolution, we can see that negotiations consist of a complex sequence of micro-interactions as the parties share information, table offers, and make concessions. These micro-interactions are profoundly nonlinear in nature, and small actions may have disproportionate impacts.[2]

Suppose Van Bolton makes Adams a specific offer to end the dispute. Will his offer provoke (1) clarifying questions, (2) a concession by the union, or (3) outrage and a breakdown in the talks? It depends on the two men's relationship, the prior history of the process, the stakes, and the offer's content and formulation. Adams's response is not fully predictable, but Bolton can exercise some control over it by building rapport with Adams, laying the groundwork for his arguments, and framing the offer. Adams in turn enjoys some control over his response: he may decide to suppress his annoyance, for instance, or fake outrage. But forces beyond his control, such as his own emotions or internal politics within the union, may constrict his ability to manage the process.

To grasp how this micro-oriented take on the process complements the macro-oriented overview, think about the flow of a river. We can predict fairly accurately how much water will flow from one point to another over a long period, but flow on a given day is much harder to predict. From a distance, the river appears smooth-flowing, but up close even the gentlest stream reveals eddies and whirlpools. Both perspectives accurately describe the river, and the macro-flow and micro-interaction views both illuminate the dynamics of negotiation.

Although unquestionably challenging to manage, order is apparent in the seeming chaos of micro-interactions among negotiators. Specifically, negotiations exhibit characteristic nonlinear patterns that can be shaped if the negotiator is aware of them and prepared to exploit them. Each of these micro-level dynamics can contribute to the creation of either vicious and virtuous cycles.

Sensitivity to Early Interactions.   How a negotiation begins tinges everything thereafter. Initial impressions, based on limited information, persist and are resistant to change, and no relationship buffer exists yet to smooth over early rough spots. If Bolton builds mutual respect and rapport with Adams up front, the likelihood of agreement increases; by the same token, bad blood at the start can poison all that follows. Similarly, promptly taking charge of the agenda and shaping the other side's views of what is at stake makes it easier to create and claim value later.

Negotiating representatives should therefore be chosen with great care, because human chemistry and sensitivity to social norms matter. Every negotiation should be thought of as a casting call. What kind of person would best manage this relationship? Demonstrations of sensitivity to cultural and social norms can powerfully affect initial impressions. If the union has a history of poor relationships with the vice president of labor relations, for example, Bolton might be well advised to lead early interactions himself, rather than reinforce a nonproductive dynamic.

Irreversibilities. Negotiators often walk through doors that lock behind them. Once a conflict has begun to fester, as in the Global-APU case, attitudes harden. And once you have made a concession, attempts to take it back may poison relationships and damage your reputation. Actions that undermine trust are particularly likely to provoke irreversible changes in peoples' attitudes toward each other. As the old adage puts it, "Once bitten, twice shy."

Irreversibility has its uses, though. If Global can persuade the union to make a small commitment to flexibility, such as about the timing of integrating Regional, it may be possible to leverage it into a more substantial commitment. This is an example of the strategy of entanglement—moving people through a series of small, irreversible commitments to do something they wouldn't have done in a single leap.[3]

Tipping Points. When a negotiation reaches a threshold, or "tipping point," even small, incremental moves result in very large shifts.[4] In escalating conflicts like this one, seemingly minor provocations may trigger a downhill slide into all-out war. If two nations are close to war, for example, even a small skirmish can trigger a broader conflict. At the same time, negotiators sometimes reach thresholds where incremental effort moves their relationship into a new, much more positive dynamic.

Bolton needs to recognize the approach of tipping points beyond which new sets of rules will apply. Has the other side been pushed to the point where they will no longer react rationally to threats or inducements? Are they close to feeling forced to adopt desperate means? Is it time to call for a break to let things cool off? Such strategies for pulling back from such thresholds belong in every negotiator's toolbox. So does awareness of your own emotional thresholds and coping mechanisms to avoid being pushed over the edge. Bolton should be very careful when raising issues that are hot buttons for the other side, such as "making the pilots whole" for the lost time during furlough or the question of who will fly Global's growing fleet of small regional jets.

Vicious and Virtuous Cycles. Once a pattern of interaction gets established, it readily becomes self-reinforcing. The result may be either a virtuous cycle that builds momentum toward a desirable outcome or a vicious cycle that spirals into breakdown. If Adams feels threatened, he may adopt defensive tactics that trigger similar responses from Bolton. On the other hand, a productive working relationship can function as a psychological buffer during the inevitable tough times.

It is instructive to approach micro-interactions with an eye to creating virtuous cycles—positive feedback loops that move the process in promising directions—and avoiding vicious cycles. Are Bolton's actions contributing to building momentum toward or away from agreement? How can he prevent undesirable momentum? How can he get Adams headed in the direction he wants? It is far easier to prevent negative feedback loops than to break them once they get established.

Path Dependence. The specific path or sequence that negotiators choose matters a great deal. This point pertains to both the starting point you choose (sensitivity to early interactions) and irreversibility (once you have started down a path, you can't go back). Some paths build momentum and create virtuous cycles.

Effective preparation on the part of all sides, for example, contributes to mutual confidence, which promotes judicious information sharing. Other paths undermine progress and initiate vicious cycles. Poor preparation on the part of any participants creates a sense of vulnerability that may lead to defensiveness and compensatory toughness. This is likely to provoke matching responses from counterparts, impeding communication and reinforcing positional bargaining.

A negotiator should therefore develop a sequencing plan, detailing in what order to talk to others and the sequence in which issues will be raised. A central sequencing question for Bolton is whether to seek federal mediation early, and hence appear conciliatory to outside audiences, or wait to see what happens in initial negotiations with the union.

Even the most skilled negotiator's ability to influence the course of events has limits. But you need to hone the ability to recognize and use nonlinearities to build momentum in desired directions by, for example, establishing a constructive tone early, encouraging incremental moves in productive directions, and engineering action-forcing events.

PRACTICAL APPLICATION: MANAGING MICRO-INTERACTIONS

Think about a recent negotiation that didn't go well:

- Did your actions contribute to the creation of vicious cycles?

- Did early interactions have a big impact?

- Were irreversibilities a factor?

- In retrospect, did thresholds get crossed that you should have pulled back from?

- If you had it to do over, would you choose a different sequence of actions?

Vicious and Virtuous Cycles

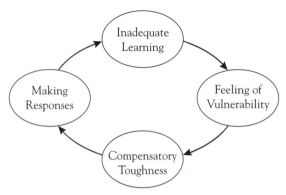

A vicious cycle: Poor preparation on the part of one negotiating team creates a sense of vulnerability that leads them to engage in compensatory toughness. This provokes matching responses from their counterparts, which impedes communication and reinforces positional bargaining.

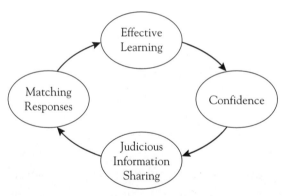

A virtuous cycle: Effective preparation on the part of both teams leads to mutual confidence, which promotes judicious information-sharing and matching responses.

The Mental Process Lens

Finally, the negotiators themselves will unavoidably leave their imprints on the negotiation. What goes on inside their heads—their mental models, motivational drives, aspirations, and emotions—is likely to shape the proceedings and the outcome, often in a decisive way. It is worthwhile to look closely at how negotiators' mental processes evolve in parallel with the flow of events and interactions.

Mental Models. Like all of us, negotiators perceive new experiences using established interpretive frameworks, or *mental models*.[5] Mental models mediate between our observations and experiences and our interpretation of them, enabling us to make sense of a novel situation. They embody our beliefs about cause and effect, others' intentions, and the lessons of history.[6] How are Adams's and Bolton's mental models likely to differ? What formative experiences have shaped their perceptions of what is and isn't desirable? How are they likely to view each other and make attributions about each other's intentions? What implications do these differences have for their negotiation?

Without mental models, we would have to figure out every new situation from scratch. But embedded mental models also promote rigidity and block learning in new situations. What will happen, for example, if Bolton and Adams consistently approach their negotiation with zero-sum mind-sets? The frameworks that negotiators use to interpret reality are often so deeply embedded in their psyches that they are unaware of their biases. As a result, they may overlook information that is inconsistent with cherished truths—a process known as selective perception. Conversely, people tend to seek evidence that confirms their biases: if union members expect hostility from management, they may devalue conciliatory gestures as tricks or traps—a bias known as *reactive devaluation*.[7] Suppose Bolton offers a concession on making the furloughed pilots whole. Will the pilots see it as conciliatory or a sign of weakness?

Motivational Drives. Negotiators are often driven by inner psychological needs or motivational drives. Because Bolton is a new CEO, still operating in the shadow of his predecessor, he may feel he can't afford a reputation for weakness toward unions. And what about Adams? How deeply does he care about maintaining control of the union? About winning the engagement with Bolton? When assessing your counterparts' motivational drives (and your own), you should think in terms of the following motivations. All are likely to be present to some degree, but which are dominant? What are the implications for how you need to manage the process?

Maintaining control: In order to feel competent, do they need to feel in control of the process and not controlled by others?

Exercising power: Do they need to "win" or to dominate their counterparts, and perhaps to demonstrate to others that they are doing so?

Preserving reputation: Are they preoccupied with maintaining a reputation as effective (perhaps "tough") negotiators?

Being consistent: Do they care about maintaining consistency (or appearing to) with prior commitments or statements of principle?[8]

Maintaining relationships: Do they care about preserving relationships and being liked?

Bolton and Adams both appear to have high needs for power, so we shouldn't be surprised if they become embroiled in an escalating quest for dominance. Alternatively, though, if one of them taps into the other's motivational drives, it can prove to be a potent source of advantage. Getting a potential ally with a high need for consistency to make a public commitment of support, for example, may create a potent block to backsliding. Offering a counterpart who is protective of his reputation a face-saving way to back down can help avoid impasse. Can Bolton help Adams to back away gracefully from his demand for immediate integration of Regional into Global and to save face? What would represent a "win" for Adams?

Aspirations. Negotiators approach the table with goals in mind. These aspirations typically take two forms: "red lines" that can't be crossed without creating psychological havoc, and outcomes that would generate delight. What are Bolton's red lines in this dispute? What are Adams's?

Because our minds tend to operate in relative rather than absolute terms, the process of setting goals is inherently subjective. Negotiators often measure success in terms of an initial reference point: Will I experience a gain or a loss relative to where I am today? Most people fight harder to avoid loss than they do to capture an equivalent gain. So Bolton should try to figure out what reference points Adams uses in setting goals. What is Adams trying to achieve? Is he really seeking immediate integration of Regional Air into Global, or would some incremental process be acceptable? Pinpointing how Adams sets goals will also equip Bolton to shape Adams's reference points, perhaps by means of anchoring tactics or threats.[9]

The solidity of the other side's commitment to its goals matters too. Negotiators who set their sights high tend to do better than those with lower aspirations.[10] However, unrealistic expectations function as a barrier to agreement. Negotiators who commit to specific goals sometimes pursue them doggedly long after it has become clear that their objectives are unrealistic. If Adams promises his constituents never to compromise, he may find himself in a box of his own making. If no agreement results when a mutually beneficial agreement was possible, the negotiators may have fallen prey to overcommitment.

The main antidotes to overcommitment are skillful learning, flexibility, and the capacity to craft face-saving compromises. Is there a formula that would allow the parties to back away from this dispute gracefully? As we have seen, you can't hope to have full information at the outset; you must learn and unlearn at the table. As you learn about the bargaining range and others' interests, you can adjust your aspirations accordingly.

But there's no escaping the fundamental tension between commitment and flexibility. This tension arises because both sides try to shape their counterparts' perceptions in such a way as to deflate their aspirations. Techniques like anchoring are explicitly designed to shape perceptions of the bargaining range. This means that learning and goal setting take place under conditions of adversity and uncertainty. Do I have to accept less than I aspire to, or has my counterpart successfully shaped my perceptions? Am I committed or overcommitted?

Emotions. Emotions, real and feigned, enter into most negotiations. A timely display of anger, for example, can demonstrate resolve so long as it is employed infrequently. At the same time, escalating disagreements and the emotions they engender can crowd out rational assessments. Emotions are certainly running high in the Global Airlines case. What can Bolton do to moderate them?

Emotions have predictable life cycles, and they also produce residues that persist and complicate the negotiation process.[11] Over the course of a negotiation, participants typically experience cycles of optimism and discouragement. Optimism builds as the process moves in favorable directions; discouragement sets in when negotiations bog down and tough choices have to be made. But optimism is not necessarily an unalloyed good, nor does discouragement presage failure. Overconfidence can contribute to impasse, and discouragement often stimulates a useful reassessment of goals and alternatives.

Intense anger often flares in negotiation. Real damage may have been done (lives may even have been lost) or a norm may have been violated (the other side could have withdrawn a concession). But negotiators are also subject to inner turmoil, and hence anger, because of their motivational drives. A sense of loss of control, for example, could trigger defensive reactions in negotiators like Adams who have a strong need for control. Feelings of shame can also trigger anger.

Once strong emotions are triggered, they dissipate slowly. The psychological and hormonal effects of anger can't simply be turned off; the result may be temporary inability to think rationally about the costs and benefits of your own actions. Time must pass before you settle down and become open to reflection and persuasion. Skilled negotiators track their own and their counterparts' emotional temperatures in order to assess when to push, when to back away, and when to let things cool off.

Care must also be taken not to let emotions irreversibly color negotiators' attitudes toward each other. A sense of betrayal or personal insult can infect the process and contribute to a vicious cycle. As Roger Fisher and William Ury note in *Getting to Yes*, the ideal stance is to "separate the people from the problem." Bolton should try to focus the negotiations on the substantive issues and adopt a problem-solving attitude. He should resist getting caught up in power games or personal attacks, even if Adams provokes him.

PRACTICAL APPLICATION: SHAPING MENTAL PROCESSES

Think of a counterpart with whom you recently negotiated:

- What role did his or her mental models play in shaping the process? Did your mental models differ, and if so how?

- What were her or his most important motivational drives, and how did they influence the negotiation? Based on what you know now, what would you have done differently?

- What role did aspirations play in your interactions? Was your counterpart undercommitted or overcommitted to a position?

- What role did emotions play in your negotiations? In retrospect, would you have managed the emotional dynamics differently?

PLANNING STRATEGY

The point of examining the negotiation process at these three different degrees of resolution is to equip you to manage at-the-table interactions more productively. If agreement is your objective, the fundamental goals at the table are twofold: (1) to learn about your counterpart's interests, alternatives, and bottom lines and (2) to shape your counterpart's perceptions of what is attainable in order to gain a favorable agreement within the bargaining range. In other words, Bolton's agenda should be to learn about Adams's interests and walk-aways and to shape Adams's perceptions of what is acceptable. As we will see, efforts to learn and to shape perceptions inevitably come into conflict; that's what makes face-to-face negotiation so compelling.

In planning what to do at the table, Bolton and his team should think through (1) what they want to learn from the union side, (2) what changes they want to bring about in the other side's perceptions, and (3) what strategies they will use. Bolton should also try to anticipate what Adams will try to find out and how Adams will try to shape his perceptions.

Learning

As you hypothesize about your counterparts' interests, think about how you will test your hypotheses at the table. You can learn a lot from strategic questioning and active listening. Bolton should draw up an initial list of questions for Adams and then keep probing. What really concerns Adams about this merger? A useful tactic is to ask the same question in different ways and triangulate the responses. Bolton could ask Adams, "What are the most important things you need to get to walk away happy?" and "How important is the issue of making your furloughed people whole?" and "Why is rapid integration of Regional so important to you?" These are all ways of getting at Adams's interests and trade-offs among issues. Are his responses consistent or inconsistent? Bolton should also feed back what he hears to test his comprehension, demonstrate that he is listening, and explore seeming inconsistencies: "So if I understand you correctly, you need X. But earlier you mentioned that Y is important. Have I got it right?"

Your counterparts also inevitably reveal their interests in indirect ways. Each offer they make conveys information about what they want (or want you to think they want). Their concessions also convey information: big concessions signal more to give; small concessions signal resistance, real or feigned.

You can learn by making offers of your own as well. One approach is to propose multiple package deals—ideally, deals whose distinctions you are indifferent about—to find out which the other side prefers. If they respond truthfully, you will learn something about their preferences across the issues. Keep in mind that they too will learn something from your offers.

Shaping Perceptions

Shaping your counterparts' perceptions of the bargaining range is partly about framing and reframing; it's also a matter of sharing information in such a way as to influence their perceptions of interests and walk-aways, both theirs and yours.

Bolton's perception-shaping goals are to convince Adams that:

- The positions he is taking cannot lead to agreement.

- Creative agreements can meet both sides' needs if Adams is willing to be more flexible.

- He can back away honorably from his public commitment to immediate integration.

The arsenal with which negotiators shape their counterparts' perceptions at the table consists largely of a handful of classic techniques of persuasion:

- *Anchoring.* Your initial position strongly influences the other side's perception of the bargaining range. An offer that is high (or low) but not so extreme that it triggers a breakdown of negotiations or dismissal of the offer can anchor your counterparts' perceptions in a favorable way. In response to Adams's demand for immediate integration of Regional, Bolton could try to anchor high.

- *Patterns of concessions*. Substantial early concessions followed by progressively smaller concessions signals increasing resistance. This tactic can be used to shape the other side's perception of your walk-away position. Having anchored high, Bolton could make a series of concessions that end with a final offer that meets his aspirations.

- *Threats*. Threats are promises to do harm, typically used to shape others' perceptions of the consequences of no agreement. Threats have to be credible to be effective. Even if credible, they can provoke irrational resistance and escalation. Bolton could threaten to continue to expand the use of regional jets by Global Focus.

- *Warnings*. Warnings are milder than threats and hence less likely to trigger escalation.[12] Instead of saying "If you do that, I will punish you," a warning says, "If you do that, bad things [not caused by me] will happen to you." Bolton could stress the financial impact of any agreement on Global's ability to remain competitive in the industry.

- *Commitments*. Commitments are self-imposed costs. Negotiators commit to a course of action (perhaps by putting their reputations or credibility at stake) to convince their counterparts that their hands are tied. The risk, as we have seen, is overcommitment and impasse. Overcommitted negotiators stand firm long after it has become apparent that their objectives are unachievable. Bolton could make a final offer, stressing that his board of directors would never approve anything more.

- *Action-forcing events*. Deadlines, meetings, and other key events can be invoked to move the process forward. Bolton could establish a deadline for agreement, beyond which he will simply proceed with his own plan to integrate the airlines.[13]

Managing Fundamental Tensions

As Bolton seeks to manage the process, he will confront some built-in tensions. These tensions arise because he and Adams each have private information that the other doesn't possess and because both will try to claim value. As a result, both of them will share and withhold information strategically to try to shape each other's perceptions. This maneuvering vastly complicates the learning process.

Suppose Bolton and Adams were engaged in a purely distributive negotiation over pay increases for the Regional pilots. Then suppose that Adams had somehow learned the maximum that Bolton was willing to offer, while Bolton remained in the dark about the minimum Adams would accept. Adams would enjoy a huge tactical advantage: he would be in a position to shape Bolton's perceptions using offers and counteroffers, but would himself be immune to Bolton's perception-shaping efforts. Adams could peg his initial offer high enough to anchor Bolton's perceptions without causing negotiations to break down, followed by a series of concessions, and then a commitment to a "final offer" he knows is marginally acceptable to Bolton and highly attractive to the union. Clearly, information is power in the sense that it allows you to shape the other side's perception of the bargaining range.

Now suppose instead that Bolton and Adams are both uncertain about each other's walk-aways. Bolton is hobbled in his efforts to learn about the union's bottom line because he doesn't know the extent to which Adams is trying to manipulate his perceptions. The greater his uncertainty about Adams's interests and alternatives, the more he needs to learn—but the more he is vulnerable to having his own perceptions manipulated.[14] The same is true for Adams. This conundrum is known as the *learning-shaping dilemma*.

In integrative negotiations, a similar dilemma arises: your efforts to learn about the other side's interests and trade-offs in order to create value conflict with your efforts to shape their perceptions in order to claim value. If Bolton is to propose mutually beneficial trades, he needs to learn about Adams's true interests and trade-offs and judiciously share information about his own. But if Bolton is truthful about his own interests, he will be vulnerable to the union leader's value-claiming tactics. And if he conceals or misrepresents his own interests and the other side responds in kind, the potential for joint gains dissolves. Bolton is thus confronting what David Lax and Jim Sebenius have termed the *negotiator's dilemma*.[15] (See the table below.) If he shares information about what he really needs in order to create value, he risks having Adams claim value from him. But if he misleads Adams about his true interests, he risks not identifying opportunities to made trades and create value.

Tailoring Tactics to Type of Negotiation

Bolton's tactics for managing the process ought to be tailored to the nature of the negotiation. Any negotiation can be positioned on a spectrum ranging from purely distributive to purely cooperative (joint problem solving in which incentives are perfectly aligned).

If the negotiation is truly distributive, Bolton has little to gain by being open about his interests; the key is to be adept at shaping the other side's perceptions and claiming value. If, on the other hand, both sides' interests are largely congruent, little is lost by sharing information and jointly exploring options to create value.

The Negotiator's Dilemma

	Goal	
Activity	*Create value*	*Claim value*
Learning	Share information about your interests to find opportunities to create value.	Gather accurate information about the other side's walk-aways. Use anchoring and commitment tactics to claim value.
Shaping perceptions	Reframe the negotiations to emphasize value-creation possibilities.	Mislead your counterparts about your priorities to claim value in trades.

The Competition-Cooperation Spectrum

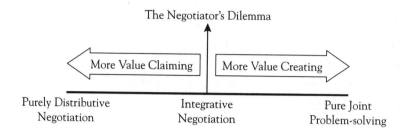

Integrative negotiations, with their mix of value creating and value claiming, occupy the middle ground. It is in the integrative arena that the negotiator's dilemma is most problematic.

To manage the negotiator's dilemma, Bolton ought to think hard about what information he reveals. He should neither share his walk-away position nor specify his exact trade-offs among issues. But he could tell Adams that he is more reluctant to pay retroactive wages than he is to give the pilots furloughed in the 1990s pension credit for the furlough period. This revelation could set the stage for a mutually beneficial trade. The central point is that information sharing should be reciprocal, not one-way. It is wisest to proceed incrementally—sharing some information, seeing what you find out in exchange, and rigorously testing it for plausibility.

PRACTICAL APPLICATION: LEARNING AND SHAPING PERCEPTIONS

Think about a negotiation in which you are engaged right now:

- What are the most important things you need to learn at the table? How will you go about learning them? What would your counterparts most like to learn about you?

- How has the other side tried to shape your perceptions about the bargaining range? How successful have you been at shaping their perceptions so far?

- Are there ways you can better manage the tension between creating and claiming value in this negotiation?

BUILDING MOMENTUM

Having diagnosed the situation and strategized about learning and shaping perceptions, the next step is to devise a tactical plan. The rough road map shown here outlines how you want the interaction with your counterpart to proceed. It blocks out your approach to building momentum toward your desired outcomes.

How should Bolton approach learning about and shaping the perceptions of Adams and his team? First, he should recognize that he can neither fully control the process nor anticipate all possible contingencies. The best he can do is to get the negotiation off to a good start and concentrate on moving it in favorable directions. He should try to anticipate and plan for the union leadership's reactions, but beyond that he has to be flexible and adapt to developments.

As a first cut at a process plan, Bolton might think in terms of the rough sequence of activities illustrated in the accompanying figure.

- *Task 1: Building the relationship.* Bolton should begin by working on the strained relationship with Adams and the APU leadership. Otherwise, the negative feelings generated by their previous encounters will continue to poison the proceedings. He needs to build up some relationship capital; he might need it to spend if the going gets tough later on. Bolton could, for example, raise Adams's strained relationship with his predecessor and say that he hopes that he and Adams will be able to work together more productively.

Process Planning

- *Task 2: Negotiating the process.* Bolton shouldn't expect to jump directly into the substance of the dispute; this is a common mistake that inexperienced negotiators make. Instead, he should spend some time negotiating the process with Adams. Agreeing on an agenda also offers an opportunity to shape the union leadership's expectations about what will be accomplished. He might say, for example, "I think we should concentrate on exploring whether there is a basis for going forward" and "We won't be making any specific offers today. I want to see if we can identify some creative options for addressing our concerns."

- *Task 3: Changing the frame.* Bolton is now in a position to begin to reframe the negotiation, prodding Adams and his colleagues to embrace a more integrative view of the possibilities. He might start by saying that there will be no basis for agreement if they continue down the same road. Then he could highlight potential joint gains by saying, "It seems to me that our needs for flexibility in integration and preservation of the scope clause in the contract [which gives union pilots the exclusive right to fly all Global Airways's aircraft] need not be incompatible."

Bolton could then work to transform Adams's perception of his interests by deftly informing Adams of his openness to separate negotiations on the timing and terms of payment of the damage award the court imposed on the union. He might also broaden the agenda to include issues like pension credit for the pilots' furlough period.

- *Task 4: Testing hypotheses.* Bolton could then move on to finding out as much as possible about the interests that underlie the union's position. His earlier analysis of Adams's interests yielded hypotheses that have to be tested and validated at the table. He should ponder carefully which information he needs most and how to elicit it. He might begin by asking, "What are your biggest concerns about the Regional acquisition?" and then practice active listening, carefully summarizing what he hears both to show that he understands and to test his comprehension.

• *Task 5: Finding the formula.* The stage is now set for Bolton to move from the diagnostic phase to the formula phase and to begin to explore potential trades with Adams. These trades will jointly constitute the formula for the deal—the overarching framework for agreement. Once a promising formula has been identified, management and the union can move on to hard bargaining over the details.

Drawing on his prior analysis, Bolton could introduce multiple potential trades. For instance, he could suggest the following as potential bases for a deal:

- Partial compensation to Regional pilots for the interval since Global took over
- Partial credits to furloughed pilots for pensions and benefits
- Impartial arbitration of the effective date of takeover
- Follow-on negotiation of a "fair process" for consultation on integration of future acquisitions, perhaps with the help of a mediator
- An extended payment schedule for the damage award if the union does not engage in further sick-outs

• *Task 6: Creating a sense of urgency.* The final step is to create a sense of urgency. Movement toward (or away from) agreement tends to be turbulent, with periods of deadlock or inaction punctuated by bursts of progress. Negotiators for Global and the APU may make initial progress, but they will inevitably arrive at difficult choices, such as whether to make concessions that will disappoint internal constituencies or whether to cross psychologically important red lines. Negotiations may stall until accumulating costs become intolerable, or an action-forcing event like a deadline compels the participants to make concessions or break off negotiations. If some or all of the parties decide to improve the terms on offer, accumulated tensions get released, and momentum builds toward agreement.

Managing the flow of negotiations is like influencing the flow of a river. You may seek to advance your interests by damming the flow in places, letting it loose in others, and channeling it in desired directions. The flow toward agreement can be dammed by purposefully engineering impasses; tension can be released and channeled by proposing a new formula or face-saving compromise. In the process, the more patient and creative negotiator may be able to create and claim substantial value.

If Bolton believes that the union incurs substantial costs for delay (because of the lawsuit) and is unwilling to negotiate in a more integrative manner, it may be worth delaying the process to let pressure build. On the other hand, if the dispute over Regional Air is a time-consuming distraction for a management team that is grappling with serious strategic challenges, it may be worthwhile to propose an attractive formula for settling the dispute.

PRACTICAL APPLICATION: BUILDING MOMENTUM

Think further about a current negotiation:

- Did you spend time up front on the relationship?
- Did you negotiate the process?
- Were you able to shape or change the frame favorably?
- Did you test hypotheses about the other side's interests and learn effectively?
- Did you work to identify a promising formula?
- Were you successful at instilling a sense of urgency in the other side?

PUTTING IT ALL TOGETHER

Managing the process calls for awareness of the multiple levels at which negotiations unfold. Your negotiations will recapitulate predictable stages, but those stages will be filled with turbulent microinteractions, and the participants' mental processes may twist and turn dramatically. Armed with that understanding, you can begin to craft strategies to learn and to shape perceptions and a tactical plan to manage interactions and build momentum.

Bolton reached agreement with Adams on the integration of Regional Airlines. Bolton devoted significant time to wide-ranging discussions with Adams about the future of the airline and somewhat improved the relationship. "Stuart and I came to see each other as reliable partners," Bolton recalled, "even though there was no love lost between us." Bolton also postponed negotiations over payment of the union fine to avoid creating the appearance of linkage. At the same time, he indicated to Adams his "openness to negotiating a long-term payment plan."

Bolton then unblocked negotiations by offering to submit the effective date of takeover to impartial arbitration, an offer the union leader accepted. By setting that potentially toxic issue aside, Bolton and Adams were able to focus on the issues of wages and seniority. Their eventual agreement extended the Global pay scale to the Regional pilots and gave full seniority credit to the oldest Regional pilots and partial credit to the younger ones. The issue of pension credit for time on furlough was deferred until contract negotiations, with the understanding that management would seriously consider offering partial credit. Several months later, Bolton offered Adams an extended payment schedule for the damage award, with the implicit understanding that the union would not engage in further sick-outs. The union accepted, and Bolton avoided the crisis that bankrupting the union might have precipitated.

4

Assessing the Results

Once a negotiation is under way, you should step back periodically to evaluate how you are doing. It comes most naturally to step back between negotiating sessions, but it can (and should) also be done in the heat of battle. The ability to "go to the balcony," as William Ury put it, to look at your situation from a distance, can be cultivated.[1] Difficult at first, it gets easier with practice. Keep asking yourself, "What would outside observers say about what is going on here? What would they suggest I do to get things back on track?"

Appraising an ongoing negotiation is partly about whether you are meeting the specific goals you set for yourself. Clearly identifying your goals while preparing to negotiate is only half the battle; you have to keep those benchmarks firmly in mind as you go forward. Research shows that negotiators perform best when they set ambitious stretch goals and then strive to meet them, as long as they don't get overcommitted and fail to accept agreements that are better than their BATNAs.[2]

Negotiations are so fluid that it's dangerous to adopt a rigid once-and-for-all approach, and stepping back can also help you stay as flexible about means as you are firm about goals. Describing his successful negotiations to end the war in Bosnia, Richard Holbrooke defined his approach as "very flexible on tactics, but firm on goals."[3] General Dwight D. Eisenhower elaborated the point: "A sound battle plan provides flexibility in both time and space to meet the constantly changing factors. . . . Rigidity inevitably defeats itself, and the analysts who point to a changed detail as evidence of a plan's weakness are completely unaware of the characteristics of the battlefield."[4] Plans are not an end, but they are an essential means.

The insights that result from stepping back will sharpen your diagnosis of the situation and reveal new opportunities to shape the structure and manage the process. After all, how can Daniel Riley, or Claire Prescott, or Van Bolton hope to negotiate effectively if they don't evaluate how they are doing and take corrective action?

Ultimately, judging success is about more than whether you do well in your current negotiation. It's also about its impact on your reputation and relationships, as well as your success at learning and your adherence to ethical principles that are important to you. This means you have to keep a broader set of criteria in mind as you evaluate your performance.

This chapter provides a suggested set of questions for assessing your progress at diagnosing the situation, shaping the structure, and managing the process. You should review these questions at the end of each negotiating session. Over time, as you internalize them, asking them during the negotiation as well will become second nature.

QUESTIONS ABOUT DIAGNOSING THE SITUATION

When you step back to assess the adequacy of your efforts to diagnose the situation, you will in effect be diagnosing your diagnosis. Ask yourself the following questions.

Question 1: Do You Have a Clear View of the Situation?

A clear view of your situation is the bedrock on which you build your strategies and tactics. If your take on the situation is flawed or incomplete, you are likely to be blindsided or to underperform. This is what happened to Daniel Riley in his negotiations with Ken Gourlay, described in Chapter One. Because he wasn't sufficiently self-conscious about probing his situation, he missed opportunities to create and claim value.

Diagnosing your diagnosis calls for periodically returning to the basic diagnostic elements we discussed in Chapter One:

Parties: Who will participate, or could participate, in the negotiation?

Rules: What are the rules of the game?

Issues: What agenda of issues will be, or could be, negotiated?

Interests: What goals are you and others pursuing?

Alternatives: What will you do if you don't reach agreement?

Agreements: Are there possible agreements that would be acceptable to all sides?

Linkages: Are your current negotiations linked to other negotiations?

Ask yourself whether anything has happened to make you question your original assessment of each element. Have new parties gotten involved, or could that happen? If so, what are the implications? Are the rules of the game what you thought they were? Are the agenda of issues and other players' interests and BATNAs what you predicted they would be? Do you see any new implications for the types of agreements that are possible? Do you understand the full set of existing and potential linkages?

Question 2: Have You Been Efficient and Effective in Your Learning?

More preparation is not always better. Diagnosis involves making a sound investment of your scarce resources to gather and analyze information. Daniel Riley failed at this: he squandered numerous opportunities to learn more at very low cost by talking to other entrepreneurs and venture capitalists and simply by asking more questions.

The more thoroughly you diagnose a negotiating situation, the more prepared you are likely to be. But trade-offs are inescapable, and you will have to contend with some limits:[5]

> *Resource limits.* Unless you have no constraints on your time, expertise, money, and access to documents and other data, you will have to make cost-benefit calculations: Is the information that could be unearthed with more research worth its cost?
>
> *Informational limits.* Even with unlimited resources, you could not collect all the information you want. Negotiations are always games of incomplete information, because of uncertainty and deliberate efforts to conceal or mislead. Remember that there's no point in beating your head against a brick wall.
>
> *Cognitive limits.* Intense preparation could rigidify your definition of an acceptable agreement.[6] You could also guess wrong about the other side's interests, distorting the way you gather and interpret information, and reinforcing your misconceptions.[7]

For all these reasons, you need to plan your investments in diagnosis. Take the time to step back and ask: Can I see any inexpensive opportunities to acquire more insight? Have I reached the point of diminishing returns, and would my resources be better spent on learning from my counterparts at the negotiating table?

QUESTIONS ABOUT SHAPING THE STRUCTURE

Breakthrough negotiators refuse to take the situation they confront as a given. Instead, they work to transform the situation's components in ways that make good agreements possible. Here, too, discipline yourself to step back and assess your success at shaping the structure by asking the following questions.

Question 3: Are You Involved with the Right People?

A highly favorable agreement with the wrong people can be of less long-term value than a good agreement with the right people. Are you dealing with the people whose participation offers you the best opportunities to create and claim value? Could you negotiate a better deal with a different mix of people? Can your counterparts be trusted to implement the terms of the agreement?

Think about Claire Prescott's negotiations with Eric Mersch, described in Chapter Two. She probably could have done better by seeking out other sources of funding for the project and by negotiating with competitors of BargainMart. Doing so would have strengthened Claire's ability to create and claim value.

Question 4: Are You Building Your BATNA?

A strong BATNA builds bargaining power. Have you done all you can to build your BATNA? Do alternatives exist that you haven't yet explored? Can you build coalitions or harness the power of competition? Are there linkages whose creation (or elimination) would strengthen your alternatives to agreement? What about your counterparts' BATNAs? Could you make their alternatives to negotiated agreement less attractive without triggering irrational resistance on their part?

In her negotiations with BargainMart, Claire neglected several opportunities to strengthen her BATNA. She could have negotiated to extend the option on the land, built a coalition of satellite tenants, and promoted competition between BargainMart and its competitor ValueShops. These and other initiatives would have substantially bolstered her bargaining position.

Question 5: Are You Shaping the Issue Agenda?

Focusing on the right set of issues enhances your ability both to create value and to claim it. Ask yourself periodically whether there are issues you could add to the agenda that would expand opportunities to create value. If so, how could you accomplish this? Are toxic issues impeding progress or poisoning the potential for value creation? If so, how can you defer them or remove them permanently from the agenda?

In the negotiation between Global Airways and the pilots' union described in Chapter Three, Van Bolton's agenda-shaping strategy was central to his success in managing the dispute. Bolton was able to defer the issue of payment of the damage award, and by broadening the agenda to include issues like pension credit for the pilots' furlough period, he both created and claimed value.

Question 6: Are You Winning the Frame Game?

Your goal in framing is to persuade your counterparts (and other influential parties) to accept your definition of "the problem" and "the options." In other words, you must find a way of framing the situation that has face validity and resonance with the target audience. Have you managed to accomplish this? If not, what are the competing frames, and what makes them more compelling? How might you hone or alter your framing to make it resonate with your audience?

Both Daniel Riley and Claire Prescott could have done a better job of framing. Daniel was in a position to bring a fully functioning design team to a new company, and he should have framed his negotiations in those terms. Instead, he let Ken Gourlay frame the situation as an ordinary job negotiation and thus claim value. Claire would have done better if she had framed her negotiation with Eric in terms of her external constraints: "If I can't find financing and attract good satellite tenants, we will both lose a very attractive opportunity."

Question 7: Are You Channeling the Flow?

Channeling the flow of a negotiation is like directing the course of a river: you can dam it or you can reroute it. Have you engineered action-forcing events that compel your counterparts to make tough choices? Can you use linkages to force action? Have you raised the cost of delay for the other side and lowered it for yourself? Would it be productive to engineer an impasse or defer commitment?

By letting Ken Gourlay determine the pace of the negotiations, Daniel Riley put himself in a weak position. Ken used the need to approach venture capitalists as an action-forcing event. Rather than defer commitment, which would have increased the pressure on Ken, Daniel allowed himself to be swept along.

QUESTIONS ABOUT MANAGING THE PROCESS

The goals of managing the process are to channel the macro-flow, shape key micro-interactions, and influence the mental processes of your counterparts. To assess your success in managing the process, ask the following questions.

Question 8: Are You Moving the Process Through the Right Phases?

There are better and worse ways to structure the flow of the negotiating process. It's usually a mistake, for example, to jump to negotiating details of the substance without first building rapport with your counterparts and negotiating the process itself. This is easy to say, but hard to do when you are in the grip of a time crunch or enmeshed in an emotion-laden conflict.

You have to discipline yourself to step back and ask: Have I been successful in reaching agreement with the other side about how the process should be structured? Are the phases through which I envision proceeding likely to build momentum? If not, how can I reshape the macro-flow of the process to remove unnecessary barriers to agreement?

Daniel Riley didn't think about the phases through which his negotiations with Ken should proceed, so he was unable to adjust his posture accordingly. Van Bolton, on the other hand, did an outstanding job of thinking through the progression of the process. By focusing first on the relationship, then on immediate issues raised by the merger, and finally on the damage award, he created and sustained momentum.

Question 9: Are You Creating Value as Well as Claiming It?

Nearly all negotiations have some potential for value creation. Even in the highly contentious negotiations between Global Airways and the pilots' union, opportunities arose to make mutually beneficial trades. To be realized, this potential must be identified. Naturally, you can't do this single-handedly. But you can periodically step back and ask yourself whether there are potential joint gains that are going unrealized and, if so, what you might try to do.

Of course, it's not enough to create value; you must claim an appropriate share of it. But be sure not to sacrifice your own interests in pursuit of joint value creation. Negotiators can err by placing too much emphasis on either value claiming (thus driving out the potential for value creation) or value creation (creating lots of value for their counterparts).

The key is to maintain both a judicious openness to value creation and caution about having value claimed from you. As we have seen, it's often difficult to tell how successful you have been at creating and claiming value: potential joint gains can easily get left on the table. But it's still worth periodically asking whether you are doing all you can to create value and whether you are giving up value too easily.

Question 10: Are You Accumulating Negotiating Capital?

Goodwill matters in any ongoing relationship. Claire Prescott can expect to negotiate with BargainMart on a multitude of issues for many years to come, as can Daniel Riley and Ken Gourlay, and

Van Bolton and Stuart Adams. A good relationship will minimize the need for monitoring compliance and facilitate future agreements. The negotiation process can create or deplete a reservoir of goodwill; it is possible to create and claim a lot of value but still squander resources or sully your reputation.

You will feel pressure to do well in the current negotiation, but you should also consider the impact of your behavior on future negotiations. So ask yourself: So far, have you accumulated or spent negotiating capital in this negotiation? Have you begun to build the foundation for a productive working relationship or poisoned the well?

Question 11: Are You Crafting Sustainable Agreements?

You can negotiate with the right people and do a good job of creating and claiming value and still fail. One way to fail is to drive such a hard bargain that the resulting agreement sets the stage for your counterparts to renege or renegotiate or cheat in implementation. The other side has to claim an acceptable share of value too.

In part, crafting sustainable agreements means anticipating and dealing with contingencies. Some contingencies are unforeseeable (the market for software solutions for managed care companies collapses, a new communication technology dramatically reduces the need for air travel), but others can be anticipated and prepared for (BargainMart refocuses its business or declares bankruptcy, Omega Systems gets acquired by another company). Ask yourself: Does the agreement you've reached accommodate foreseeable contingencies? Does it establish mechanisms (such as dispute-resolution processes and mediation-and-arbitration provisions) for handling unforeseeable contingencies?

Question 12: Are You Upholding Your Ethical Standards?

"Negotiation ethics" may strike some people as a contradiction in terms. But negotiators have to live with the consequences of their actions, and failure to adhere to your core beliefs is corrosive. It's no defense to hide behind your role as representative of an organization. In the end, you have to live with yourself. Step back occasionally to make sure that you aren't sacrificing your standards in the heat of battle.

Negotiation is shot through with tough choices. By and large, truth telling, fairness, and balanced representation of parties absent from the table present the biggest challenges. Truth telling has to do with acts of commission and omission in the sharing of information. Where does shaping perceptions end and lying begin? Do you owe it to your counterparts to reveal information they haven't asked for? Is it simply a matter of caveat emptor?

Issues of fairness are inescapable in negotiations. Should you aim for the most favorable agreement your power enables you to achieve? To what extent should notions of fair division shape your thinking? Even if you want to be fair, there are no objective criteria for fairness. Where you stand depends on where you sit.

Finally, negotiations often affect the interests of people who don't have seats at the table. You may represent others' interests and also your own. Whose interests come first? Sometimes even the interests of unborn generations must be balanced against those of today. To what extent can and should you consider the interests of those absent from the table?

Question 13: Are You Learning, Both Individually and Organizationally?

Finally, every negotiation is an opportunity to learn and to become more adept. But learning happens only if you invest in capturing the lessons of experience. This means taking the time to reflect on the lessons you learned. What went well? What should you do differently next time? What did the other side do well, and what can you learn from them? It is a useful discipline to write an after-action report summarizing decisive events and lessons. Doing this will help you avoid the same sticking points in the future, perhaps by beginning to shape the structure earlier. We will discuss this step in more detail in the Conclusion.

CLOSING THE LOOP

These thirteen questions are a template for evaluating your own performance and progress in any negotiation. They are summarized in the table on pages 113–114. Use the Actions column to address any weaknesses that you identify in the Assessment column.

Before proceeding to Part Two, flip back to the Introduction and briefly review the core elements of the framework: diagnosing the situation, shaping the structure, managing the process, and assessing the results. Then think about how to apply these ideas to a negotiation in which you are involved, focusing on what you will do both at the negotiating table and away from the negotiating table.

Template for Judging Performance

Question	Assessment			Actions
Diagnosing the Situation				
1. Do I have a clear view of the situation?	not at all	adequate	absolutely	
2. Have I been efficient and effective in my learning?	not at all	adequate	absolutely	
Shaping the Structure				
3. Am I involved with the right people?	not at all	adequate	absolutely	
4. Have I built my BATNA?	not at all	adequate	absolutely	
5. Have I shaped the issue agenda?	not at all	adequate	absolutely	
6. Am I winning the frame game?	not at all	adequate	absolutely	

Template for Judging Performance (*continued*)

Question	Assessment			Actions
7. Am I controlling the flow?	not at all	adequate	absolutely	
Managing the Process				
8. Am I moving the process through the right phases?	not at all	adequate	absolutely	
9. Am I creating value, as well as claiming it?	not at all	adequate	absolutely	
10. Am I accumulating negotiating capital?	not at all	adequate	absolutely	
11. Am I crafting sustainable agreements?	not at all	adequate	absolutely	
12. Am I upholding my ethical standards?	not at all	adequate	absolutely	
13. Am I learning, both individually and organizationally?	not at all	adequate	absolutely	

PART TWO

Building the Breakthrough Toolbox

Now that you are familiar with the foundations of the breakthrough approach, you are ready to augment your toolbox and try putting it to use. The following five chapters will present strategies and tactics for dealing with common challenges that confront real-world negotiators:

Overcoming power imbalances: What do you do when you are on the wrong side of a power imbalance? You will probably have to deal at some point with counterparts who enjoy substantially more bargaining power than you do. Chapter Five offers guidelines for such situations.

Building coalitions: When a negotiation involves many interested parties, influential coalitions spring up and shape outcomes. How do you build supportive coalitions and prevent opposition from coalescing against you? Chapter Six lays out how to analyze influence dynamics and build coalitions.

Managing conflicts: Many negotiations involve disputes rather than deals. What do you do when conflict is, or could be, a barrier to negotiated agreement? Chapter Seven looks at how to manage conflict while negotiating.

Leading negotiations: Negotiators are often called on to represent others who are absent from the table and to lead teams of people. What does a skilled negotiator need to know about leadership in such situations? Chapter Eight looks at the negotiator as a leader.

Negotiating crises: Finally, managers inevitably confront crises, but few are well prepared to deal with them. The skills of negotiation and coalition building turn out to be central to effectiveness in crisis situations. Chapter Nine looks at how to prepare for and negotiate your way through crises.

As you begin to apply these ideas to craft specific strategies and tactical plans, always keep in mind that negotiations are by nature fluid. Strategies need to be carefully designed, but they also need to be flexible enough to allow for changes in tactics in response to evolving circumstances.

5

Overcoming Power Imbalances

A start-up has a promising technology or product. It has secured early-stage funding, assembled a solid management team, and developed a prototype that clearly demonstrates commercial potential. Now it faces a big hurdle. To get to market, the young company must make investments in product development or operations or distribution that are beyond its reach. Perhaps the company's product is an enabling technology, such as a new composite material, or a component to be embedded in the products of much larger companies with established brands. Perhaps the start-up lacks the expertise to shepherd the product through convoluted product development or regulatory processes. Regardless, it has no choice but to negotiate deals with much larger companies. And that's when life can get very hard indeed.

How can a mouse negotiate with an elephant? This is a life-or-death question for many entrepreneurs (and anyone on the wrong side of a power imbalance). If they can't do those early deals to demonstrate to investors that they are on track, they crash and burn. Plenty of advice is available on negotiation, but there is surprisingly little on how to negotiate when you are a mouse dealing with elephants. This chapter will show you how to apply the techniques outlined in Part One.

THE LIFE AND DEATH OF GO COMPUTER

To illustrate how hard it can be to negotiate with elephants without getting crushed, consider the untimely death of GO Computer. As chronicled in CEO Jerry Kaplan's memoir *Startup: A Silicon Valley Adventure,* GO was founded to develop a small computer that would be operated by stylus rather than a keyboard, an early personal digital assistant.[1] With initial funding from a gold-plated group of investors including Mitch Kapor of Lotus Development and John Doerr of the Silicon Valley venture capital firm Kleiner Perkins, Kaplan assembled an outstanding team of software and hardware developers who quickly put together an impressive functional prototype. The prototype attracted interest from State Farm Insurance for an auto claims estimating application. Kaplan was sure they were off to the races.

But after a promising start, things started to unravel. State Farm insisted that GO team up with one of its conventional computer suppliers, IBM or Hewlett Packard (HP). Kaplan concluded that IBM would bring more weight to GO's efforts to establish its pen-based computer as a standard and decided to negotiate an alliance. The result was a year-long nightmare in which Kaplan was passed from person to person in IBM while GO's cash burned. The deal that was ultimately signed placed onerous oversight restrictions on GO and held its intellectual property hostage to performance. It became evident that some individuals within IBM viewed GO as a source of technology at best and a potential competitor to be crushed at worst. Persistent problems in the relationship ultimately contributed to GO's bankruptcy.

GO made some classic mistakes in its negotiations with a much larger partner. Management didn't understand how to leverage its core technology to negotiate deals with multiple potential partners, leading to overreliance on a single partner. Worse, the choice of partner was unfortunate: HP had been anxious to work with GO, but IBM didn't really need the start-up and was in no hurry to do a deal. IBM could afford to wait while GO depleted its resources and then impose very unattractive terms. Perhaps worst of all, some people within IBM viewed GO as a threat. Kaplan never found an internal champion or identified a group within IBM that had a lot to gain by working with GO. At bottom, he simply didn't understand how to dance with an elephant. GO ended up paying the price.

The GO case is only one of many stories of mice failing to negotiate effectively with elephants. Often the outcome is less dramatic than outright bankruptcy: the mouse gets swallowed by its larger partner at terms unattractive to its shareholders. By giving away too much too early, it prematurely caps its ability to reach critical mass.

THE MILLENNIUM EXPERIENCE

The difficulty of negotiating with elephants doesn't mean it can't be done. A biotechnology start-up, Millennium Pharmaceuticals, faced a situation very much like GO Computer's in the mid-1990s and the outcome couldn't have been more dissimilar.[2] Millennium's founders had developed a promising genetics technology for early-stage drug discovery, and they intended to leverage the technology to build a full-line pharmaceutical firm. Their strategy was to create a technology platform that would enable the company to develop and sell information assets—initially drug targets, later drug leads, and eventually elements of the technology itself. The company set out to exploit the new knowledge base produced by the Human Genome Project to speed drug discovery.

To realize this ambitious vision, the founders of Millennium had to raise the necessary capital. At the time, the venture capital community was wary of the high risks and long time frames of biotech product development; so was the public investment community. A typical successful biotech company burns through between $500 million and $1 billion in capital before it becomes profitable, and product-based revenues typically do not begin to flow for at least a decade.

Management concluded that Millennium could not secure venture funding at the right terms and decided instead to negotiate strategic alliances with established pharmaceutical companies, both to gain access to capital and to validate the company's technology in the eyes of the investment community. The new firm would take advantage of the industry's thirst for new drug candidates to engage in targeted collaborations. The revenue generated by contract research would provide funding to develop the technology platform and eventually to produce and market products.

Strategic deal making was at the core of this ambitious vision. Millennium not only had to produce knowledge valuable to the pharmaceutical companies; it had to extract maximum value for that knowledge while building the base necessary to develop its own products. Otherwise Millennium would degenerate into a contract research shop. The company also had to develop a diverse customer base or risk losing its independence and becoming a captive research subsidiary of one of the large pharmaceutical companies.

In short order, Millennium negotiated alliances with eight of the world's ten largest pharmaceutical companies. These alliances yielded about $130 million in equity financing, over $200 million in targeted funding for research, $600 million in licensing fees to support technology development, and valuable rights to future milestone payments and royalties, as well as a growing base of retained intellectual property to support the company's own drug-development efforts. This string of deals was capped by a 1998 joint venture with Bayer that qualifies as the largest biotech deal of all time. By 2001, Millennium's market capitalization had grown to close to $5 billion.

DANCING WITH ELEPHANTS

Millennium's success was founded on a set of principles for negotiating with much larger partners. These principles represent ways that smaller players can deftly shape the structure and manage the process when facing a negotiating partner of greater perceived power. Sometimes there is no substitute for heavy artillery, but you can do a lot to level the field of battle.

Principle 1: Never Do All-or-Nothing Deals

The biggest mistake a small player can make is to enter into a single make-or-break negotiation with a larger partner. Doing so just reinforces the elephant's perception of its own strength and inevitably leads to disadvantageous deals. This was the hard lesson GO learned: reliance on a single large partner can lead to dependence and then to absorption or extinction. GO focused on developing a single application for one customer, and so was limited to doing a deal with IBM or HP. GO might have survived if it had defined its technology platform as a pen-based operating system, which has many potential embedded and stand-alone applications.

This is why it is essential for weaker players to shape the structure of the situation in such a way that everything is not riding on a single negotiation. A primary objective, then, is to *diversify partner risk* so that no single large negotiating partner can exert monopoly power over you.

One way to do this is to enter into complementary relationships with several larger counterparts. Millennium decided at the beginning to create a balanced network of alliances with larger players. If the company could negotiate a portfolio of roughly balanced relationships with larger pharmaceutical companies, the loss of a partner wouldn't be fatal, and no single partner could hold the company hostage.

Millennium had to figure out how to negotiate early deals with large companies without precluding other future deals. Otherwise, it risked selling the crown jewels early and getting locked into too narrow a set of partners. Avoiding this misstep called for leveraging the company's core assets to generate what the founders called "partnerable applications" that would create value for a range of potential partners. Millennium decided to invest in developing promising leads in five distinct disease categories: obesity and diabetes, cardiovascular, central nervous system (CNS), respiratory, and oncology. The company then did a separate deal in each of these areas, with Hoffman-LaRoche (obesity and diabetes), Eli Lilly (cardiovascular and oncology), Astra (respiratory), and American Home Products (CNS). A deal for diabetes with LaRoche didn't preclude a deal with Lilly for cancer targets. These deals all leveraged Millennium's core gene-based technology platform and met important needs on the part of the chosen partners. Millennium reinvested the proceeds of these deals in the technology platform to create still more partnerable applications.

Even if you believe that you can negotiate a strong, mutually beneficial relationship with one reliable partner, it's essential to diversify partner risk: the partner's strategy can change, or your champions within the partner company can leave, or internal competitors for your offerings can emerge.

Principle 2: Make Them Smaller

A second classic mistake is to treat a larger partner as a single unified entity. The notion of big-company-as-powerful-monolith fails to recognize that large companies are made up of smaller units led by people with their own incentives and interests. This is increasingly true given large companies' trend toward increasing decentralization of responsibility and accountability.

The point here is that the mouse should negotiate with the elephant's leg or the trunk rather than the whole beast. This means looking for individuals and units within the larger company likely to have a vivid interest in what you have to offer and to champion a deal upwards. Your task is to pinpoint potential alignments of interests and then to work your way up the chain of authority to someone with real clout and to get them on board. GO never found such a champion within IBM. Perhaps there was none, in which case GO shouldn't have been negotiating with IBM. But it's equally plausible that a champion could have been found if Kaplan had relentlessly searched for one, perhaps by leveraging his connections to people like Mitch Kapor and John Doerr.

Millennium, by contrast, understood this principle well. It designed its deals to be attractive to the leaders of specific subunits within large pharmaceutical companies. This required creativity in structuring deals. More important, it called for a thorough grasp of how the larger partner was organized and how the performance of its key people was measured and rewarded. By framing its early deals in terms of disease categories, Millennium was able to negotiate with managers inside the big pharmaceutical companies who cared only about diabetes drugs, or cancer drugs, or cardiovascular drugs. Because an alliance with Millennium would generate a lot of value for these managers, they were willing to advocate internally on behalf of deals with the company.

Millennium's negotiators structured deals to give these managers what they needed but still claimed a lot of the value that got created. Specifically, Millennium retained rights to the intellectual property that got created and the right to pursue multiple, complementary sources of funding. Millennium committed to producing a certain number of target genes or drug candidates, granting exclusive rights for certain disease categories and nonexclusive rights for others. Steven Holtzman, Millennium's chief business officer, put it this way:

> One of the key principles was the notion that the major goal of [units within the large pharmaceutical companies] was the acquisition of targets for small-molecule drugs. What the CNS guys care about is developing CNS drugs. What the cardiovascular guys care about is developing cardiovascular drugs. That's where their bonuses lie. And they have budgets to fund it. So you can go in and say, "We will undertake a program of research which is going to generate a bucket of knowledge, lots of different molecules, only some of which will be relevant for CNS. You will have the right to exploit

those targets to develop small-molecule drugs for central nervous disorders. All the bits of knowledge that don't become CNS targets, we own. If it turns out the target is also relevant in cardiovascular disease, we have the right to exploit it." So we could structure deals where they got targets for small-molecule drugs for specific disease conditions. We retained the rights to use that knowledge for many other applications.[3]

A corollary principle is: *Don't try to negotiate deals that require approvals from multiple powerful groups inside the larger player.* Such deals are a recipe for trouble because cross-unit decision-making processes are inherently political and time-consuming. They may also lead the other side to adopt lowest-common-denominator positions that limit your opportunities to create and claim value. So keep it clean: structure the deal so that it's within the purview of a single unit within the larger company, led by someone whose interests are aligned with yours.

Principle 3: Make Yourself Bigger

There is strength in numbers. So a mouse dealing with an elephant should focus hard on *building coalitions* to buttress its bargaining power. An effective coalition can be built with one or a few large players or a lot of smaller players: it is essential to diagnose the situation carefully, identify promising allies, and build alliances with them. The larger player must come to see that you, in conjunction with your allies, are a force to be reckoned with.

A related technique is to play balance-of-power politics adeptly. This means finding other large players that can act as counterbalances in negotiations—finding a gorilla, if you will, to help keep the elephant in check. GO could have used this strategy but didn't. It had a very eager potential customer in State Farm Insurance but never exploited this relationship in its dealings with IBM. Kaplan decided to go it alone rather than, for example, convening a joint steering committee of representatives from GO, State Farm, and IBM to set objectives and oversee negotiations. This was a big mistake.

Having built a coalition, of course, you have to expend effort to maintain it. Otherwise, you risk seeing your supporters slip away, leaving you alone in the spotlight. Assume that the elephant will try to blunt your coalition-building efforts and even break your alliances.

Principle 4: Build Momentum Through a Sequence of Deals

As David Lax and Jim Sebenius have noted, negotiating the right deals early makes it easier to negotiate subsequent deals at better terms.[4] But early deals with the wrong partners can make everything that follows an uphill battle.

A small company usually has two objectives in negotiating deals with larger players: building its reputation and acquiring resources (funding, technology, distribution) at attractive terms. In early deals, the reputation-building component looms large. Millennium's initial deal with Hoffman-LaRoche, for example, put the company on the map as a serious biotech player. It also generated resources to develop the company's technology platform further, allowing the company in turn to negotiate alliances with Eli Lilly, Astra, and American Home Products. Clearly, reputational gains from early deals can be leveraged in negotiating later deals.

The first major deal is the crux because it defines whether the company is playing in the big leagues. That's why GO chose IBM over HP: IBM had the resources to make the company's pen-based computer a standard. So it is advantageous to do the first deal with a big player, even if smaller ones would provide more attractive terms.

The risk is that a very strong first partner who negotiates very attractive terms could set a problematic precedent for future deals. The ideal first partner is thus the "wounded elephant"—the one that has the most to gain from access to the small company's offerings. In the case of Millennium, the wounded elephant was Hoffman-LaRoche, which was falling behind the curve in gene-based drug discovery and hence was eager for an alliance that would propel it to the forefront.

When you think about sequencing your negotiations with elephants, ask yourself these questions:

- With which set of potential partners would I like to do deals?

- Which companies within the set have the most to gain from doing a deal with me? Pursue these partners first.

- Which potential partners would want to see that I have done deals with credible partners? Pursue these partners later.

- What is the most promising sequence in which to approach potential partners?

Principle 5: Harness the Power of Competition

Trying to dance with several elephants at once may sound like a dangerous undertaking for a mouse. But a mouse who cultivates competition among the elephants gains bargaining power. This is a classic example of creating linkages among negotiations to shape the structure of a situation favorably.

If successful, the mouse may be in a position to demand denial value. When elephants realize that you will do a deal with a competitor if they don't do a deal with you, some will be willing to pay a premium to prevent you from falling under a competitor's sway. Millennium cultivated and exploited this status: competing pharmaceutical companies that did not want each other to enjoy a leg-up bid up the value of Millennium's offerings.

Of course, it is difficult to harness the power of competition in your earliest deals when you have no reputation. So unless the potential impact of your offering is relatively certain, massive, and well recognized, it's tough to attract multiple bidders early on. That's why it's important to do an early deal with a wounded elephant.

Once you are on the map and have done the first couple of deals, things change. The watershed appears when you have developed a reputation and people recognize the value of what you have to offer. Potential partners who begin to fear that you will do a deal with a key competitor may seek you out preemptively. As Steven Holtzman of Millennium explains, you can cultivate such fear by strategically sharing information:

> Whenever we feel there's a possibility for a deal with someone, we immediately call six other people. It drives you nuts, trying to juggle them all, but it will change the perception on the other side of the table, number one. Number two, it will change your self-perception. If you believe that there are other people who are interested, your bluff is no longer a bluff—it's real. It will come across with a whole other level of conviction.[5]

Spreading the word that you may do a deal with someone else sets the stage for judicious use of competition in negotiating the terms of deals. As Holtzman points out, competition for your business also bolsters the self-perception of your negotiating team. If you believe that there are other people who are interested, "your bluff is no longer a bluff—it's real" and it comes across with much more conviction. After its initial deal with LaRoche, every opportunity that Millennium explored involved negotiations with multiple potential partners before converging on a single deal.

Principle 6: Constrain Yourself

Most people resist constraints. But when negotiating with elephants, you need plausible rationales for why the elephant can't have everything it wants. "I'm sorry but you can't have my cheese" probably won't cut it. Far more convincing is, "Much as I would like to, the terms of my contract with Company X prevent me from giving you that cheese."

This is why you may want to constrain yourself, by entering into binding prior agreements, to buttress your bargaining power with elephants.[6] Millennium's network of relationships with pharmaceutical companies functioned this way. Its early deals pinpointing specific diseases imposed contractual restrictions on what Millennium could offer to other partners, effectively reinforcing its strategy of narrow deals with multiple large players.

The same constraints also protected Millennium from hostile takeover. Acquisition by one of the large pharmaceutical companies would require unwinding a complicated web of agreements. In effect, Millennium had a built-in blocking coalition that would sustain its independence.

The price of using constraints as a source of bargaining power is, of course, that they are constraining. They can come back to bite you: if you aren't careful, you can become so constrained by prior commitments that you have no room to breathe. Smart mice carefully balance the benefits of commitments that constrain negotiating partners against the costs of lost flexibility.

Principle 7: Hold the Informational High Ground

The right information, processed and organized for easy access, is a potent source of strength in negotiations with elephants. Negotiation positions are built on supporting rationales and arguments: you have to build a solid foundation of fact for your position while you attempt to knock supporting pillars out from under the other side. It's therefore essential to be better prepared than the elephant and to gain and hold the informational high ground in the negotiation.[7] Ask yourself: What information would most strengthen my negotiating position? Can I acquire it from prenegotiation research, or must I learn it at the table?

Start by thinking broadly about the types of information that will leverage you at the negotiating table. You obviously need a firm handle on your own assessment of the economics of the situation so that you are prepared to argue the merits. But in order to anticipate where the ZOPA will lie, you also need to understand how the other side is likely to see the economics. "Remember there's often a wide window there," says Millennium's Holtzman. "Partly it's the intrinsic value of what you have. But there's also the value to the other side. . . . We spend a lot of time trying to understand how they are modeling it, so that we know whether we can fall within their window."[8]

You also need to understand who you will be dealing with and how decisions will be made within the larger firm. What parts of its anatomy will be involved? Who will make the final call? What are the key decision makers' interests and incentives? GO's Kaplan was never able to answer these questions about IBM. Millennium, by contrast, raised this form of intelligence gathering to a high art. "We spend a lot of time thinking about the person on the other side of the table," says Holtzman, "and how he is going to have to go sell this deal to the boss."[9]

Collecting information is just the beginning. You also have to analyze and organize the information in such a way that you can deploy it deftly at the table. Suppose you are negotiating to sell your company to a much larger player and you foresee a potential environmental liability on a piece of your property. Identifying the issue is just the beginning: you must also generate a list of ways to deal with it. Alternatives might include a reduction in price, indemnification for the buyer, a take-back of the affected land, or a restructuring of the transaction as an asset purchase with the tainted parcel excluded. What is the cost of each alternative? Which, on balance, is preferable? The arguments for your preferred option, and the downsides of the others, must be outlined and quantified before meeting the other side. Which option will the other side prefer? Where are you willing to compromise? All of this information ought to be easily accessible to you.

In summary, keep in mind that your core goals in managing the process are to learn and shape the other side's perceptions. Effective learning helps you gain and hold the informational high ground, which in turn equips you to share or withhold information in order to create and claim value.

Principle 8: Take Control of the Process

If, as a small company, you are at a significant disadvantage in terms of BATNAs and resources, it is essential to take control of the process. If you let the elephant select the music and lead the dance, you are probably in big trouble.

GO's Jerry Kaplan slipped into this trap: at each stage, he allowed IBM to call the tune, reacting to its moves rather than designing a process favorable to him. When he was shuttled from person to person within IBM, he dutifully tried to deal with each new player. When IBM sought to impose more and more onerous terms, he failed to respond.

Millennium's negotiators, by contrast, skillfully controlled the sequencing of the process, shepherding it through successive stages to build momentum. As Holtzman explains:

> First we would establish that there was this valuable thing that we could make together, "a bucket of gold." Then at the right time we shift to a dialogue of "Gentlemen, at some point we really need to establish whether we are in the same ballpark, on the same block, in the same city, in the same hemisphere, on the same planet" in terms of monetary expectations.[10]

Articulating the reasons that both parties came to the table in the first place establishes an initial sense of momentum. Then, Holtzman says, "We always make the first offer. We want to define the playing field."[11] The more complex the deal, the more cautious he was to flesh out the offer thoroughly and work out the basic structure of the deal (who would get what intellectual property and rights) before even raising the subject of money.

Millennium also paid close attention to logistics, including where the negotiation would take place. Holtzman insisted that every individual on the other side who needed to vet the deal be at the table and sometimes even locked the players into a room for days until the deal was done. Millennium also drafted the agreements. "We always do the drafting, partly because we think we are better at it," Holtzman notes. "These are very complex deals, and you have an advantage if you know how to deal with the complexity."[12]

Process control is not a panacea. It can't compensate for lack of a credible BATNA or failure to cultivate competition or build coalitions. But it can have a substantial impact on the margin, especially in combination with the techniques already described.

Principle 9: Negotiate with Implementation in Mind

It's one thing to negotiate an agreement with an elephant and another to get it implemented satisfactorily. Mice often become vulnerable after a deal is signed because they have let go (often irrevocably) of alternatives. In effect, the strength of their BATNA erodes once the process moves from deal making to implementation.

As GO discovered with IBM, when the elephant has you all to itself and gets access to more information about what you are up to, it can really get in your face. This is also a juncture when internal competitors or opponents within the other side can intervene to slow or even stymie implementation of the deal.

So what can a mouse do to reduce its vulnerability in the implementation phase? In brief, try not to burn your bridges, and try to preserve the strength of your BATNA in case serious problems arise during implementation. This is easier said than done, which is another reason not to put yourself at the mercy of a single large partner.

Second, give your champions within the other side as big a personal stake as possible in successful implementation of the deal. They need to own it in a visceral way. Entangle them, cognitively and emotionally, in making the deal work. As Holtzman puts it, "There are three things to making deals: you have to move minds, hearts, and bodies. You have to move someone's mind; the deal has to make sense. But you have to move their heart too. They have to believe that the deal is good in an emotional way. Then you have to move the bodies to close the deal."[13]

A related technique is to negotiate a formal structure for overseeing implementation as part of the deal and, crucially, build a network of personal relationships that will supply you intelligence about what is going on and social capital to draw on if things get tough. GO didn't build a formal implementation structure or good working relationships, and repeatedly it got blindsided. Millennium, by contrast, established multilevel governing structures up front, not just a joint management team with each partner but a joint steering committee composed of higher-level executives from both companies. Millennium also fostered informal relationships at multiple points of contact. That network provided Millennium with an early-warning system about changes in partners' direction and intentions. "That was something which we saw becoming more important over time," says Holtzman, "especially as companies change people. We need to be able to maximize the value of the relationship, even through the changes."[14]

Finally, leverage the coalitions you build during negotiation into implementation of the deal. For example, GO could have invited its champions at State Farm to participate much more actively in implementation of the deal with IBM.

Principle 10: Build Superior Organizational Capabilities

To apply the first nine principles, you will need specialized organizational capabilities. The foundation is getting the right technical and business people on board, and then setting up the right team structures and coordination mechanisms. Beyond that, it is essential to forge relationships with skilled external advisers, such as lawyers and investment bankers.

These are the necessary conditions for success, but they are not sufficient. You must be organized to learn rapidly as you do more deals with elephants. Fast learning is a dynamic source of advantage for small players: if you can learn from past negotiations, capture the resulting insights, and, crucially, share these insights among yourselves, you will increase your overall negotiating effectiveness. But unless you put specific mechanisms in place to capture and disseminate learning, valuable knowledge will be lost. Given the press of business, it requires real discipline to set up and maintain organizational learning processes. But the rewards well outweigh the costs.

It is particularly important for small players to cultivate organizational capabilities and not just individual competence. Otherwise, you will run the risk of being dependent on one or a few people and suffering greatly if you lose them. The starting point is to ask some basic questions: How can those newly hired learn to negotiate? Are insights from past negotiations captured and shared? How is knowledge preserved and forgetting prevented? Particularly in organizations with substantial turnover, the risk of losing institutional memory is very high. Memory loss can be avoided only by self-conscious management of the acquisition and dissemination of knowledge.

Collective knowledge sharing and reflection could take the form of postnegotiation debriefings that distill and share lessons learned or reports that summarize specific negotiations. Person-to-person transmission is usually more flexible and time efficient than written documentation. Flexibility and time efficiency are important because of the pace at which most negotiators operate. Busyness—a given in small organizations—is often the enemy of learning.

NEGOTIATING AS AN ELEPHANT

It seems only fair to close with a few thoughts on how elephants ought to deal effectively with mice.

Elephants' most common mistake is overreliance on their power (a strong BATNA and lots of resources) to impose terms on weaker players. Power may work, but it is likely to provoke resistance on the part of mice who don't like being dictated to. It may also provoke reactive coalition building, prompting the mouse to seek out allies. Even the best-intentioned elephant can fall into this trap, because the mouse is likely to feel on the defensive before the negotiation even begins. It takes only small slights to activate the mouse's expectation of being taken advantage of.

A second mistake is to get nibbled to death by many mice. At the height of the Internet frenzy in the late 1990s, a large soft drink company was approached by many small firms eager to leverage the big company's core brands. The small companies were applying a principle we endorsed earlier: make overtures to interested individuals and units within a larger company seeking to cut a deal. Chaos threatened, so the soft drink company created a central point of contact to keep track of and vet deals. Individuals in the line organizations remained champions of individual deals, but the central group represented the corporate interest in selecting partnerships and conducting negotiations.

Beyond using power deftly and maintaining a companywide perspective, how you approach deals with mice flows from a basic strategic decision: Will you try to preserve and deploy your power to extract very favorable agreements, or will you position yourself as the partner of choice for smaller players? If the former, you should work to blunt the tactics that we have urged mice to employ. If the latter, you should cultivate the reputation and capabilities to negotiate and sustain deals with smaller and more vulnerable partners.

Many negotiations match stronger and weaker parties: entrepreneurs deal with venture capitalists, suppliers deal with customers, and small companies are acquired by conglomerates. In these situations, it is essential to be realistic about whether you are a mouse or an elephant and to condition your approach to negotiation accordingly.

6

Building Coalitions

After fifteen years of steady advancement at a leading durable-goods manufacturing company, Dana Monosoff decided to move on. Recruiters had long been calling her, and she soon had several attractive options. Ultimately, Dana became the new chief operating officer (COO) of White Goods, Inc., a struggling maker of high-end kitchen appliances.

Several years of flat sales at White Goods prior to Dana's arrival had precipitated the departure of her predecessor. Nimbler and more aggressive competitors had begun to chip away at the firm's traditional quality advantage by introducing new materials and production technologies. Even more ominous, how products were sold and distributed was changing. While White Goods continued to rely on a network of independent dealers, its most formidable competitors had begun to establish long-term ties with large retail stores; some had even begun to manufacture private-label appliances. Dana expected these trends to accelerate.

Dana was the first senior executive in fifteen years to be brought in from outside the company. When White Goods's chief executive officer, Paul Schofield, hired her to get growth back on track, he promised Dana that if she did well, she would succeed him as CEO within a few years. But Dana was convinced that producing moderately priced products for large stores was the way to go, and such a move would not be an easy sell. A decision to market through large outlets would anger the dealers and could erode White Goods's tight control over sales and servicing channels. Moreover, producing lower-priced offerings was at odds with White Goods's proud tradition of manufacturing premium products.

Assuming that Dana is correct about the direction White Goods should go, how should she build support for needed change? Take a few minutes to think about how you would approach this situation.

Dana cannot hope to accomplish the changes she desires by relying on the authority vested in her position. She needs to be able to persuade people to go along with her. To be effective, leaders like Dana need to master five core coalition-building tasks:

Task 1: Mapping the influence landscape—identifying who needs to be persuaded and how to do so

Task 2: Shaping perceptions of interests—influencing others' beliefs about what they want

Task 3: Shaping perceptions of alternatives—influencing others' beliefs about the options open to them

Task 4: Gaining acceptance for tough decisions—increasing the likelihood that difficult choices will be accepted

Task 5: Persuading at a distance—achieving a broad impact through mass persuasion

TASK 1: MAPPING THE INFLUENCE LANDSCAPE

Sometimes it is sufficient to convince a single person, but more typically leaders like Dana must build supportive coalitions of interest groups to secure support for their initiatives. Often it is also necessary to neutralize opponents and prevent blocking coalitions from forming. Before beginning to design a persuasion strategy, it is essential to map the influence landscape.

Dana's ultimate goal was to build support for her strategy and to prevent opposition from coalescing. Simply dictating change would have bred resistance, undermining her position. It could even have cost her job. Consequently, she set out to identify people and groups whose support was crucial, as well as potential opponents. The CEO, Paul Schofield, would obviously have to be on board. But other top-level executives would influence him, so she wanted to pinpoint who else in the organization she needed to persuade.

Identifying Targets of Influence

The first step is to identify the groups within which support must be built and opposition neutralized. Such groups typically include:

- Organizational units of employees bound together by shared training and expertise or by shared tasks and supervision
- Identity groups, bound by occupation, age, gender, race, or social class, that protect shared interests and promote mutual solidarity
- Power coalitions of people who have banded together opportunistically to advance or protect shared interests, but who may not otherwise identify with or socialize with each other[1]

Dana's analysis persuaded her that she needed to build support in top management, the sales and distribution division, and the manufacturing workforce. Persuading top management would require that she cultivate and retain the confidence of the CEO, her peers, and top-level subordinates. The changes Dana envisioned would call for shifts in power relationships that could create winners and losers among key players who enjoyed longstanding relationships with the CEO and with each other. She would also need to deal with likely opposition from White Goods's sales force and network of independent dealers. Her third task would be to build a base of trust and respect with the workforce to convince them of the need to manufacture less expensive (and less prestigious) products.

Analyzing Influence Networks

The next step is to analyze influence networks—configurations determined by who defers to whom on crucial issues.[2] This level of analysis identifies opinion leaders who exert disproportionate influence on decision making.[3] Convincing these pivotal individuals translates into broad acceptance, and resistance on their part could galvanize broader opposition.

Dana's analysis of influence networks within top management at White Goods convinced her that Todd Simpson, vice president of sales, was pivotal. A career employee strongly invested in the company's traditions, Todd had risen through the sales ranks to become a trusted adviser to Schofield. Todd's support for Dana's proposed change initiatives was crucial. He would be influenced by his direct reports, the regional sales directors, who would in turn come under pressure from White Goods's independent dealers. But Todd was also respected by both groups and capable of influencing them.

Dana concluded that she would also need to win the support of Sarah Wolverton, vice president of manufacturing, and Nathan Simon, vice president of engineering, to move down-market to lower-priced products. Both were influential with the CEO, though less so than Todd, and both deferred to Todd on matters pertaining to company culture and traditions. Dana had begun to develop a relationship with Nathan but barely knew Sarah. The resulting influence network is illustrated in the figure on page 139, with the strength of existing relationships represented by the thickness of the connecting arrows.

Identifying Supporters, Opponents, and Persuadables

Some people will endorse the leader's agenda right away because it advances their own interests. But enlisting people as supporters doesn't mean that you can take them for granted. It's never enough simply to elicit support; you have to maintain it to ensure that support doesn't slip away in the night. Leaders must devote energy to

Influence Diagram

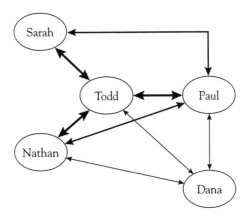

buttressing and deepening the commitment of their supporters, and to expanding their own persuasive reach by helping allies become more persuasive. In the words of Owen Harries, "Preaching to the converted, far from being a superfluous activity, is vital. Preachers do it every Sunday. The strengthening of the commitment, intellectual performance, and morale of those already on your side is an essential task, both in order to bind them more securely to the cause and to make them more effective exponents of it."[4]

Meanwhile, other important players will oppose your efforts whatever you do. But identifying people as opponents does not mean that you can ignore them. To analyze your opponents, ask yourself the following questions: How long have efforts to organize opposition been going on? Is the opposition united by longstanding relationships and shared interests or by short-term opportunism? Are there linchpins whose conversion or neutralization would substantially weaken resistance?

Because persuasion consumes time and emotional energy (which should not be wasted on the irrevocably opposed), it is essential to assess early who can be persuaded. If Todd were not persuadable, Dana would be well advised to start elsewhere and aim to bring him on board later. But Dana perceived Todd as a thoughtful, forward-looking person; she considered him persuadable. She was confident that she had a strong case and could support it with logical arguments and sales trend data, but she also knew that Todd might still oppose change.

Assessing Targets' Interests

The next step is to zero in on the targets' interests. What do Todd and the regional sales managers care about? Put yourself in their shoes; your aim is to grasp what they *perceive* their interests to be, not what you believe they *should* be. Faced with the change Dana envisioned, Todd and others could resist for a variety of reasons:

- *Loss of a comfortable status quo.* They see no reason to change in ways that might cut their earnings or alter established patterns of social interaction.

- *Challenge to one's sense of competence.* They fear feeling incompetent and unable to perform well in the postchange environment.

- *Threats to self-defining values.* They believe that change will produce a culture that discredits traditional notions of value and rewards behaviors antithetical to their self-image.

- *Potential loss of security due to uncertainty about the future.* They misunderstand or fear the intended consequences of a proposed change.

- *Negative consequences for key allies.* They fear the consequences for others they care about or are beholden to.

Dana foresaw that Todd might oppose a dramatic shift in distribution strategy out of concern for White Goods's premium image and the impact on his organization. She knew that Todd would come under strong pressure from others. Many regional sales directors would oppose a change that could undermine their status and affect their compensation. Todd would also hear from dealers who would view a decision to sell through large stores as a threat to their businesses. Clearly, she faced an uphill battle to gain Todd's support.

Assessing the Driving and Restraining Forces

People facing tough decisions experience psychological tension as opposing forces push them in conflicting directions.[5] The source of tension might be internal conflicts (Do I want X more than Y? Should I do what I want to do or what I think I should do?) or social pressures, such as competing prior commitments or worry about what respected people will think.[6] Ultimately, a person decides that the benefits of one path outweigh the costs of renouncing others.

You can deepen your analysis by probing the driving and restraining forces at work on prospective targets of your influence. Driving forces push people in the direction you desire; restraining forces push them elsewhere. The goal is to strengthen the driving forces or weaken the restraining forces, or both. Dana's analysis of the driving and restraining forces acting on Todd is illustrated in the force-field diagram. The driving forces that would lead Todd to support Dana's initiative include the logic and data that support her case and, perhaps, reluctance to oppose her openly. Restraining forces include his desire to protect White Goods's culture and the pressures exerted on him by sales directors and dealers. On the face of it, the driving forces look like thin reeds arrayed against the powerful restraining forces.

Identifying Targets' Alternatives

The next step is to evaluate how key people perceive their alternatives. For Dana, this means predicting the actions that Todd and other potential opponents might take. Specifically, is resistance to persuasion likely to be overt or covert? Todd could simply withhold his support or, more subtly, raise questions about the risks of

Balance of Driving and Restraining Forces

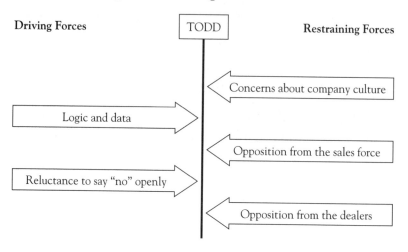

Dana's proposals. He could act alone or in concert with others, such as the regional sales managers. A blocking coalition of Todd and the regional sales managers would seriously threaten Dana's change agenda.

Todd's influence with Paul, the CEO, is sufficient to stall Dana's efforts, but not everyone with reason to resist change has the power to do so. Ask yourself: Is the resistance of opposing coalitions likely to be active or passive? What forms might it take? More generally, how do key people perceive their alternatives? How might these perceptions be altered? A clear grasp of the latter will sharpen your influence strategies.

TASK 2: SHAPING PERCEPTIONS OF INTERESTS

The next step is to try to shape others' perceptions of their interests—what they care about and the goals they want to achieve. Strategies for transforming perceptions of interests are altering incentives, framing decisions, drawing on the power of social influence, and engaging in quid pro quo negotiation.

Altering Incentives

Changing the incentive systems within which people operate—introducing rewards or disincentives or both—can alter their perceptions of their interests. To the extent that people pursue the rewards or avoid the disincentives, their behavior (but not necessarily attitudes) will change.

Measurement systems, compensation plans, budgets, and even mission statements and strategic plans can all function as levers to influence behavior in organizations. By setting expectations and defining rewards and punishments, they push people in desired directions. Such measures can be especially effective in the short term, and they are usually necessary when prompt and significant behavioral change is called for.

Dana should think through how compensation might work for the regional sales directors under the new system and how incentives could be structured for dealers. A proposal that responds positively to their objections would weaken a potent restraining force.

Framing Decisions

Framing is the use of argument, analogy, and metaphor to promote a favorable definition of the problem to be solved and the set of potential solutions. Framing has been characterized as "a burning glass which collects and focuses the diffuse warmth of popular emotions, concentrating them on a specific issue."[7] Because people's interests tend to remain latent and diffuse until they face a choice, and because how people perceive their interests depends on how choices are posed, framing is a powerful tool.

Dana ought to frame her proposal in a way that elevates some interests while marginalizing other interests or leaving them dormant. She can accomplish this by linking her agenda to people's needs, wants, and aspirations and linking choices she opposes to their worries and fears. Done well, this approach excites emotions that color individuals' choices. Effective framing uses a number of techniques:

- *Invoking the common good.* This approach emphasizes collective benefits and downplays individual costs. Dana could stress the overarching importance to the organization of getting sales growth back on track and attempt to frame the costs to Todd and the regional sales directors as a sacrifice that must be made for the common good.

- *Linking to core values.* Marketers and propagandists long ago learned the efficacy of linking choices to the values that define self-identity. Cigarette companies, for example, link smoking to independence and the freedom to choose. Dana could endorse Todd's identification with the company's tradition of producing high-quality products and emphasize that sales growth would support the investment in new technologies needed to sustain it.

- *Heightening concerns about loss or risk.* Some framing techniques exploit biases in the ways that people make decisions. Many people are loss averse—more sensitive to potential losses than to equivalent potential gains.[8] Desired courses of action could thus be cast in terms of gains and undesired choices in terms of losses. Similarly widespread is the tendency to be risk averse—to prefer guaranteed gains to risky choices, even if the latter could yield much larger gains.[9] Here again, desired courses of action can be characterized as less risky, undesired choices as more risky. Dana could dwell on the risks of failing to get sales growth back on track, including vulnerability to takeover and loss of control over the organization's destiny.

- *Rejection and retreat.* Asking for a lot initially and then settling for less shapes the other side's perceptions of interests. This works because people are loss averse—more sensitive to potential losses than to equivalent potential gains.[10] Dana could propose to sell exclusively through large stores and then "retreat" to a plan to sell only midrange lines through large stores, reserving the premium lines for existing dealers. The risk is that an extreme initial request might trigger resistance and the emergence of a blocking coalition.

- *Enlarging the pie*. Choices perceived as win-lose propositions are particularly difficult to sell. Broadening the range of issues under consideration can facilitate mutually beneficial trades that "enlarge the pie."[11] Alongside her proposal to sell through large stores, Dana might put on the table issues she knows to be important to Todd. Her earlier analyses might have revealed, for example, that Todd wants to adopt a state-of-the-art sales-tracking system.

- *Neutralizing toxic issues*. As we saw in Chapter Two, progress on multi-issue initiatives can be stalled by the presence of toxic issues. Toxic issues can sometimes be neutralized by postponing them for future consideration or by making up-front commitments that allay anxieties. Dana could demonstrate her commitment to the dealer network by proposing a two-tier distribution system in which mid- to low-range products would be sold in large stores and mid- to high-range products through dealers.

- *Inoculating against expected challenges*. As far back as Aristotle, persuaders have been advised to inoculate their audiences against the arguments they expect their opponents to make. Refuting weak forms of expected counterarguments immunizes audiences against the same arguments when they are advanced in more potent forms. Dana should prepare responses to the objections she anticipates from the regional sales directors and dealers. She might say to Todd, "I know that your people are likely to be concerned about X, but the issue is really Y."

- *Providing a script for convincing others*. In addition to influencing the immediate target, successful framing provides that person a persuasive script for convincing others. As she frames her arguments, Dana should keep in mind that Todd will have to sell them to the regional sales directors and dealers; her arguments should explicitly address their concerns.

Using Social Influence

People rarely make important choices independently; most people are influenced by their networks of relationships and the opinions of key advisers.[12] Awareness that a highly respected person already supports an initiative alters others' assessments of its attractiveness, its likelihood of success, and the potential costs of not getting on board. Convincing opinion leaders to lend support and mobilize their own networks thus has a powerful leveraging effect. Likewise, a leader who has built political capital with key people can draw on reciprocity to gain a buy-in.

Todd's assessment of the costs and benefits of supporting or opposing Dana's initiative will be strongly influenced by the opinions of those in his network of relationships. It is thus important for Dana to understand the full range of pressures that could impinge on Todd. Research in social psychology has established that people prefer choices that enable them to:

- Remain consistent with strongly held values and beliefs, which tend to be shared with important reference groups. People asked to behave inconsistently with their values or beliefs experience internal psychological dissonance, external social sanction, or both.

- Remain consistent with their commitments, because failure to honor commitments incurs social sanctions. People prefer not to reverse themselves or overtly constrain their future choices by setting undesirable precedents.

- Preserve their sense of control. Choices that threaten one's position in a social hierarchy or sense of control are likely to provoke anxiety.

- Repay obligations. Reciprocity is a strong social norm, and people are vulnerable to appeals for support that invoke past favors.

- Preserve their reputations. Choices that preserve or enhance one's reputation are viewed favorably, those that could jeopardize one's reputation negatively.

- Gain the approval of respected others, such as opinion leaders, mentors, experts, and others to whom people look for clues about "right thinking."[13]

All else being equal, Todd will make choices that appear consistent with his values and commitments, maintain his status, repay obligations, enhance his reputation, and gain the approval of respected others. He will avoid choices that violate his values, require him to renege on commitments, create undesirable precedents, undermine his sense of control, make him appear ungrateful, damage his reputation, and offend respected others.

These universal preferences translate readily into effective ways to harness the power of social influence:

- *Leveraging small commitments into larger ones.* As we saw in Chapter Three, a person who has been persuaded to make innocuous commitments has already started down the slippery slope to larger ones.[14] This approach to persuasion—entanglement—presumes that people can be led from point A to point B in a succession of small, irreversible steps when doing so in a single leap would be impossible. Note too that public commitments carry more weight than private commitments. Commitments made in private offer wiggle room; you can argue that you were misunderstood or misquoted. Backing away from commitments made in front of others is significantly more difficult. This is why weighty decisions and commitments to specific goals should be made at meetings: people's reputations are put on the line. This is also why the first-mover advantage in securing early commitments is substantial; once your opponents secure commitments of support, the battle to win away their supporters is uphill. In addition to making a good case, you must also help targets of persuasion find ways to disentangle themselves from prior commitments gracefully.
- *Drawing on the power of reciprocity.* The desire to reciprocate is a strong motivating force.[15] Because Todd's relationship with his regional sales directors involves long-standing expectations of mutual support, he will be loath to betray those expectations. Dana

can begin to counter this stance by cultivating a sense of obligation in Todd, perhaps by helping advance goals that are important to him. The resulting debt is a source of capital on which she can draw when the time comes to push her initiative. Note that favors do not have to be precisely balanced. Studies have shown that small favors can be leveraged into disproportionately large reciprocal favors. It is valuable to keep this principle in mind when influencing others and when resisting others' attempts at persuasion.

• *Using behavior change to drive attitude change.* Everyone knows that attitudinal changes can translate into significant behavioral changes, but the reverse can also be true: changing someone's behavior can change the person's attitudes.[16] People have a strong need for consistency; once persuaded to try something new, they are likely to revise their attitudes accordingly. For example, Dana might ask Todd to participate in a study of ways to make a two-tier distribution system work. Having worked on the study and helped to shape its conclusions, Todd's attitudes might shift to align with his actions.

• *Sequencing through relationship networks.* Faced with difficult choices, people often look to others they respect for clues about "right thinking." They seek out opinion leaders for their expertise or experience or their access to information, or simply because they have authoritative personalities. Whatever the source of their stature, it is important to understand how opinion leaders formulate their opinions. As we have seen, this is a matter of tracing who defers to whom on key issues.[17] If Todd defers to senior people in other functions on issues of company strategy, it pays off to secure the support of these people first. As we saw in Chapter Three, Dana should draw up a sequencing plan to decide when and in what order to approach people in order to form a coalition and build momentum before she gets to Todd.[18] She should also carefully plan the sequence of individual and group meetings. Dana could meet individually with those whom Todd trusts. Having won their support, she could introduce the issue in a group meeting that Todd attends and then follow up with a one-on-one meeting with Todd.

Engaging in Quid Pro Quo Negotiation

If crucial people cannot otherwise be brought along, it may be necessary to engage them in this-for-that negotiation, agreeing to support initiatives they care about in exchange for their support of yours. Success rests on understanding the full set of interests at stake—which may include reputation and prestige as well as tangible needs—and on knowing how to craft a suitable trade. Support can often be bought. But at what cost? Leaders who don't know when to stop buying support can end up making compromises that dilute their efforts.

As illustrated in the accompanying figure, artful use of incentives, framing, social influence, and quid pro quo negotiation will strengthen the forces driving Todd in the direction Dana favors and weaken restraining forces. With careful thought and sustained effort, Dana may be able to tip the scales and get Todd to support her initiative.

New Balance of Driving and Restraining Forces

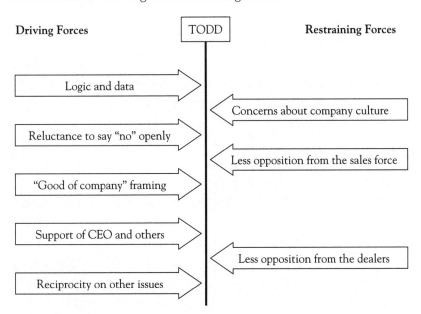

TASK 3: SHAPING PERCEPTIONS OF ALTERNATIVES

Shaping people's perceptions of their own interests is by no means the only avenue for persuasion. You can also influence their perceptions of their alternatives, the set of options among which they believe they must choose. This usually entails directing their attention toward alternatives you favor and eliminating less favorable choices from consideration.

Introducing New Options

People are likely to perceive their alternatives too narrowly: they overlook potentially attractive alternatives or construe them as nonviable, too risky, or undesirable. Often this phenomenon is a consequence of how decisions are framed. Because organizations tend to cast new choices in the same old ways, coalitions are likely to form along predictable lines.

Often one can exert influence simply by expanding the range of alternatives under consideration. Dana could stimulate innovation, for example, by encouraging people at White Goods to benchmark best-in-class organizations, thus exposing them to alternative approaches to familiar problems. Ideally, she would suggest an organization with a successful two-tier approach to sales. Introducing new options can put stress on existing coalitions, setting the stage for the creation of new ones.

Setting the Agenda

Big decisions draw on tributary processes that define the problem, identify alternatives, and establish criteria for evaluating costs and benefits.

By the time the problem and the options have been defined, the actual choice may be a foregone conclusion. This is why it is so important to shape the decision-making agenda early on. "Pay great attention to the agenda of the debate," cautions Owen Harries:

He who defines the issues and determines their priority is already well on the way to winning. . . . Diplomats, at least when they are performing effectively, understand this well, which is one reason they often appear fussy and pedantic to outsiders who have not grasped the point at issue. . . . It is just as important, and on the same grounds, to deny your opponent the right to impose his language and concepts on the debate, and to make sure you always use terms that reflect your own values, traditions, and interests.[19]

One touchstone to successful persuasion is thus simply to be there during the formative period in order to define the terms of the debate before momentum builds in the wrong direction, or irreversible decisions are made, or too much time passes. Another is to help select the information used to define the problem and the options. Dana could commission studies, for example, to explore changes in how kitchen appliances are sold and distributed.

Eliminating "Do Nothing" as an Option

It is alarmingly easy, even with the best of intentions, to defer or delay a decision. When success requires the coordinated actions of many people, delay by any single individual can have a cascade effect, giving others an excuse not to proceed. A leader must therefore work to eliminate "do nothing" as a viable option. Dana must decide when the time is ripe and then push for a decision on distribution systems.

One approach is to schedule action-forcing events—events that force people to make commitments or take actions. Meetings, review sessions, and deadlines can all provide impetus. Those who do make commitments should immediately be locked into timetables that specify incremental implementation milestones. Regular meetings to review progress and tough questioning of those who miss agreed-on goals increase the psychological pressure to follow through. A caveat: avoid pressing for closure until the balance of forces is tipping in the right direction.

A related tactic is progressive elimination of less desirable options, funneling the decision-making process toward the choice you favor. People are rarely willing to make difficult decisions before they have exhausted less painful options. Sometimes it makes sense to let them try to make these options work, especially if you are reasonably certain that they will fail. If Dana finds Todd strongly opposed to her plan, she could suggest that he produce a plan for changing the distribution system and see what he proposes. If his plan isn't feasible and the CEO rejects it, she will be in a position to say, "Okay, now we try it my way." Pruning of options is often necessary to provide a defensible rationale for a decision, diffuse responsibility for unpleasant outcomes, and lead others to the point of readiness to commit. The downside is that valuable time gets consumed.

TASK 4: GAINING ACCEPTANCE FOR TOUGH DECISIONS

Leaders often have to make unpopular decisions. When someone's pet project is shut down, spending is curtailed, or someone is deprived of responsibility, the challenge is to get people to accept the consequences of the imposed decision. Although never easy, tough decisions can be made more palatable by paying careful attention to process.

Creating a Fair Process

People at White Goods are more likely to accept the consequences of Dana's decision if it is perceived to be the outcome of a fair process.[20] When people believe that the decision-making process was legitimate and that their views were taken seriously, they are more likely to support implementation. Leaders who gain reputations for being thoughtful and deliberative enlarge the scope within which people will accept and support their choices. Those known for arbitrariness, thoughtlessness, and apparent disregard for equity fuel resistance and furnish focal points around which opposition can mobilize.

Engaging in Shared Diagnosis

Involving people in the diagnosis of organizational problems is a form of entanglement: participation in the diagnosis makes it more difficult to deny the need for tough decisions. By the end of such a process, people are often willing to accept outcomes they would never have accepted at the outset. This is another reason for Dana to engage Todd in an analysis of changes in how appliances are distributed.

Consulting Before Deciding

Consultation promotes buy-in. Dana should consider consulting throughout White Goods about the emerging challenge from competitors and the role of large retail stores in the market. The knowledge gained could promote acceptance of the eventual decision and deepen her grasp of the state of play in the organization.

Good consultation means active listening.[21] Posing questions and encouraging people to voice their worries, then summarizing what you have heard, signals that you are paying serious attention. The power of active listening as a persuasive technique is vastly underrated. By channeling people's thinking and framing choices, active listening can promote acceptance of difficult decisions. Because the questions leaders ask and the way they summarize and feed back responses powerfully affect people's perceptions, active listening and framing are a particularly potent persuasive pairing.

Giving What Is Asked For

It is disconcerting to be asked what you would need in order to accomplish something difficult and then to be given it. Having made a difficult decision, the leader asks those responsible for implementation what resources they will need. After carefully probing their assessments, the leader then says, "You have it! Let's get going." This tactic is a variation on persuading people to make a commitment and then holding them to it.

TASK 5: PERSUADING AT A DISTANCE

Finally, leaders can't possibly communicate individually with everyone they need to persuade, so they must be proficient at persuading from a distance—communicating themes and priorities in speeches, memos, and other forms of one-to-many communication. In addition to persuading top management and the sales organization, Dana also has to win the support of the larger workforce; they are justifiably proud of the high-quality products they produce and may resent a decision to move down-market.

Constructing Reliable Communication Channels

Just as nature abhors a vacuum, informal networks spring up to fill communication voids in organizations. In the absence of reliable formal communication, people rely on the grapevine for information. The problem, of course, is that the grapevine introduces distortion into the communication process. Some of this distortion is unintentional, a product of error and omission in person-to-person transmission. But those seeking to advance partisan goals can intentionally distort information. As Garth Jowett and Victoria O'Donnell put it, propaganda functions by "withholding information, releasing information at pre-determined times, releasing information in juxtaposition with other information that may influence perceptions, manufacturing information, communicating information to selective audiences, and distorting information."[22]

Whatever their intentions, the people at focal points in these informal communication networks have substantial power to shape messages. Thus, leaders like Dana must preempt the grapevine by building reliable formal communication channels. Whether this means publishing a new newsletter or writing memos to the workforce or convening town meetings, the goal is direct access to the target audience.

Good communication channels transmit the right information in a timely and responsive way. It is easy to fall behind the communication curve, especially when the decision in question has negative consequences. It may seem easier to withhold bad news, particularly if the full picture is not yet available. But doing so sets up a vicious circle in which official statements come out in bits and pieces, reactively, and never catch up with the grapevine. It is wise to assume that bad news will leak out quickly; plan to be there first so you can shape the message and avoid triggering resistance unnecessarily.

Focus and Repetition

Leaders who try to communicate too many messages at once often end up with a muddle. One of the core insights of research on persuasive communication is the power of focus and repetition.[23] Dana's persuasive messages are most likely to take root in the minds of White Goods's workforce if they consist of a few core themes, repeated until they sink in. It is a sure sign of success when people begin to echo your themes without knowing they are doing so, and focus and repetition are effective means to this end. By the third or fourth time we hear a new song on the radio, for instance, we often cannot get it out of our minds. Of course, we may also grow irritated by repetition: using precisely the same words over and over is likely to annoy and insult your listeners and will make it apparent that you are trying to persuade, which can provoke backlash. The art of effective communication is to repeat and elaborate core themes without sounding like a parrot.

Dana had to craft the message that a move down-market need not compromise quality. In early tours of White Goods plants, Dana had learned that the workforce was proud of its products but ashamed that the company sold only to wealthy customers. Dana could tap into this sentiment by subtly emphasizing that the new products would be affordable for workers and their families.

Matching the Medium to the Message

Decisions about how to communicate a message shouldn't be made lightly. Leaders have at their disposal a variety of forums and media, including speeches, small-group meetings, town meetings, newsletters, memos, interactive videoconferences, videotapes, and Web pages. News is nearly always best delivered in an interactive forum, such as a meeting at which people can ask questions, but complex technical and data-intensive arguments are best conveyed in written form.[24] Speeches and live videoconference and town meeting presentations are ideal for communicating broad goals, values, and inspiration. Prerecorded video presentations, though useful for disseminating information about the progress of initiatives, can seem contrived when used to communicate a new vision. In developing her communication plan, Dana should take into account how White Goods employees feel (or could feel) most comfortable interacting with top leadership. Do senior managers meet regularly with employees in town hall formats? Are such meetings viewed as open and risk-free opportunities to ask questions or as one-way streets for management to tell employees how it's going to be? If the latter, Dana could send a message by running a more open process.

Building Personal Credibility

Personal credibility is an important persuasive resource. Numerous studies have found the persuasiveness of a message to be strongly linked to the perceived credibility of its source.[25] This is not a new observation; as Aristotle pointed out in *Rhetoric*:

> Of the modes of persuasion furnished by the spoken word there are three kinds. The first kind depends on the personal

character of the speaker; the second on putting the audience in a certain frame of mind; the third on the proof, or apparent proof, provided by the speech itself. Persuasion is achieved by the speaker's personal character when the speech is so spoken as to make us think him credible. We believe good men more fully and readily than others; this is true generally whatever the question is, and absolutely true where exact certainty is impossible and opinions are divided.[26]

Just so. Leaders with a reputation for integrity are listened to because they are respected, considered trustworthy, and perceived to possess the experience to make good judgments. They are also more persuasive when their approval is highly valued. Leaders who demand and reward excellence, and who spotlight and condemn inadequate performance, are likely to find their approval a rare and sought-after commodity. A leader who takes this too far might earn a reputation for never being satisfied, but a reputation for not being tough enough is probably more damaging.

OUTCOME FOR DANA

In the end, Dana successfully transformed White Goods. She employed shared diagnosis to convince top management, including a reluctant Todd, of the need for change. This initiative led to the selection of a project team to plan changes in the product development process and, in turn, to two pilot projects for midrange offerings. As these projects began to bear fruit, but substantially before they were ready for launch, Dana began communicating extensively with the company as a whole about the need to move in the direction of midrange appliances. She made the case for change in a series of in-person meetings and written communications, and emphasized that the proposed new offerings would bring the company's products within the reach of everyone. She also highlighted the likely downside of not moving in this direction: progressive erosion of the company's competitiveness.

The final piece involved placating salespeople and the network of independent dealers. Working closely with Todd, Dana met directly with groups of salespeople and dealers to explain the decision to sell midrange products directly through large retail stores under a different brand name. Though upset, they were relieved to be reassured that the company was committed to retaining the dealer network for higher end products.

HONING YOUR DEFENSES

Efforts to persuade are a pervasive part of life. Negotiators and leaders don't merely need to know how to persuade; they must also know when to permit themselves to be persuaded and when to resist. The former calls for understanding your own biases and blind spots and how they might impede openness to good arguments. The latter calls for understanding others' persuasive techniques and honing your defenses.

All the approaches to persuasion that we have surveyed are as likely to be used *on* leaders as *by* leaders. People will strive to frame arguments, employ entanglement, and exploit the power of reciprocity; they will seek to alter perceptions of alternatives and artificially constrain choices. Recognizing these strategies is the most potent defense: forewarned is forearmed. The next best defenses are to broaden options and defer commitment. Slowing down the pace of events and thinking things through are bulwarks against making decisions you will come to regret.

Techniques of persuasion are inherently neither benign nor malign. Like many other tools, they can be used for good or ill, and without them leaders would be unable to lead.

7

Managing Conflict

After years of supplying fuel and lubricants to operators of medium-sized fleets of trucks, Foster Fuels decided to expand its offerings to include engine coolant, procured in bulk from a reputable manufacturer. Foster approached its existing customers, including Robert Wood of the Wood Construction Company. Wood operated a fleet of over one hundred dumptrucks, loaders, and other vehicles. Chuck Foster had supplied Bob Wood for seven years, and the relationship had been cordial.

Things changed fast after Wood's decision to buy the coolant and install it in half his fleet. The vehicles with the new coolant began to experience engine problems, including leaky cooling hoses and corrosion of metal fittings. Because only the trucks with the new coolant were affected, Wood blamed it for his problems. Ultimately, his mechanics found such severe damage in twenty-one vehicles that their engines had to be replaced. Thirty-five more had the coolant flushed and replaced and new hoses and fittings installed. Only time would tell whether there was internal damage to their engines.

Wood calculated the costs of this debacle—replacement and maintenance costs, lost business, and damage to existing contracts—at close to $450,000. He sent a bill for this amount to Chuck Foster, demanding payment for the damages. Foster retorted (accurately, it later emerged) that none of his other customers had experienced coolant problems and suggested other possible causes, such as other chemicals used by Wood's mechanics or some unusual interaction.

Enraged, Wood threatened to sue and to tell others about Foster's irresponsibility. Foster replied that he would sooner roast in hell than take the blame for Wood's problem.

Wood terminated his contract with Foster, found a new fuel-and-lubricant supplier, and sued for damages. He also told his story to other Foster customers, leading two of them to break with Foster. Foster countersued for the cost of lost business and damage to his reputation.

Foster also informed his insurance company, Mutual Fidelity. His policy was such that the insurance company would pay any damage award less than $250,000. Mutual assigned the case to an adjuster, who engaged the services of a lawyer. The lawyer told Foster that Wood's case was weak and advised against agreeing to a negotiated settlement.

The contract between Foster and Wood required nonbinding mediation prior to going to trial. An experienced commercial mediator, Dwight Golann, met separately with the parties and found both to be deeply dug into their positions.

After a joint meeting with the parties to set the agenda and lay the groundwork, Golann set up proximity talks: the parties sat in adjoining rooms and he shuttled between them. This approach avoided further escalation and allowed him to control communication. Golann emphasized the costs in time, money, and aggravation of going to court and then probed the positions and interests of the two sides.

After several hours of back-and-forth discussion, Golann concluded that neither side was being realistic about what would happen if the case went to court. Wood's case was stronger than Foster was willing to admit, but weaker than Wood believed it to be. Wood's damage claim was also out of line. If the lawsuit went Wood's way (a fifty-fifty proposition, in Golann's opinion), he predicted an award in the range of $290,000. That outcome would mean that Foster would be out of pocket about $40,000, plus the time and aggravation of the lawsuit and damage to his reputation. Golann suspected that the Mutual representative assessed the situation similarly, but saw little risk in taking a hard line. If Foster won, Mutual would pay nothing other than the remaining cost of defense (estimated at $25,000). If Foster lost, Mutual's liability would be capped at $250,000.

Golann narrowed the gap between the parties but failed, after six hours of discussion, to get them to agree. He then took a chance and offered them his own assessment of what would happen at trial. Golann told Wood that he had a 50 percent chance of winning and that if he won, the award would be in the $300,000 range. If Wood lost, he could be liable for the lost business Foster had suffered, plus the cost of the suit. Wood responded by offering to settle the case in the $200,000 range if Foster dropped his countersuit.

The conversation with Foster and the lawyer for Mutual Fidelity proved more contentious. The lawyer rejected Golann's prediction of the outcome, and Foster appeared to realize that he and Mutual Fidelity had differing interests. Foster offered to settle and to drop his countersuit provided that the damage award was less than $250,000, he did not have to admit liability, and Wood agreed not to discuss the case with anyone.

Golann took another chance and put a package on the table: a settlement of $190,000, withdrawal of Foster's countersuit, and a commitment by Wood not to discuss the case. When Mutual Fidelity's lawyer protested, Golann reminded him privately that if he refused to settle and the trial went against Foster, Mutual could well be sued. After several hours, Mutual agreed to pay Wood $175,000, and the case was settled.

UNDERSTANDING SIMPLE DISPUTES

The starting point for managing conflict is to understand the difference between a simple dispute and a self-sustaining conflict system. Although unpleasant, the dispute between Foster and Wood was essentially a simple one: it proceeded relatively smoothly from eruption to a definitive resolution. Later in this chapter, we will look at an example of a self-sustaining conflict at Seneca Systems.

The Phases of a Simple Dispute

According to Jeffrey Rubin and his colleagues, simple disputes like the one between Wood and Foster proceed through distinct phases of escalation, deescalation, stalemate, and settlement, as outlined in the table below.[1] Escalation is an often-abrupt increase in the intensity of conflict between contending parties. Conflict may persist, but its intensity typically declines; in other words, deescalation occurs. Over time, the parties may reach a stalemate in which neither is able to win outright. If stalemate continues and the parties come to prefer resolution to continued contention, they will move toward a definitive negotiated settlement.[2]

Escalation. Escalation is a vicious circle of provocation, reprisal, and counter-reprisal that ratchets up hostility between the parties.[3] The escalatory process typically begins with a provocative action (such as Foster's insulting remark to Wood) that triggers a perception of insult or injury in another party. The injured party's

Phases of a Simple Dispute

Escalation	The dispute's intensity accelerates. Other interested parties get drawn in. The issues in dispute proliferate from specific to more general and deeper grievances.
Deescalation	The parties act to prevent conflict from escalating further. An explicit or implicit agreement over a "cease-fire" may be reached, sometimes with the help of outside intervention.
Stalemate	Neither party prevails, and both realize that neither can win by force.
Settlement	The contending parties agree to a negotiated resolution.

response is likely to be disproportionate—to cause more damage than the triggering event; for instance, Wood sues and encourages Foster's other customers to withdraw their business. This stance elicits another reaction—Foster launches a countersuit—and the cycle continues to build. The conflict-spiral model of escalation is illustrated in the figure below.[4]

As a dispute escalates, Pruitt and his colleagues noted, the behavior of the contending parties changes in predictable ways:[5]

- *From light to heavy tactics.* Foster and Wood began with attempts to influence each other, including arguments. As the conflict heated up, they moved to heavier tactics. Reasoned argument was replaced by insults; insults gave way to threats. Eventually, the parties turned to whatever weapons were available, including lawsuits.

- *From specific to general issues.* The disagreement between Foster and Wood began over specific issues. But as the conflict escalated, the participants invoked deeper and more global grievances.

The Conflict-Spiral Model of Escalation

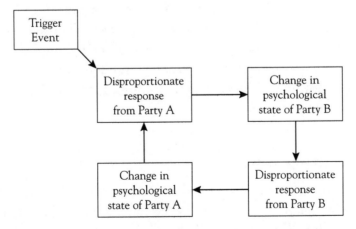

Source: Adapted from J. Z. Rubin, D. G. Pruitt, and S. H. Kim, *Social Conflict: Escalation, Stalemate and Settlement,* 2nd ed. (New York: McGraw-Hill, 1994). Reproduced with permission of The McGraw-Hill Companies.

- *From modest to large commitments of resources.* As the conflict escalated, the parties invested more and more of their energy and resources. The decisions by Wood and Foster to launch lawsuits, for example, involved potentially very large commitments of money and precious management time.
- *From few to many participants.* With Wood's effort to pull other Foster customers into the dispute, the conflict infected and polarized the social system within which it erupted. Other parties felt pressure to choose sides, and became part of the conflict dynamic.

Deescalation. Few disputes escalate completely out of control. Instead, something happens that promotes deescalation. In the case of Wood and Foster, the parties took a sober second look at their BATNAs and backed away from further provocative actions. In other cases, interested outside parties may intervene to suppress the conflict.

Stalemate and Settlement. Eventually the parties may reach a stalemate and realize that no one can win through use of contentious tactics. If the parties are suffering unacceptable losses, the situation is a "hurting stalemate."[6] This situation may propel them to the negotiating table in pursuit of a settlement. The dispute between Wood and Foster was damaging both companies' abilities to conduct business, costing revenue, and consuming precious management time. Recognizing their losses, both decided to seek a negotiated settlement.

Barriers to Agreement

Just because a dispute is simple doesn't mean that it's easy to deal with. As a mediator between Foster and Wood, Golann had to confront and overcome several difficult barriers to agreement that can complicate efforts to resolve disputes.

Overconfidence. Contending parties are prone to believe that future uncertainties will be resolved in their favor.[7] When both sides in a lawsuit believe that they will prevail in court, one and possibly both are falling prey to overconfidence that tends to discourage out-of-court settlement. Overconfidence is a manifestation of a desire to feel competent and secure. Max Bazerman and Margaret Neale have pointed out how what they call "need-based illusions" and "self-serving biases" can contribute to irrational behavior.[8]

Loss and Risk Aversion. As we saw in Chapter Six, people tend to be loss averse—more resistant to potential losses than they are eager for equivalent gains.[9] Situations that require people to accept losses—whether they involve money or power or status or territory—therefore tend to be more difficult to manage than the divvying up of gains. Similarly universal is the tendency to be risk averse—to prefer guaranteed gains to risky choices, even if the latter could yield much larger gains. Both loss aversion and risk aversion can seriously complicate efforts to forge negotiated settlements in disputes.

Principal-Agent Issues. Differences in interests between principals and agents also hinder agreement in simple disputes.[10] Think of the lawyer representing Mutual Fidelity in the Foster Fuels case: ostensibly present to advise Chuck Foster in the settlement negotiations, he is in reality representing the interests of the insurance company. Foster could face a similar problem with his own lawyer if she prefers a quick settlement to a trial so she can move on to other cases.

Agents may enjoy expertise and access to information unavailable to those they represent, allowing them to see the outlines of a deal more clearly and to shape perceptions accordingly. But when agents' own interests are not fully aligned with those of their principals, they may use their expertise and information to advance their own interests.

UNDERSTANDING CONFLICT SYSTEMS

Some disputes don't get resolved. Once sparked, they evolve into bitter, ongoing conflicts among contending parties who have no choice but to continue to interact. This transformation occurs when some or all of the parties take actions that cause irreversible hostility. Such actions could involve loss of life, or a mortal insult to character or integrity, or a searing loss of face. Combined with the need for ongoing interaction, hostility transforms simple disputes into self-sustaining conflict systems. In such situations, illustrated by the following case, the goal is conflict management, not dispute resolution.

Ron Emmons, president of Seneca Systems, a large manufacturer of microcomputers, wasted no time when his marketing people reported a surge in warranty claims on the company's newly launched Phoenix computer. After running successfully for three to four months, a significant percentage of Phoenix machines experienced systems failures requiring replacement of the main printed circuit board.

Emmons immediately called Desmond Lovell, vice president of Seneca's Assembly Division. Lovell already had his quality engineers working around the clock, and he told Emmons that they had traced the problem to the PowerMiser microprocessor chip supplied by Seneca's Data Devices Division. The engineers believed the problem to be due to static charge–induced failures of the PowerMiser chips caused by weak insulation. Microprocessors are unusually sensitive to slight static electrical changes that break down internal insulation between circuits.

Emmons then contacted the vice president of Data Devices, David King, who denied responsibility for the problem. Outside customers for the same chip had not complained, King told Emmons, and his staff attributed the problem to damage done to the chips at Lovell's assembly plant due to inadequate training and equipment. King intimated that Lovell was lying to avoid blame.

Lovell and King had clashed before. Lovell was an engineer from a working-class midwestern family who had risen through the ranks. King, the son of a Nobel Prize–winning scientist, had a Ph.D. in physics from Stanford. Both were superb at their jobs, but the two disliked each other at a visceral level. Their ongoing conflict had been stoked by the company's measurement-and-incentive system, which strongly rewarded the two vice presidents for promoting growth and keeping costs down in their individual units. Lovell and King were also vying to succeed Emmons as CEO.

The result was a history of strained interactions between the two over pricing, product schedules, and a host of other issues. Disputes erupted periodically. Over time, the conflict had spilled over to provoke bad feelings between employees of the two divisions, impeding communication and cooperation. But it hadn't yet had a harmful impact on the company's performance.

Emmons called in Lovell and King and read them the riot act. "If you two can't work out this problem, and fast, I'm going to find people who will," he said, adding, "I don't care who's at fault. I want the problem fixed, and I want it fixed now." As for whose budget would pay for the repairs, Emmons said, "If you can't work that out between the two of you, I'll split the baby." Lovell and King appointed a task force of senior people from their groups to fix the problem and recommend a formula for splitting the costs. The team ultimately attributed 40 percent of the problem to Data Devices and 60 percent to Assembly and proposed apportioning the cost accordingly. Data Devices would also provide technical advice to the Assembly Division. Without ever speaking to each other directly, the two vice presidents signed off on the proposal, and things quieted down.

Self-Reinforcing Conflict Systems

Self-sustaining conflicts like this one remain mired in a state of low-level hostility, impervious to efforts at resolution. It is useful, in fact, to think of longstanding conflicts as self-reinforcing systems stuck in a permanent state of cold war—low-level contention and friction that is neither all-out war nor durable peace.[11] Periodically, something will trigger a bout of escalation. Usually, however, escalation doesn't result in all-out violence. At Seneca Systems, for example, the two vice presidents' disagreement flares, then dies down.

Meanwhile, however, attempts at peacemaking get undermined. At Seneca, efforts by lower-level people to improve relations between the two divisions foundered. Bitter disputes can thus persist in a cold war equilibrium, punctuated by occasional escalatory episodes and failed peacemaking efforts.

Persistent conflict of this kind results from a dynamic tension between forces militating for escalation and those resisting escalation. Think of a longstanding labor dispute between a union and a company. The union numbers both radicals and moderates. Moderates prefer to address ongoing disputes through the contractual grievance mechanism (a restraint on escalation), while the radicals periodically act more confrontationally (promoting escalation). When management provokes them, the radicals may respond with work slowdowns, sick-outs, and even sabotage. The radicals are seeking to wrest political power within the union, and they miss no opportunity to deride moderates' efforts at conciliation as a sellout to management.

Management too has its hard-liners and moderates. The hard-liners are virulently anti-union, a stance that has only hardened over time. Given the choice, they would respond to the union radicals' actions with every provocative tool at their disposal, including legal actions and lockouts. The moderates within management want to improve the company's relationship with the union, but find their efforts undermined by hard-liners who deride them as weak. Over time, the company and the union have engaged in low-level contention, punctuated by war in the form of long and costly strikes. Both the company and the workers have suffered.

The conflict system model in the figure on page 169 illustrates these dynamics.[12] Think of the curve in the center of the figure as a series of hills and valleys. The three valleys represent possible stable states: peace, cold war, and war. The hills represent forces that

The Conflict System Model

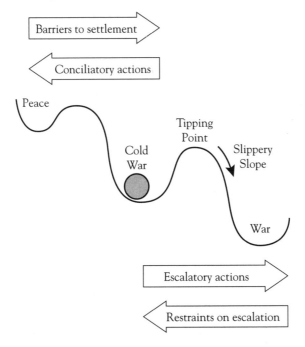

resist change in one direction or the other. The ball at the bottom of the valley labeled "Cold War" represents the equilibrium state of a self-sustaining conflict: neither war nor peace.

Driving and Restraining Forces

Events and people that propel conflict out of the cold war valley toward either war or peace are driving forces. Escalatory actions (such as a work slowdown) push the conflict up the hill to the right, toward all-out war in the form of strikes and lawsuits. Conciliatory actions (such as efforts to negotiate new workplace arrangements) push the ball up the opposite hill toward peaceful coexistence.

Longstanding conflicts like the one between Lovell and King develop built-in regulatory mechanisms that resist change in either direction. As driving forces push the system toward war or peace, they are met by restraining forces that act to maintain the cold war equilibrium. These forces are represented in the figure by the slopes surrounding the cold war valley; it would take an uphill push to reach a state of either peace or war. Escalatory forces are restrained by forces that moderate conflict. Likewise, peacemaking efforts are met by efforts to block resolution.

As the forces that militate for war gather strength, so do the restraining forces—at least at first. As tension in the system rises, however, the conflict reaches a tipping point beyond which a slight additional push can cause rapid acceleration toward a new state.[13] These tipping points are represented by the tops of the hills in the figure. As long as escalatory forces fail to reach some threshold, restraining forces will tend to pull the conflict back to its cold war equilibrium. At the threshold, however, a small increment can accelerate a slide down the slippery slope to full-scale conflict.

The dynamics of a particular conflict depend on the relative balance of driving and restraining forces. If the restraints on escalation are weak, the slope on the right will be low and violence will be easily ignited. For example, if outside parties like Ron Emmons can't intervene effectively, we can expect conflict to flare more frequently and escalate more seriously.

Irreversible Psychological Transformations

Self-sustaining conflicts provoke irreversible psychological changes in the contending parties that discourage peacemaking efforts. Managing such conflicts requires an understanding of these psychological changes, particularly partisan perceptions, reactive devaluation, and groupthink.

Partisan Perceptions. When conflicts become embittered, the parties begin to gather and interpret information about each other in profoundly biased ways.[14] Their perceptions get distorted in three ways. First, partisans assume that they themselves see things objectively, whereas their opponents have extreme and distorted views.[15] Second, partisans tend to misjudge the other side's motivations, underestimating the situational pressures their counterparts face. Third, as illustrated in the accompanying figure, partisans consistently overestimate the distance between themselves and the other side. At the same time, individual partisans tend to see themselves as more moderate than typical members of their own group. Robert Robinson calls this the "lone moderate" phenomenon.[16] The net result is marked exaggeration of the actual differences between the sides.

As a consequence, the parties indulge in selective perception—Lovell and King, for instance, interpret each other's actions in ways that confirm their preexisting negative beliefs and attitudes. They even unconsciously overlook evidence that challenges their stereotypes. They may also adopt a zero-sum mentality that casts the negotiation in purely distributive terms. Finally, their behavior may contribute to self-fulfilling prophecies.

Partisan Perceptions

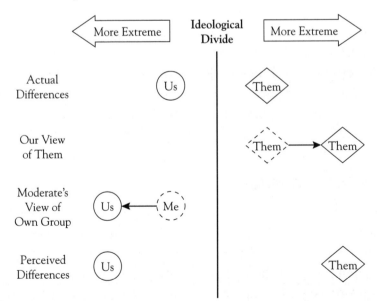

Reactive Devaluation. As we saw in Chapter Three, gestures intended to be conciliatory are often discounted or ignored by the other side, a phenomenon known as *reactive devaluation*.[17] If Lovell believes King to be untrustworthy and totally self-interested, any conciliatory gesture will be treated with profound suspicion, as either a trick or a sign of weakness. Any other conclusion would require a fundamental reassessment of the other side. If the overture is interpreted as a deception, the typical response is counterdeception or rejection. If it is seen as a sign of weakness, the response may be to press forward aggressively.

Groupthink. Conflicts between groups, such as the divisions at Seneca Systems, stimulate shared psychological transformations within the opposing sides—a phenomenon that Irving Janus has termed *groupthink*.[18] Internal cohesion increases within groups in conflict. A two-sided worldview develops: we represent truth and justice, desire only security and self-respect, and respond reasonably to provocations, while they are bent on our destruction and are essentially evil.

These attitudes infect communication between the groups. Contact is discouraged, and any communication is treated as a concession. The perceived need for solidarity results in suppression of internal dissent, in part through pressure to conform but more perniciously through self-censorship. Moderate leaders get pushed aside by radicals. Individual inclinations toward overconfidence get magnified, and an illusion of invulnerability can take hold.

HANDLING CONFLICT

When you seek to resolve a dispute or manage a conflict, you have an array of tools at your disposal. You can pull in third-party intervenors to change the pattern of communication and the parties' perceptions of their BATNAs. You can design momentum-building processes to help override barriers to agreement. And you

can work to change the game by altering the balance of forces acting on the contending parties.

Third-Party Intervention

Third-party intervenors (we use the terms *third-party* and *intervenor* interchangeably) can play constructive roles in disputes and
sustained conflicts. Note that we said *intervenors*, not *mediators*.
Traditional mediators, like Dwight Golann in the Foster-Wood
dispute, are just one type of intervenor. The others are *arbitrators*,
whose coercive power equips them to impose settlement terms on
the contending parties, and *negotiators*, who pursue their own
interests by bargaining with the contending parties to end the
dispute. Ron Emmons of Seneca Systems is an example of an arbitrator. Although he didn't exercise it, he had the power to impose an agreement on Lovell and King.

Intervenors' Interests

To understand the roles that intervenors can play, it is useful to
explore why third parties intervene in conflicts and to identify
the sources of their power. Why do outside parties decide to intervene in conflicts? Like Golann, they may be invited in. But even
seemingly impartial mediators may be pursuing personal or institutional goals, such as enhanced reputation. And many otherwise
neutral mediators (who have no preexisting bias toward one or
another of the disputants) nonetheless have a substantial bias toward settlement.

Other outside parties insert themselves into a conflict because
it threatens their vital interests. Seneca's CEO Ron Emmons might
have intervened in the conflict between Lovell and King for this
reason. If a conflict spills over, affected outside parties have a powerful incentive to minimize the damage. And outsiders partial to
one of the disputants try to influence the conflict in favor of their
allies. Emmons had not revealed whom he favors as his successor,

but his preference could easily have influenced how he approached the conflict between Lovell and King.

Intervenors' Sources of Power. Third parties can wield three types of power, and their roles in conflicts are strongly shaped by their sources of power:

- *Facilitative power.* Intervenors' facilitative power derives from their status, legitimacy, process management skills, and persuasiveness. These are the prime sources of influence that traditional mediators like Dwight Golann draw on. The techniques that mediators can use to implement their facilitative power are summarized in the accompanying table.

There are limits to how much third parties can accomplish with facilitative power alone. A mediator alone cannot coerce the parties or offer tangible incentives. Thus, the contending parties must be willing to make peace but may be unable to overcome residual barriers on their own.

To gain entry to a dispute, a mediator needs permission from the contending parties. Initially, both parties try to dominate the choice of intervenor. When one party is far more powerful than the other, however, the only possible way to move forward may be for the weaker party to accept a "biased" intervenor. Upon gaining entry, the mediator automatically becomes a target of influence attempts: both parties try to sway the mediator (or to discredit a mediator they consider biased).

- *Coercive power.* A third party with coercive power can unilaterally impose terms of settlement. The intervenor may be in a position to punish the contending parties or to block their access to crucial resources. As CEO of Seneca, for example, Ron could have coerced Lovell and King to come to an agreement.

When a third party wields coercive power, control over decisions shifts away from the disputants. Intervenors with facilitative power enjoy only as much influence as the parties are willing to concede, but coercive power is innate and independent of the

Mediation Techniques

Technique	Description
Enhancing and shaping communications	An intervenor opens up a communication channel by shuttling between the contending parties, as Golann did in the Foster-Wood case, or by convening face-to-face meetings in neutral locations. A third party can also relay messages, soften language, raise the salience of potential common ground, and otherwise shape communications.
Setting up action-forcing events	Third parties may impose deadlines that call for hard choices. The parties then have to decide whether to let the intervention "fail" or make the necessary compromises. Golann could, for example, have imposed a time limit on his own involvement.
Critiquing the parties' positions	A third party can provide a reality check by assessing both sides' positions. By throwing cold water on unrealistic and incompatible aspirations, the intervenor may move the parties toward a settlement. Golann did this when he assessed the likelihood of each side prevailing in court and the size of the damage award.
Proposing creative options	An intervenor can suggest trades that create value for both parties. Because of reluctance to reveal their interests, communication barriers, and differences in frames, the parties may have overlooked shared interests or been unable to move in mutually beneficial directions. An intervenor may also enable the parties to back away from mutually incompatible commitments without loss of face.
Persuading the parties to make concessions	The parties may make concessions to an intervenor that they could not make to each other. Dwight Golann could have asked Foster

Mediation Techniques (*continued*)

Technique	Description
	and Wood, "If the other side made this concession, would you make a countervailing concession?" and promised not to reveal either side's response unless both agree.
Absorbing anger and taking blame	An intervenor may allow the parties to blow off steam and otherwise serve as an emotional buffer. In the Seneca situation, both Lovell and King can aim some of their anger at Emmons instead of each other.
Serving as a guarantor of agreements	A third party can act as guarantor of an agreement in order to make it more sustainable. This role is especially important when one or more of the parties may back away from full implementation or "reinterpret" the agreement strategically.

Source: For further discussion of intervenor's power, see C. W. Moore, *The Mediation Process* (San Francisco: Jossey-Bass, 1996). See also J. Bercovitch and J. Z. Rubin, *Mediation in International Relations: Multiple Approaches to Conflict Resolution* (New York: Macmillan, 1992); and M. Watkins and K. Winters, "Intervenors with Interests and Power," *Negotiation Journal* 13, 2 (1997).

parties. In disputes with significant spillover potential, outside parties may feel justified in imposing outcomes, and even punishing the disputants, to deter future eruptions. Direct coercion has potential costs to the intervenor, however. For one thing, coercion is often costly.[19] And a settlement that is imposed on the disputants is inherently unstable. One or both will view the settlement as illegitimate and may feel free to violate its terms. Coercion thus necessitates postsettlement monitoring and enforcement: the intervenor has to be willing to act as its guarantor and enforcer.

For these reasons, a third party with coercive power often chooses to exercise power in more indirect ways. One option is to threaten intervention as a way of spurring the parties to negotiate. This is what Ron Emmons did in the conflict between Lovell and King.

- *Bargaining power.* A third party with bargaining power is in a position to reward the disputants for making peace. The intervenor with bargaining power effectively becomes a party to the negotiation and manipulates the combatants' perceptions of their alternatives by enlarging the pie. Suppose it had been not Ron Emmons but rather Kelsey Madden, Seneca's vice president of marketing, who mediated between Lovell and King. If she had had funds of her own to contribute to solving the problem, she would have been an intervenor with bargaining power. She could have used those funds to speed up a settlement but would have had to bargain with Lovell and King over who would pay what.

Bargaining power is a mixed blessing. As soon as an intervenor becomes a party to a negotiation, attitudes toward her shift. If the disputants suspect that the intervenor is willing to offer compensation, they will be less open about their interests and bottom lines. The intervenor in turn will be less able to generate creative options and more likely to be drawn into bargaining.[20] Furthermore, disputants who agree on little else often cooperate in extracting a high price for peace when they know the third party has interests at stake and resources to bargain with. Thus, Kelsey Madden may be vulnerable to implicit cooperation between King and Lovell to extract value from her. Both would be happy to see her use her resources to help pay for their problem.

Intervention Roles. Now that we understand intervenors' sources of power, we can think about the intervention roles that third parties play in disputes. As a starting point, let us look at three "pure" roles:

- *Mediator.* A pure mediator, such as Dwight Golann, is an impartial and mutually acceptable third party whose goal is to help resolve the dispute. The mediator has no bias toward either party and no self-interest in achieving or preventing a settlement.

Although mediators lack power to coerce or bargain, they can use facilitative power to influence disputants. To gain entry to the dispute, a mediator must be accepted by the contending parties.

• *Arbitrator.* A pure arbitrator, such as Ron Emmons, is an impartial third party with the coercive power to impose terms of settlement. Arbitrators are not biased toward either party, and they subordinate their own preferences to some set of rules or values. Nor does a pure arbitrator have a personal stake in the outcome sufficient to engage in bargaining with the disputants.

• *Negotiator.* A pure negotiator, such as Kelsey Madden, has well-recognized interests in the outcome, either in getting a settlement (substantive interests) or in seeing one of the disputants prevail (relationship-coalitional interests). Negotiators lack coercive power, but may use bargaining power to gain entry and advance their own interests.

In practice, intervenors often play a mixture of these three pure roles. Mixed third-party roles can be characterized by referring to the two-dimensional intervention role grid in the figure on page 179.

On the vertical axis, mediator and negotiator are poles on a continuum of extent of stake in the outcome. At the bottom is the impartial mediator (Dwight Golann) who seeks a mutually acceptable resolution to the conflict; at the top is the partisan negotiator (Kelsey Madden) pursuing self-interests or those of an ally. Neither mediator nor negotiator has coercive power, and both have facilitative power to influence the disputants. But the mediator is disinterested, whereas the negotiator is highly interested and possessed of bargaining power. Between the poles are various stances that combine a desire to help resolve their dispute with an interest in achieving desired outcomes. At the center is the mediator-with-an-interest.

On the horizontal axis, mediator (Golann) and arbitrator (Ron Emmons) are poles on a continuum of extent of ability to impose outcomes. Both seek to resolve the conflict, and neither has a strong personal stake in the outcome or incentives to bargain. How-

Intervention Role Grid

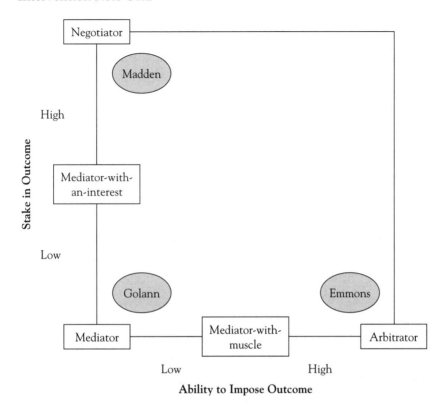

ever, an arbitrator can coerce a settlement, while the mediator must be acceptable to the disputants and must rely on facilitative power to influence them. Between the mediator and the arbitrator are roles with varying degrees of coercive power. At the center is the mediator-with-muscle, who exercises some ability to coerce the disputants but cannot simply impose an outcome on them.

Goal and Method Dilemmas. If you intervene in a dispute, you will inescapably confront tensions over the goals you pursue and the methods you use. These tensions will vary with the role you adopt.

• *Dilemmas for mediators*. Conventional mediators such as Dwight Golann face a difficult choice between narrow and broad goals. They may stay focused on the presenting problem—the positions and issues that are the focal point of conflict. Or they may try to address the systemic root causes—the underlying interests, history of grievances, and structure of interactions—in hope of a long-term resolution.[21] Premature efforts to tackle root-cause issues can open old wounds, weaken constituent support, and cause the entire process to stall or break down. By contrast, working incrementally builds confidence and can set the stage for later broad agreements, but the resulting agreement may be unsustainable if the real causes of the conflict are overlooked.

Mediation methods pose another dilemma. A mediator must choose between merely facilitating the disputants' efforts to communicate and working more actively, as Golann did, to evaluate positions and identify options for mutual gain.[22] Mediators who limit themselves to facilitation alone forgo opportunities to help the disputants abandon entrenched positions. The more activist approach, however, can be risky if the parties fail to claim full ownership of the agreement or get too far ahead of their constituencies and lose credibility. This can cause the negotiations to collapse in acrimony.

• *Dilemmas for intervenors with interests*. Intervenors with an interest in the outcome, like Kelsey Madden, experience an additional goal dilemma: how aggressively to pursue their own interests versus the best interests of the contending parties. Because Sheila is directly involved in creating and claiming value in a multiparty negotiation with Lovell and King, she is also likely to confront a methods dilemma: a version of the classic negotiator's dilemma discussed in Chapter Three.[23] If she tries to claim value, she will have trouble creating joint value. Conversely, if she works to create joint value, she risks having value claimed from her.

• *Dilemmas for intervenors with coercive power*. Intervenors with coercive power, like Ron Emmons, are prone to a different goal-related dilemma: putting a stop to the immediate flare-up (whatever its form) tends to short-circuit a longer-term resolution. Employing coercion to stop escalation may work against a sustainable resolution because it lowers the costs to the parties of continuing contention, and hence sows the seeds for future eruptions. This tension arises because coercion can control disputants' behavior but can't change their attitudes. There is usually a limit to an intervenor's staying power to police terms of settlement, and there is a limit to the intervenor's ability to observe the actions of the disputants. Intervenors with coercive power also experience a classic methods dilemma concerning ends and means. Emmons may suppress conflict using means that damage his credibility or reputation or set unfortunate precedents.

The figure on page 182 illustrates these goal-and-methods dilemmas in terms of the intervention role grid. In the middle of the grid, mediators-with-an-interest *and* -muscle must manage all of these goal-and-methods-related tensions.

Momentum-Building Processes

When your goal is to build momentum by bootstrapping a conflict-wracked negotiation, the design of the process merits a fresh and hardheaded look. Circumstances determine whether it makes sense to conduct a shuttle or a summit, a multistage agreement, or secret back-channel diplomacy.

Shuttles and Summits. Shuttles and summits bring utterly different dynamics to bear on building momentum in negotiations, but are sometimes used at different stages of the same conflict. Think about a negotiation involving many parties, and ask yourself why you might decide *not* to bring them all together to negotiate as a group. If the parties can't meet because of geographical or political constraints, for example, a shuttle can serve as a bridge for purposes of communication. When the parties still lack a shared definition of the problem or haven't truly absorbed the consequences of no agreement, a shuttle can be a way to nudge them

Goal-and-Methods Dilemmas

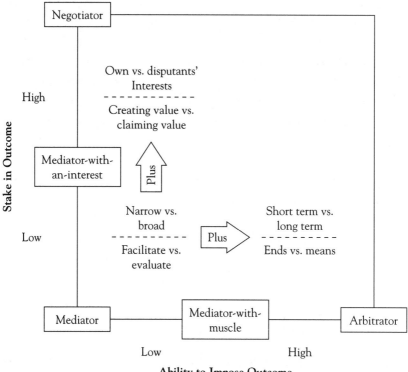

toward a common definition of the problem and the options before bringing them to the table. Skillful framing and information control are needed as well.

When it isn't clear whether there is a bargaining range at all and differences appear insurmountable, a face-to-face meeting of the parties could break down entirely. A shuttle in this situation is an opportunity to learn: to gather information about interests and positions, figure out where the sticking points are, and perhaps begin to identify a promising formula for a deal.

A fourth reason to opt for a shuttle is the risk that bringing the parties together too early will simply encourage escalation. A classic example is the negotiation in the early 1990s between the government of Ecuador and the oil giant Conoco over oil field development in a tract of ecologically sensitive rain forest. Conoco was promoting itself as a green oil company, committed to ecologically sound oil drilling and waste disposal methods. Confident that environmental groups and indigenous inhabitants of the rain forest would prefer Conoco to a less enlightened company, the firm called a summit of all the major parties at an isolated location on the Rio Napo in Ecuador. The meeting was a disaster. The environmental groups and indigenous groups were implacably opposed to any development and didn't understand that drilling was virtually inevitable. The process got poisoned, and Conoco withdrew. Ultimately, the drilling concession went to a smaller company with fewer resources to mitigate environmental damage: a lose-lose outcome. In retrospect, a carefully sequenced shuttle might have paved the way for a winning coalition.

The party who is shuttling back and forth should approach supporters of agreement early, explaining how other supporters see the issues and keeping opponents in the dark. Whatever its rationale, a shuttle offers unmatched control over the process in the form of opportunities to frame the issues, control the flow of information, and manage the sequence of interactions. This is especially true if other parties do not communicate directly with each other.

If shuttles are this potent, why might you want to bring all the parties to the table at all? The most important reason is that in multiparty negotiations, agreements are rarely reached through a shuttle. Understandably, the parties will refuse to make their final concessions until everyone is present and a deal can be hammered out. Otherwise, they run the risk that another party will hold out to claim a final slice of value. Ultimately, the negotiating must be simultaneous rather than sequential.

A summit is also an occasion for learning of a very different type than occurs during a shuttle. Specifically, summits afford opportunities to learn about the relationships among the parties, as apparent in patterns of deference and dislike.

Concessions made at private meetings are more easily withdrawn than concessions made in public, so a summit helps to seal the deal and to prevent backsliding. This is one reason that the timing of summits is important: the process must have ripened enough for agreement to be a likely outcome.

Finally, a summit is a way of focusing peoples' attention and acts as an action-forcing event. By getting parties together, it is often possible to force uncommitted people to take a position, a kind of action-forcing event in itself. The objective of Conoco's Rio Napo meeting was to situate the parties in an isolated hot-house environment to aim a lot of energy at reaching agreement. If the parties view failure of the summit as an undesirable outcome, they experience pressure to make the necessary difficult choices. As the Rio Napo meeting illustrates, the process has to have ripened or the result may be breakdown.

A summit meeting is less controllable than a shuttle situation, but the organizer can wield influence by deciding who gets invited, controlling process details, and setting the initial agenda.

Clearly, shuttles and summits play complementary roles, and it shouldn't be surprising that they are often used in tandem. A shuttle is time-consuming, but when employed to learn, hammer out a shared definition of the problem, and establish a zone of agreement, it can set the stage for overcoming sticking points and locking in gains at a summit meeting.

The same pattern of progress from one-on-one to group negotiation is employed in many negotiating situations. A business leader pressing for organizational change often employs a shuttle-like process to educate and elicit initial buy-in from influential individuals. The next step is usually group meetings to obtain public commitments to specific courses of action. Then the leader holds further one-on-one meetings to press for implementation.

Multiphase Agreements. Multiphase agreements share an essential logic: the parties negotiate relatively easy sets of issues first, implement that agreement, and then move on to progressively tougher issues. In one common form of phased agreement, the parties first negotiate the guiding principles for a mutually acceptable settlement. These principles then serve as a basis for negotiating more specific agreements and more divisive issues.

Once guiding principles are in place, attention typically shifts to a general framework agreement and then to details of implementation. The overarching rationale is that the experience of reaching agreement alters the parties' attitudes toward each other and creates personal investment in the process. These changes in attitude and perception then kick in to overcome remaining barriers to agreement when the time arrives to tackle the hardest issues.

A phased approach can have drawbacks, though. Settling the easy issues first leaves only the hard issues to be worked out at the end, and the parties will find that they remain hard. More crucial, the process may turn out not to build trust. Implementing the early agreements can inflame internal opposition and sour the relationship. The contending parties may build momentum only to run straight into a brick wall. Efforts to build momentum through phased processes must therefore be undertaken with care, ensuring that enough issues remain on the table for the parties to craft some mutually acceptable trades in later phases.

Secret Diplomacy. Leaders sometimes choose to craft an agreement using secret or back-channel diplomacy and then present it to their constituencies for ratification as a fait accompli. Secrecy effectively transforms a two-level (internal-external) negotiation into a simpler bilateral process, delaying the internal negotiations and marginalizing opposition. As international negotiation expert Fred Iklé explains:

> Secrecy has two major effects in diplomacy. First, it keeps [internal] groups ignorant of the process of negotiation, thereby preventing them from exerting pressures during successive phases of bargaining. Second, it leaves third parties in the dark and thus reduces their influence. The exclusion

of the public may help overcome domestic opposition to concessions or threats before negotiations are completed.[24]

Secrecy also insulates the parties from media attention so they can forgo posturing and concentrate on the substantive issues.

Like phased agreements, secret diplomacy has potential drawbacks. Its very secrecy will tend to legitimate protest by those who are excluded from the process. Marginalizing such groups may have been necessary in order to move forward, but their opposition makes it particularly urgent to sell secret agreements once the ink is dry. The goal is to create and sustain a supportive coalition of the middle.

Changing the Game

By definition, simple disputes get resolved. In conflict systems, definitive resolutions are far harder to achieve. But some union-management relationships have been fundamentally changed for the better, and even nations with long histories of war have embraced peaceful coexistence. There is reason for optimism.

Suppressing Escalation. It's difficult to settle a bitter dispute if escalatory episodes continue to erupt. Each bout of escalation sets back efforts to negotiate a resolution. Three approaches to discharging escalation—all involving shaping the parties' perceptions of their BATNAs—are effective:

Avoidance. Help the parties to avoid each other. Avoidance is a substitute, and sometimes an effective one, for resolution of a dispute. But while Foster and Wood can decide never to interact again, it is not always possible to separate the combatants. Lovell and King are inextricably intertwined with each other unless one leaves the company.

Mutual deterrence. Help the parties build a regime of mutual deterrence. The capacity to visit pain on each other will act as a brake on escalation. This is the logic of mutually assured destruction. In the case of Foster and Wood, the costs and uncertainties associated with lawsuits acted as a restraint on escalation.

Coercive intervention. Pull in outside parties to shape the disputants' perceptions. By putting Lovell and King on notice that their actions were damaging the corporation, Emmons implicitly threatened both with loss of their shot at leading Seneca.

Altering the Balance of Forces. Suppressing escalation is a good first step, but it doesn't change the basic dynamics of a conflict system. The dispute simmers, always ready to boil over again. Conflict suppression can go on and on without changing the underlying reality.

True resolution of a sustained dispute requires changing the game—eliminating underlying causes and transforming the driving and restraining forces in the conflict system. A general guideline to doing this is to weaken incentives for competition and strengthen incentives for cooperation. At Seneca, for example, the conflict between Lovell and King was fueled by the company's incentive system, which rewarded individual rather than collective performance. By altering rewards to emphasize overall company results, CEO Emmons could change the balance of forces in the conflict system. Over time, Lovell and King (and their subordinates) may cooperate more because it is in their interests to do so.

TRANSFORMING CONFLICT SYSTEMS

Fundamental transformation of a conflict system always involves dealing with deeply internalized feelings of grievance. Often all sides cast themselves as victims and use this stance to rationalize their actions. They may even vigorously compete to convince outside parties of their victimization. Transformation of a conflict calls for cutting the Gordian knot that binds the parties in a mutually reinforcing, destructive relationship and providing opportunities to move from contention to rebuilding. In between, the parties may need to come to terms with their losses, give up on efforts to seek revenge, and become psychologically ready to move forward. This process takes time and a lot of patience.

The tools presented in this chapter are applicable to personal conflicts as well as business negotiations. You probably experience conflict, or observe its effects, almost daily with family, friends, neighbors, or coworkers. The approaches to dispute resolution and conflict management described here are no panacea, but employing them skillfully can make a difference.

8

Leading Negotiations

Ben Fiorentino had long been expecting an offer to buy his family's business. FHE (originally Fiorentino Heavy Equipment), founded by Ben's father, Tony, was an Indianapolis-based regional distributor of industrial equipment. With annual sales of $220 million and just under three hundred employees, FHE had thrived under family management for nearly forty years. After his father's death fifteen years earlier, Ben had taken the reins as chairman and CEO, leading the company through a period of sustained growth.

But Ben could feel the winds of change in his industry. Larger companies were buying and consolidating regional distributorships like his to gain advantages of scale—the classic rollup strategy. It had become clear to Ben that FHE could not survive long term as an independent business. He could stave off competition for a while, but it was just a matter of time.

When Ben was approached by Argus Corporation, a leader in the trend toward consolidation, it was almost a welcome development. Argus already owned a similar distributorship in an adjacent region (and sometimes competed with FHE at the intersection of the two regions), so FHE was a natural fit for them.

Although pained, Ben concluded that it would be best to sell—and relatively soon, while he could still get a good price. His father had wanted, above all, financial security for the family. Tony had always seen the business as a way to achieve that, not an end in itself. Properly invested and overseen, the proceeds of the sale could sustain the family for the foreseeable future, and probably less divisively than the business had. As the family had grown and the third generation had joined the company, conflict had increased (though it was scrupulously confined to biannual family meetings and never aired in public). Ben was also ready to move on himself. In his early fifties, he was prepared to spend a few more years running the business but wanted to pursue other interests.

Getting the family to agree to sell would be an uphill battle. Ben's two siblings were emotionally attached to the business and to its employees. His sister, Leslie, had never been active in the company, and she and Ben were close. But her husband had been CFO until his sudden death three years earlier, and he had been strongly invested in its success. Two of Leslie's three children also worked for the company, and the oldest planned on a career there. (Ben's own two children had gone into other professions.)

Potentially more problematic was Ben's brother, James, who held a midlevel position in the company. James had no higher aspirations, but his older son worked at FHE and aspired to run it. James's position in the business had anchored him through a turbulent personal life, and a decision to sell would represent a profound change for him. Ben and James rarely saw eye to eye on business issues, politics, or anything else. Legally, Ben needed the support of either Leslie or James, not both, to sell the business. But a decision based on anything less than consensus would be wrenching.

Then there was the related question of whether and how to involve the third generation in the decision. As part of an estate planning initiative, FHE had created two classes of stock. The nonvoting stock, which represented 70 percent of the economic value of the business, had been split evenly among the members of the third generation. Ben, Leslie, and James had retained all the voting stock, evenly apportioned among them. This arrangement gave them control, but their shares represented just 30 percent of the economic value of the company.

The seven members of the third generation, all in their late teens and twenties, thus had no clear-cut legal right to participate in the decision-making process, but they would have an influence. Three were active in the business and had expressed varying degrees of interest in running in it. The other four showed no interest in the company other than receiving dividends. Ben believed that they would be happy to see the business sold, since their financial futures would be secured and the increasingly divisive family meetings would end.

Finally, there was the question of the role that FHE's professional managers should play. After the death of Leslie's husband, Ben had hired an experienced outside manager as CFO. Vice presidents of sales, operations, and human resources also reported to him. All earned competitive salaries and participated in the profit-sharing plan Ben's father had established twenty years earlier.

Even if he could elicit buy-in from the family to negotiate a sale—which was not a foregone conclusion—it was unclear to Ben how to go about managing the process. He had no prior experience with mergers and acquisitions, nor did anyone else at the company. Who should participate in the negotiations? What external advice, if any, should he solicit? How should the process be run? What role should he play?

This chapter will explore leadership in negotiation, looking in particular at how negotiators lead when they represent others and when they orchestrate teams.

REPRESENTING OTHERS

When a negotiator represents the interests of others, those who are absent from the table could be principals with decision-making power (such as the CEO of a company being represented by a business-development executive) or constituencies who expect the representative to lead them (such as the members of a union bargaining unit being represented by their elected leader).[1] The internal interests being represented may be monolithic or fractious. And the representative may function as a pure agent or pursue personal interests in tandem with others' interests.

Whatever the scenario is, the representative functions as a bridge between internal decision making and external negotiations.[2] When negotiators participate in shaping their mandates, have an unwavering vision of what they want to achieve, and work to shape perceptions internally and externally, they maximize their ability to advance their side's interests—and their own.

Representational Roles and Dilemmas

Negotiators who represent others enjoy considerable leeway in how they exercise leadership.[3] To be effective, though, representatives have to understand the roles available to them and shape the roles they play.[4] This is largely a matter of confronting and managing several characteristic dilemmas that test their leadership.

Representing Others Versus Representing Oneself. Representatives may or may not have their own legitimate interests in the outcome of a negotiation. At one extreme, as illustrated in the figure on page 193, a representative is a mere agent of others with no independent interests; at the other extreme, the representative is the principal decision maker, someone who has the legitimate authority to participate in making decisions. In between, a representative operates as a partner of other decision makers who are not at the table, representing both their interests and his or her own. This is the role that Ben would play in a negotiation with Argus. He has decision-making authority as well as his own interests, which may not be perfectly aligned with those of his siblings or the company's professional managers.

Operating in the middle of this spectrum, Ben is certain to confront a *principal-agent problem:* his interests and the interests of

Representing Others Versus Representing Oneself

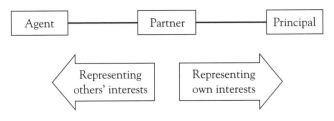

those he represents are not perfectly aligned.[5] His ability to control the flow of information and shape perceptions could allow him to create and claim value in ways that serve his personal interests and not those of other constituencies. This enviable position may generate distrust on their part. The more he tries to create value at the table by identifying creative trades, for example, the greater the likelihood of generating suspicion in his constituents that he is doing so to further his own interests. Given the long-standing tension between Ben and his brother, James, and the potentially incompatible interests of the third generation, Ben must prepare to confront this dilemma.

It is likely, for example, that a deal with Argus will provide for Ben to stay with the company for a couple of years to ensure continuity. He has a personal interest in maximizing his salary and performance-based bonus, but must avoid the appearance of giving Argus too favorable a deal in return for a good package.

Representing Stated Interests Versus Best Interests. At one extreme, as shown in the accompanying figure, a representative acts as a mere agent, seeking only to gain a mandate and to understand his principals' stated interests and instructions. He acts on these instructions and conveys at-the-table offers to the principals for ratification or revision.

At the other extreme, the representative acts as a visionary leader, profoundly shaping his constituents' perceptions of their best interests in response to external realities. Between these two

Representing Stated Interests Versus Best Interests

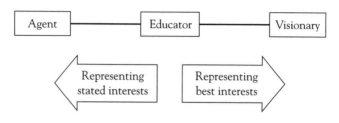

poles, the representative functions as an educator to help the principals understand what their best interests are. Because Ben must convince his family and the professional managers that selling the business is in their best interests, this is the role that he must play in any negotiation with Argus.

Representatives in a position to shape their constituents' perceptions of their interests encounter another dilemma. If Argus viewed Ben as unable to budge his constituents, he could plausibly portray their positions as rigid and could use the need to satisfy them as a tool for claiming value. But it would be hard for him to create value because he wouldn't be able to demonstrate flexibility in exploring options without damaging his credibility.

Conversely, if Argus viewed Ben as highly influential with his constituents, he would come under increasing pressure from Argus to influence them. He would be in a stronger position to create value, but less able to claim value by using ratification tactics.

To the extent that Ben is seen by the family and FHE's managers as having a personal interest in the outcome of the negotiation, his ability to influence their perceptions will suffer. If his constituents don't trust him to act in their best interests, they are likely to resist his efforts to educate them about external realities.

Representing Unified Interests Versus Incompatible Interests.
When internal interests are unified, a representative can simply act as a straightforward agent of those interests. If internal interests

Representing Unified Interests Versus Incompatible Interests

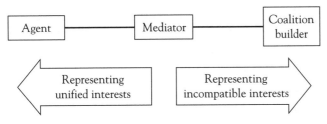

are fractious, as the accompanying figure illustrates, the representative has to act as a coalition builder, allying with some subset of people inside. Between the two extremes, the representative acts as an internal *mediator* in an effort to craft consensus positions.

Ben will initially act as a mediator in an effort to gain support for selling the business. He will try to integrate the interests of all family members, develop creative options, and craft a consensus position on sale of the business. But what if some members of the family implacably oppose a sale? What does he do then? One option is to drop the plan to sell. But Ben believes that this outcome is not in the best interests of the family. It would also hold everyone hostage to the veto of the most opposed family member. Ben might have to shift to building a coalition that alienates some members of the family.

It is essential that Ben establish workable decision rules governing how the family will reach closure on a decision to sell. This means drafting a set of rules that is perceived as fair and getting the family to agree to them. Because the decision rules are likely to have a decisive impact on the ultimate outcome, Ben must craft them with care and expect vigorous debate. The battle may be lost or won here. He should therefore (1) use arguments about fairness to shape family members' perceptions of their interests, (2) raise the cost of disagreement by building a coalition in support of exploring options, and (3) isolate the opponents.

Ben's efforts to build internal consensus could constrict his flexibility in external negotiations: the terms on which the family reaches consensus may be too extreme for the other side. For this reason, it might be best for Ben to postpone trying to build internal consensus. The risk of postponement, however, is vulnerability to being divided and conquered. Ben will have more flexibility in his negotiations with Argus if he doesn't push for early consensus, but he will face more internal disagreement when he brings the family a proposed deal. Conversely, if he pushes for early consensus within the family, he will enjoy less flexibility in external bargaining but will have an easier job ratifying a proposed agreement.

This dilemma is most acute when a representative attempts to function as a mediator. If Ben has to reconcile diverse internal interests, he may want to maximize his internal flexibility by undertaking exploratory talks with Argus and developing an attractive package before pressing for internal consensus. But he will risk looking unprepared or weak in external negotiations. Ben may decide instead to abandon hope of an internal consensus and work at building a partisan coalition in the family to maximize his external flexibility.

The Representational Role Grid. The three dimensions along which representational roles vary can be combined and depicted in the three-dimensional grid on page 197. All three dimensions are anchored by the role they share: that of agent. The situation confronting representatives can be diagnosed by first identifying where they lie on the three axes and then assessing the corresponding challenges. Because of his role in the family, Ben will have to operate close to the middle of the representational role grid. He will act as a partner, representing his own interests as well as others'. He will have to educate his constituents about their best interests. And he will function, at least initially, as an internal mediator.

Shifting Among Roles. As the negotiation proceeds, Ben may decide to shift roles. If he concludes that consensus is impossible and

Representational Role Grid

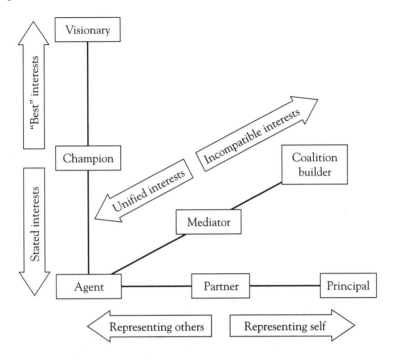

that less-than-unanimous agreement is more desirable than no deal, he might stop acting as an internal mediator and become a coalition builder. He must be careful, however: shifts among roles are not always reversible. Once he has sided with a particular coalition in the family, it will be impossible for him to revert to being a neutral mediator.

With a better understanding of the representational challenges Ben faces, take a couple of minutes to think about what you would do in his situation. What would your goals be, and what actions would you take, in what order, to achieve them?

Building Momentum

Ben's ultimate goal is to sell the business at a good price. To build momentum toward that goal, he should structure the process in three phases: securing a mandate from the family, getting the professional managers on board, and then structuring and leading the team in negotiations with Argus (and possibly others).

Securing a Mandate. In the first phase, Ben's objective is to secure a mandate to explore sale of the company, without anyone having to commit to do so. It will be hard for opponents of a sale within the family to argue against simply exploring options. Once exploration is under way, it is likely to create its own momentum; this is a splendid example of entanglement.

Ben should begin to educate his family about the risks of not selling the business and make the case for doing so at the right price. Above all, he wants to discourage early formation of a blocking coalition. Such a coalition could consist of James, James's son, and one or more of Leslie's children. But because there is no sign of implacable opposition at this point, Ben should avoid actions that will generate reactive coalition building.

Ben should use a mix of shuttles and summits to build momentum. He should probably begin with one-on-one discussions, first with Leslie and then with James, followed by a three-way meeting. Then he should organize a full-family meeting to solicit approval to explore a sale.

Before meeting with Leslie and James, Ben should think about how to frame the argument for each. Leslie will probably trust Ben's assessment of the business realities, but she may feel emotionally resistant to selling her father's company. Ben should stress that, above all, their father wanted financial security for his family and that it is their financial security that is at risk; he could remind her of specific remarks their father made. She will also be concerned about her son's future. Ben should stress that a sale would have to include a transitional arrangement for family members to continue to work in the business for a year or more.

Ben should use similar arguments with James. But he should stress the need for outside assessments of the future of the business in order to blunt possible suspicion that Ben simply wants to get out. He should also spell out the financial benefits of a sale at the right price. Assuming that the business could be sold for a price of roughly 1 × annual sales, it would net roughly $200 million. Since the company has negligible debt, this price would translate into $20 million each for James and his children.

Meeting individually with every member of the third generation would take too much time and might create the appearance that Ben is playing politics. Instead, he should ask his siblings to discuss the issues with their children. (They would do so anyway.) He should then convene a family summit meeting as soon as is practical (leaving no time for misperceptions to build up or coalitions to form). Meanwhile, he should talk with his own children to be sure they are on board. If his children are friendly with cousins who don't work in the business (and who thus might be more likely to support sale), he could encourage his children to sound them out; they should wait a few days to do so, to give Ben's siblings time to talk with their children first and to avoid the perception that Ben is coalition building. This will help Ben get a sense of where things stand.

Ben's goals for the family summit meeting are to (1) present a clear picture of the business's current situation and details of Argus's overture, (2) lay out the potential costs and benefits of a sale, (3) get buy-in for hiring advisers and exploring possibilities, and (4) agree on decision rules for the ultimate decision. The issues should be dealt with in this order. Ben should stress that none of these steps commits them to sell the business, but that they need clarity about what their options are.

The crucial step, as we have seen, is to secure agreement on the decision rules. Ben could accomplish this by framing the first key decision—whether to hire professional advisers to help the family value the business and to advise them on dealing with Argus—and using that decision to engineer agreement on a decision process. Specifically, he should propose a decision rule of sufficient consensus, not unanimity. Otherwise, the most opposed individuals can veto sale of the company. Sufficient consensus could consist of a two-thirds majority of the family, including both the second and third generations. Because each individual effectively owns 10 percent of the company's value, he can argue that this is a fair way to proceed. This rule would shape opponents' perceptions of their alternatives; they would not be able to unilaterally veto a move to go forward, and hence might well prefer to be part of the agreement rather than isolate themselves and lose control. This rule would also make Ben's life easier if he has to shift to coalition-building mode.

Ben could say, "I believe that we should at least explore the potential for selling the business. To do that, we should get some professional advisers to assess the company and the industry and give us a sense of what we can hope to secure in a sale, as well as the consequences of waiting. I suggest that we agree to make this decision, and subsequent decisions concerning the sale, through an open vote with a two-thirds majority of the family required to approve an action." This proposal has a good chance of carrying the day.

Suppose, however, that one or more family members, such as James's older son, strongly oppose exploring a sale or, more likely, balk at Ben's decision rules and demand full consensus on all decisions. What should he do? This is a battle he has to win. He can argue that full consensus would be unfair because it would hold the entire family's future hostage to the demands of a small minority. He should also point out that the alternative to a two-thirds majority is the legal standard for decision: a majority of the second generation, which has the controlling shares. If push really comes to shove, he can express willingness to resign over the issue, secure in the knowledge that no one else in the family is ready to run the business. Although it may come at a cost, he will win.

Getting Management on Board. Assuming Ben wins family support for moving forward, his next step is to secure the value of the business by getting the company's professional managers on board. To accomplish this, he will need to shape their perceptions of their alternatives and interests. He should meet with his key direct reports and lay out Argus's overture and the family's decision to explore a sale. The decision to explore options should be presented as a fait accompli, to make clear that the status quo is not an option.

At the same time, Ben should put an incentive package on the table for senior managers in order to align their incentives with the family's. Above all, he needs to prevent necessary people from jumping ship, because they represent part of the value to be sold. He also wants to prevent some or all of the managers from siding with family members who decide to oppose sale. This is particularly critical, because the managers will have access to information that Ben might want to share selectively.

Ben should point out that any buyer is likely to want to retain the professional management team and will almost certainly offer attractive retention packages. He should also offer the senior managers a sales bonus, both a fixed sum that each will receive if the business is sold and a variable amount linked to the sale price of the business. This move will give the managers an interest in maximizing the sale price and prevent them from implicitly siding with the buyer to get attractive financial packages for themselves.

Having secured internal commitment to moving forward, Ben can turn to the next phase: assembling a team of internal people and external advisers and preparing to negotiate. This brings us to the subject of leading teams.

ORCHESTRATING TEAMS

Representation is about negotiating on behalf of others; leading teams is about negotiating in concert with others. Even if Ben were the sole decision maker, he would still have to assemble and lead a team to negotiate with Argus (and other potential buyers). So he has to understand the opportunities and potential pitfalls of team negotiation.[6] He also has to assemble the right people, assign them appropriate roles, and deploy them effectively.

Strengths and Weaknesses of Teams

Ben needs a team because he lacks the necessary expertise about the company and the acquisition process to negotiate single-handed. Teams are valuable precisely because they bring together people with complementary expertise. The trick is to assemble a critical mass of knowledge without creating too large a team: the larger the team, the greater the difficulty and cost of coordination.

There are reasons other than expertise that you might decide to assemble a negotiating team. If the negotiations require buy-in by key constituencies who do not fully trust you to represent their interests, they may need to be represented at the table. You can also assign distinct roles and responsibilities to team members, such as analysis or observation of the other side or note taking. As lead negotiator, you may pace yourself better if you can sometimes shift the burden of talking to another member of your team. Team negotiation also gives you extra tools to control the flow of the process. If the tide is running against you, for instance, you can interrupt the negotiation to caucus (consult with your team) in order to regroup.

At the same time, a team can unquestionably be a source of weakness if the wrong people are involved or if they are insufficiently trained, organized, and disciplined. One trap is unintentionally making internal differences visible. The other side is likely to play a divide-and-conquer game in order to claim value, forcing you to play defense to keep value from being claimed from you and hindering you from identifying and pursuing creative options. ("Good cop–bad cop" scenarios are sometimes effective in claiming value, but they are very difficult to pull off convincingly. Experienced negotiators will not be fooled.)

A related problem is lack of clarity about who is leading the team. A negotiating team needs a clear-cut lead negotiator to function effectively. But if your team includes representatives of constituencies with differing interests, they may engage in a dysfunctional competition for leadership at the negotiating table. This jockeying will be exploited by the other side, so you have to be prepared to exert discipline.

Negotiating teams often include technical experts inexperienced at negotiation. If the members of your team are not instructed on how to keep their guard up, the other side can learn a great deal from inadvertent information leakage. Leakage can occur during formal negotiation, but the biggest risk is uncontrolled side encounters with counterparts who have been coached to extract information from unsuspecting members of your team. Team members have to be sensitized to the dangers of inadvertently giving away important information.

One way to exploit the benefits of a team while avoiding its pitfalls is to use a team to prepare for negotiations but to conduct the at-the-table interactions alone. Simply asking a couple of knowledgeable people to critique your preparation—the military calls this exercise a "murder board"—can significantly enhance your performance. In this case, however, Ben needs the expertise of key team members at the table during negotiations.

Selecting Team Members

Think of every new negotiation as a casting call. What are the roles to be enacted? Who are the right players (inside and outside the organization) to fill them?

Selecting the Internal Team. For Ben, selecting the right people from inside the business is quite straightforward. He himself will be the lead negotiator, or deal manager. Because Ben exercises formal authority over the members of his team, he will play quite a different role than he would if he were acting as a coordinator. (Coordinators often have little control, for example, over who is on the team and may have to contend with other members who seek to exert leadership.)

Ben will want all of his direct reports—finance, operations, human resources, and sales—on the team. Their operating expertise will be needed when a potential buyer initiates due diligence on the company. It is therefore essential for them to be on board and motivated to help Ben get a good deal.

Choosing External Advisers. Selecting external advisers requires more work. The company's accounting firm should definitely participate. The accountants have to make sure that the accounts are spotless, and they should walk potential buyers through anything out of the ordinary.

Ben will also need legal advisers to oversee the drafting of agreements. The company has a longstanding association with a law firm, but extra legal support will almost certainly be required. Ben needs someone who specializes solely in merger-and-acquisition transactions, which probably means someone situated in a financial center like Chicago or New York. Referrals are helpful here. If Ben knows people in his industry who have sold their businesses, he can ask which lawyers they worked with and how satisfied they were.

Does Ben need the services of an investment banker? If he plans to look for potential buyers other than Argus, the answer is almost certainly yes. Lawyers will not structure a sale process for him, and he is unlikely to have the time or expertise to do it himself. Running a sale process involving multiple potential buyers requires a great deal of work that can distract managers from running the business precisely when it is most urgent to ensure that everything runs smoothly.

Even if Ben plans to negotiate only with Argus, there is still a good case for involving an investment banker. A good banker will have expertise at conducting negotiations and can help value the business accurately and provide detailed information about comparable transactions in the industry. A banker would also lend seriousness to the process and put Argus—and the family—on notice that Ben plans to drive a hard bargain.

The interests of any investment banker are strongly aligned with Ben's: the banker's fee is based on the size of the transaction. But Ben must select a banker who sees his transaction as potentially lucrative enough to merit a significant investment of time. At roughly $200 million, his transaction is large enough to interest top-tier investment banks that operate middle-market practices and smaller firms that specialize in medium-sized transactions. Ideally, he will find someone who specializes in rollups in his industry. Once again, people in the industry who have sold their businesses are a good source of leads.

Finally, if the sale of the business involves complicated technical issues, there may be a role for consultants. If some of the company's sites raise environmental issues, for example, Ben may need the services of an environmental consultant. If the family has a trusted adviser on tax and estate issues, he or she should be consulted and participate as necessary. If not, Ben should probably seek out such a person.

Assembling the Cast. The full cast of participants in an acquisition can be very large, especially when external advisers are taken into account. The table on page 206 summarizes the roles and responsibilities of the individuals involved.[7]

Matching Posture to Process

As we saw in Chapter Three, negotiations tend to proceed through distinct stages. A merger and acquisition transaction like Ben's typically consists of five distinct stages: partner selection, initial agreement, due diligence, final agreement, and closing.[8] Each will demand a different negotiating posture and a different configuration of the various internal and external players.

Partner Selection. The goal at this stage is to identify, and elicit interest from, attractive potential partners. It is unlikely that Argus is the only potential buyer for FHE. Ben's investment bankers should help him survey the consolidation trend in his industry, pinpoint firms that are doing rollups, and analyze their goals and strategies. This survey will reveal the likelihood of generating competition

Members of a Negotiating Team

Inside Participants	Role	Possible Outside Complement
Decision makers (the family)	Oversight, direction, final approval.	Investment bankers, lawyers
Deal manager (Ben)	Overall management of process. Setting strategy and making tactical decisions.	Investment bankers
Internal financial staff (CFO)	Valuation, review of tax and accounting treatment. Financing of transaction. Accounting and financial due diligence.	Investment bankers, accountants
Legal staff (company lawyer)	Verification of assets and liabilities in due diligence. Ensuring adherence to regulatory requirements. Keeping records of the negotiation and drafting agreements.	Lawyers
Operating management (operations, sales, and human resources)	Operating due diligence.	Specialist consultants (for example, on environmental and tax and estate issues)

to buy the business. Argus may be willing to pay a premium, for example, to prevent a competitor from acquiring Ben's company. A survey will also reveal whether financial buyers, such as private equity firms, might be interested.

Ben will not want to auction the company formally. An auction would call for an up-front commitment to sell—not feasible given the resistance within the family—and he would lose control of the process. Needed employees could also become demoralized and quit if they perceive that they are "on the block." Ideally, he and his team would engage in quiet linked negotiations with two or three potential buyers.

Meanwhile, Ben should work with his investment bankers to estimate the potential value of the business. A discounted cash flow valuation analysis and comparable transactions should produce a target sale price for the company.

This is also the time for Ben to bring his management team up to speed. They should be pressed to consult with external advisers on questions that potential acquirers will ask during due diligence and assigned specific responsibilities and deadlines for collecting supporting information. This preparation process should help to build relationships between the internal management team and the external advisers.

Initial Agreement. The next step is to reach an initial agreement with one potential buyer. An initial agreement is a shared commitment to proceed with the deal as long as no unpleasant surprises emerge in due diligence.

Initial agreement is the time for both sides to put their "must-haves" on the table. Ben and his team must therefore be on the same page concerning "must-haves." The buyer will almost certainly want commitments from management to stay on for a minimum transition period. The buyer will also make certain that FHE's contractual arrangements with its suppliers are in good repair and that there are no environmental time bombs. For his part, Ben will want to structure the transaction financially to ensure maximum security for the family; he is likely, for example, to insist on doing the deal in cash rather than stock. He will also want assurances of employment during the transitional period for the family members and professional managers currently on the payroll.

Ben should not expect firm agreement on price at this juncture; neither he nor the potential buyer will have enough information. The goal is to exchange enough information to ensure that both sides are thinking within the same price band. At this stage, the focus should be less on the numbers than on the broad structure of the deal—the key issues and financial structure.

This is also the time for the two sides to get to know each other. A sophisticated buyer will use this opportunity to take the measure of FHE's management team. Ben should prepare his team for scrutiny and should coach them to take the measure of the other side as well. He and his team should also be working to build a reservoir of goodwill with their counterparts, to draw on when the going gets tough.

Due Diligence. Due diligence is much more than fact checking. Experienced acquirers use interactions during due diligence to assess the abilities and personal agendas of the target company's managers. Do they have a command of operational details? Do they work well as a team? Are they easily flustered or hostile when challenged? Are they enthused by the transaction or mainly concerned about their personal futures?

Ben's team should be prepared not just to provide the requested information in a timely manner, but to understand the broader goals of potential acquirers at this stage. The work that Ben did earlier to align the team's incentives will pay off at this stage, but he must keep working to bolster the team's solidarity and sense of purpose.

Final Agreement. This is the stage at which the two sides and their advisers negotiate on price and other specifics. It is important to stay focused on the most critical issues at this juncture. Otherwise, talks could get stalled on relatively trivial items, exhausting the hard-won goodwill gained in earlier stages.

Ben should think hard about how to build momentum by sequencing both issues and interactions. He should probably try to start with a few easy-to-resolve issues, postponing the toughest few issues (including price) to the end and dealing with them as a package. This tactic will leave him some flexibility to create value through trades.

Ben should also plan to break up the team into two or three separate negotiating groups—managers, lawyers, and perhaps investment bankers—during this phase. Division of labor has important benefits. First, it allows for parallel processing. The legal team, for example, can work on the acquisition agreement, while the bankers address the terms and structure of the financing. Meanwhile, the managers can focus on strategic and personnel issues, stepping into the other negotiations only to help unblock impasses.

Negotiating through multiple channels also facilitates sending informal messages. Without conceding anything, Ben's investment banker or lawyer could float ideas about different ways to address particular concerns.

Finally, negotiation at several levels simultaneously isolates acrimony. The bankers and lawyers can deliver hard messages or take inflexible positions without poisoning Ben's relationships with his counterparts. He may, after all, have to work with them for several more years.

Once the deal is done and approved by the family, the managers on the team must begin to sell it aggressively. Each senior manager should be given responsibility for informing employees and outside constituents and promoting the agreement to them. Not everyone will be happy with the deal. FHE's employees will worry about adapting to a different operating culture, and they may have legitimate worries about job security. Customers will wonder whether the acquirer will damage long-established relationships.

Closing the Deal.   Once the ink has dried, it is easy to think that a deal is done. But a surprising number of deals fall apart between final agreement and closure, the last stage of the process, because of glitches that arise in the target business like an undisclosed environmental liability or new operating problems. Ben should focus now on getting the deal closed as quickly as possible. Prompt closure is a way of showing employees, suppliers, and customers that the deal will work. While Ben and his external advisers ensure that no barriers to prompt closure arise on his side, the attention of the managerial members of the team should be redirected toward ensuring that the business continues to post good operating results.

INTEGRATING REPRESENTATION AND TEAM LEADERSHIP

At the same time Ben is leading the team, he has to continue to represent the family and to lead its members through the deal-making process. Winning the family's agreement to explore potential deals was an important first step, but hardly guarantees eventual support for a sale. Even a highly attractive opportunity to sell could come to naught if Ben does not adequately inform and consult with the family throughout the negotiation. He has to think both about how to get ratification for a deal he believes serves their best interests and how best to lead the team in order to advance the family's best interests.

Structuring Consultations

Ben should not inform the family about every detail of his team's preparation and negotiations. Instead, he shares information with the family in a structured and planned way. Because Ben wants to continue to nudge the family in a series of small steps from exploration of a potential sale to sign-off on a deal, information sharing should be synchronized with the stages of the negotiation process. Information should also be released to everyone simultaneously, to head off suspicions of coalition building.

Before approaching anyone other than Argus during the partner selection stage, for example, Ben should feed back to his family (remotely, such as by telephone or e-mail, not at a meeting) the investment bankers' assessments of industry trends, the value of the business, and potential partners. He should say that he plans exploratory talks with other potential partners and urge family members to bring him their questions and concerns. Ben should also allow (and perhaps even encourage) family members to talk directly with the investment bankers and members of the management team if the conversations would help reassure them.

At the end of the partner selection phase, Ben should meet with the entire family to recommend negotiating an initial agreement to sell the business. This will be a crucial meeting. The team can play a central role: if the entire management team supports sale by this time, the task of convincing the family will be vastly simplified. Ben should now seek approval to explore the terms of an initial agreement to sell. Once again, he should rely on the logic that the family is not being asked to commit to sell, just to see what they can get. This decision should be put to a vote using the established decision rules.

Immediately after the meeting, Ben should begin talking individually with family members who work for the business about their concerns and transitional arrangements. In effect, he should conduct follow-up shuttle diplomacy to seal the commitments he got at the summit.

The terms of the initial agreement (which do not include a definitive price) also should be brought to the family for approval. The deal should be structured to yield a high level of financial security, take care of employees, and provide family members with acceptable transitional arrangements.

Before the final step—presenting the family the terms of a definitive agreement to sell—Ben should make efforts to shape their expectations about price. This means being sure that they are being realistic about what the business will fetch and perhaps even deflating their expectations a little. Ideally, the family will be pleasantly surprised by what Ben has managed to secure for the business.

Leading from the Middle

Ben is fortunate that he can largely separate the two roles of representative and team leader: the people most likely to resist the deal are not on the team, and the team is likely to help him sell the agreement to the family.

When, unavoidably, members of the team represent powerful constituencies that are predisposed to oppose any agreement, the leadership challenges are far greater. In this situation, there is no way to separate representation from team leadership. The likelihood that information will leak at inopportune times, or be distorted and used to foster opposition, is also much greater. Managing this complex representational situation requires much more attention to information control and coalition building within the team itself. Success depends on in-depth understanding of alignments of interests among team members, the relative power of the constituencies they represent, and the communication channels they use. The leader should abandon hope of consensus in favor of coalition building within the team and among the constituencies that must ratify agreements.

In the end, Ben won approval to sell the family business. The family elected to take cash rather than stock and received $190 million. Ben agreed to stay on for two years to help with the integration, and the other members of the family in the business were guaranteed positions for up to three years. All but one of the senior professional managers decided to stay with the company, encouraged in part by Argus's proposed stock option plan.

Although the outcome was the one that Ben believed to be best, the process did a lot of damage to relationships in the family. By the time the decision was made, Ben and James were no longer on speaking terms. Although James eventually voted for the sale, he felt that Ben had railroaded the family into the decision. James's older son remained vehemently opposed to the sale and voted against it. His relationships with his father, uncle, and cousins were seriously, perhaps irreparably, damaged.

9

Negotiating Crises

On April 29, 1995, Greenpeace activists boarded and occupied the *Brent Spar*, an abandoned Royal Dutch/Shell deepwater oil storage platform located in the North Sea.[1] At the same time, Greenpeace officials released a report to the media in London asserting that Shell's decision to dispose of the platform by sinking it deep in the Atlantic Ocean was environmentally dangerous and that other options were more attractive. They advocated a plan to bring the aging platform on shore to dismantle and dispose of it. Greenpeace timed the operation for maximum effect, occupying the platform and issuing the press release just one month before European Union environmental ministers were scheduled to meet and discuss North Sea pollution issues.

Shell officials had finalized the disposal plan after four years of study and quiet negotiations with the British government, which approved the plan in February 1995. Shell managers and engineers considered the plan to sink the *Spar* the best practicable environmental option, basing their view on over thirty independent studies and months of consultations with conservation bodies and fishing interests. The University of Aberdeen reviewed and endorsed the results of the studies; the publicly funded National Environmental Research Council deemed the plan environmentally sound. After approving the plan, the British government notified the twelve other European signatories of the Oslo and Paris Convention. No objections were raised.

As the first of dozens of anticipated disposals of North Sea oil platforms, Shell's disposal plan for the *Spar* would set the precedent for other companies. Although they considered the plan sound, some oil industry executives were upset that Shell put the *Spar* at the front of the disposal queue. The *Spar* was one of only a few North Sea platforms equipped with the large oil storage tanks that had been necessary prior to the installation of a pipeline to take the oil directly to shore. Because the *Spar*'s tanks contained oil and toxic residues that would be sunk with the platform, there were likely to be significant environmental concerns.

During the mid-1990s, Greenpeace was the world's largest nongovernmental organization; headquartered in Amsterdam, it operated in thirty-two countries. By 1995, the organization had achieved many of its environmental goals and was looking for a new high-profile mission to capture public attention. One former Greenpeace board member noted, "Greenpeace [had] a fleet of ships running around the oceans looking for something to do."[2] The organization decided to turn the *Spar* disposal into a high-visibility issue in advance of the European Union environmental ministers' meeting. It was not interested in exploring the technical merits of various disposal options. As one Greenpeace director stated, "I don't care about scientific arguments. . . . The question is how does society cope with its waste? And our message is: don't litter!"[3]

The Greenpeace operation to occupy the platform caught Shell officials completely by surprise. The company had no contingency plans in place to deal with the crisis. Shell responded instead by taking Greenpeace to court, successfully suing for trespass. After the activists were removed from the platform, Shell reoccupied the *Brent Spar* and defended it from further assaults with water cannons. Through mid-June 1995, Shell continued with plans to sink the platform. This provided Greenpeace and the world press with many opportunities to broadcast dramatic stories and images of activists fighting through water cannons in an attempt to reboard the platform as Shell towed it to its North Atlantic dumping ground. During the crisis, Greenpeace spent $2 million on its media campaign; its public relations staff of twenty-nine people provided the only press communication links from the platform.

Shell provided little effective response to the Greenpeace media onslaught. The company's decentralized, matrix management structure inhibited the company from coordinating crisis response activities and notifying employees of decisions and events. Chairman of Shell Germany Peter Duncan remarked publicly, for example, that he first heard about the planned sinking of the *Spar* "more or less from the television."[4] In addition, senior Shell managers outside the United Kingdom publicly criticized both the disposal plans and each other through the press; the company showed little ability to work with the press to educate the public or shape perceptions of the issue.

Ultimately, the crisis spiraled out of control. By June 1995, Greenpeace had organized a grassroots boycott of Shell gas stations in Germany. The boycott eventually grew violent; several Shell stations were firebombed and two hundred others damaged. With no support from the public or European governments, Shell abandoned its plan to sink the *Spar* on June 20, 1995.

What might Shell have done differently? How could negotiation and coalition-building skills have helped the company? What might they have done to organize more effectively?

The question is not if an organization will face a crisis situation but when a crisis will erupt.[5] When the inevitable crisis hits, many organizations find themselves unable to handle the situation effectively. In part, this is because a good crisis response capability usually requires different organizational structures and processes from normal day-to-day operations. As a result, it is senior management's responsibility not only to anticipate and avoid potential crises, but also to ensure that the requisite organizational capabilities have been developed and exercised.

The negotiation and coalition-building skills presented in this book are central to effectiveness in anticipating, avoiding, and managing crises. To stay ahead of the curve in crises, for example, organizations often must conduct very rapid negotiations for resources with outside suppliers. Dealing with the press also requires adeptness at negotiating the terms of engagement. Above all, managers must reach out to key external constituencies—customers, suppliers, shareholders, analysts, government agencies, and the public at large—and build supportive coalitions to sustain the organization through the duration of the crisis.

COMMON MISTAKES

Shell's performance during the Brent Spar crisis exhibited many mistakes that are typical in crisis situations.

Not Tuning into the Environment

The best crises are the ones you see coming and take action to avoid. Shell failed to scan the landscape and identify potential threats. By doing a linked negotiation analysis, for example, the company might have realized that the platform was probably a poor choice as the first large oil platform to be disposed of at sea. In addition, Shell might have realized that the more militant members of environmental groups such as Greenpeace were looking for a significant new mission and that the upcoming environmental ministers meeting made the *Spar* disposal a potential high-profile issue. If the age of the platform dictated that it be disposed of first, Shell management should have taken more aggressive and comprehensive steps to prevent the crisis from escalating. Even after Greenpeace protestors had occupied the platform and garnered significant attention from the press, Shell officials tried to stay the course and responded only with a series of civil court cases to have the protestors removed for trespassing.

Failure to Build Supportive Coalitions

Shell employed a process the company would later characterize as Decide-Announce-Defend (DAD), and this made it vulnerable to Greenpeace. As one nongovernmental organization activist put it, the proposal couldn't pass the Dracula test: it died when exposed to the light. Instead of quiet negotiations to obtain British government approval to sink the platform, it might have made the four-year decision process more transparent to the public and even encouraged public dialogue. The company later described this as a Dialogue-Decide-Deliver (DDD) process. Shell could have accomplished this by publicizing independent technical assessments and repeatedly sending a consistent message on the environmental merits of the plan to the press. By more adequately involving the public in the decision, Shell management might have anticipated the public's emotional reaction to the disposal decision and responded appropriately before the crisis started. By not paying attention to coalition building, Shell allowed Greenpeace to set the agenda.

Doing Too Little, Too Late

The crisis response actions that Shell did take were often too little, too late. The same actions or statements that may be an excellent response on Day 1 may be viewed as inadequate on Day 2 and completely insufficient on Day 3. For example, Shell developed a number of worst-case scenarios for potential *Spar* disposal problems but did not formulate any response plans until after Greenpeace had taken control of the platform. As public outrage grew over the plan to sink the *Spar*, Greenpeace published measurements of oil-related contamination levels from the *Spar* over one hundred times greater than Shell's previously published estimates. Long after Shell abandoned the plan to sink the *Spar*, it commissioned an independent assessment that showed Shell's original estimates to have been broadly correct. The report came much too late, however, to have any effect on the crisis.

Contributing to Sustaining the Crisis

Often companies that are targets of negative media attention help to sustain the damage. In addition to taking action too late, some of Shell's decisions and actions added fuel to the fire. Employing water cannons to prevent the activists from reboarding the platform and allowing Greenpeace to provide the only media communication links from the *Spar* ensured a steady stream of damaging images and stories for the world press. In addition, an earlier decision to put disposal plans on hold might have prevented the crisis from escalating. Ultimately, Shell's abandonment of its plan to sink the platform defused the crisis by denying Greenpeace its high-profile issue.

ORGANIZATIONAL WEAKNESSES

Failures to identify and respond to events effectively ensue when organizations lack structures and processes necessary for crisis response. Common organizational failures include the following.

Lack of a Dedicated Crisis Management Organization

Decentralized organizations, which are so good at helping promote innovation in normal times, prove woefully inadequate in times of crisis. Crisis demands a rapid centralized response, and this requires a very clear line of command and the ability to shift rapidly into what the military terms "war-fighting mode." Otherwise, the organization responds incoherently.

Shell's decentralized matrix management structure, although effective for normal business operations, proved to be a liability in this crisis situation, because there was no single leader or group in charge. In addition, the company lacked dedicated crisis response facilities and other infrastructure to handle the situation. Without the crisis response capabilities that could have been honed through rehearsals and simulations, the company was unable to respond to Greenpeace actions quickly and effectively.

Not Developing an Effective Communications Plan

Shell managers failed to designate a person or group to act as a public relations voice for the company. As a result, the company was unable to present an effective, coherent message to the public and lost the frame game. A single voice could have provided a channel for communication with employees, the press, and government officials. In addition, this person or group might have acted to prevent senior European Shell executives from making unhelpful and divisive statements to the press.

Although Shell's disposal plan was technically sound, the company lacked a crisis management capability that might have prevented the situation from spinning out of control. Greenpeace, for its part, had a well-developed crisis management capability, in many ways a mirror image of typical crisis management processes in that the organization's goal was to create crises rather than prevent them. Capabilities needed for effective crisis response include a crisis prevention mind-set, precrisis planning and rehearsals, an ability to identify crises in their early stages, effective structures and processes for crisis response, and an ability to bring closure to the situation and capture lessons learned.

CRISIS PLANNING

The simplest and most effective way to limit damage from a crisis is to prevent it from happening in the first place. Senior managers should constantly survey the landscape for potential problem areas and address them before they become crises. In some cases, crises are unforeseeable, caused by a bolt out of the blue. In many cases, however, with careful thought and action, crises can be averted or their impact mitigated. Senior managers, for example, can prevent problems by making sure employees follow safety procedures or by taking time to consider the range of possible public reactions to corporate decisions.

Develop Planning Scenarios

When developing crisis management plans, it is essential to identify a set of crisis scenarios.[6] By developing scenarios, the organization may come to perceive vulnerabilities that previously were obscured. In addition, the scenarios provide a concrete basis for planning responses. This is not to say that the organization should try to anticipate every contingency. Instead, the key is to identify a reasonably compact set of threats that the organization plausibly faces. Examples include shooter on site, epidemic, bomb threat, major fire, major external terrorist attack, major economic dislocation, or infrastructure failure (power grid outage coupled with extreme heat, loss of the Web or telephone lines, disruption in the water supply). This is also an opportunity to think through how opponents could try to exploit the vulnerabilities of the organization. As with Shell and the *Brent Spar*, crises are as often instigated by people as by acts of God.

Rapidly Identify Emerging Crises

Once a problem occurs, it is human nature to ignore it and hope it goes away, because it distracts from, or conflicts with, other plans. In other cases, senior leaders simply do not recognize that what appears to be a technical problem might be an emotional issue for the public. Managers must remain tuned into what is being said within the organization and where public sentiment is likely to converge. Issues to explore include the cause of the situation, current status, potential risks, and affected parties. In addition, senior leaders should assess what is controllable and what is not, how much time is available before action must be taken, the potential for an escalation of the crisis, and possible spillover effects.

Because of the potential for industrial and environmental disasters in the oil industry, Shell had a well-developed scenario planning capability. Nevertheless, the company failed to anticipate or plan for the *Spar* crisis. Shell managers' intense focus on the technical merits of the issue and the company's matrix management structure blinded the organization to the potential for a crisis.

Design Flexible Response Modules

Crises rarely replicate exactly the scenarios that were used for planning. Instead, the crisis typically involves some new scenario or a mix of anticipated scenarios. There is thus a danger that plans built on the planning scenarios will prove to be brittle—unsuited to rapid adaptation to the circumstances at hand—so it is essential to build flexibility into the organization's crisis response routines.

The most effective way to do this is to modularize crisis response plans. This means creating a set of packaged responses that leaders can mix and match as their first response to a crisis. Done well, this approach buys the organization time to craft a deeper, more customized response to the situation at hand. One example of a crisis response module is an evacuation plan. This module could be activated for many different crisis situations. Others include facility lockdowns, preset communication protocols for contacting key employees, police and fire response, press relations, and grief management. Each module should include a list of steps to be taken and resources that can be activated to help deal with the situation.

Craft Contingency Plans

Because many crisis situations can be anticipated, contingency plans can be developed in advance. This means creating a road map, linking the response modules to the anticipated crisis scenarios. For example, a shooter on site triggers an immediate facility lockdown plus a police response plus preset communication protocols to convene the crisis response team and warn staff.

This sort of preparation can hasten responses in time-critical situations, prevent confusion, and ensure that a well-thought-out and coordinated plan is put into action. Plans and procedures are especially important for companies with decentralized management structures like Shell. The benefits of decentralization, such as responsiveness to local market conditions and flexibility, become liabilities in a crisis when a fast, coordinated response is required.

CRISIS ORGANIZATION

The best plans are worthless without the right organizational structure to execute them. Following are guidelines for creating such a structure.

Set Up a Command Post

Many organizations designate a command post or "war room" in advance of a crisis situation. The command post may normally be used for other activities (such as an executive conference room), or it may be used only in times of crisis. The important thing is to have a place that is physically isolated from routine activities. A separate crisis response area means that the team can focus on the crisis without disturbing, or being disturbed by, the ongoing operations of the organization. A separate crisis response area also provides a focal point for those charged with resolving the situation, and for employees, the public, the press, and government agencies.

The command post should be outfitted with the communication tools such as telephones, faxes, video, and Internet and documentation such as telephone directories, maps, and technical information that might be needed in a crisis. To the extent possible, there should be redundancy in these channels, including backups that are not linked to the telephone system or the Web.

The command post must be prepared in advance, as it is very difficult to pull these resources together during the early hours of a crisis. If evacuation is a strong possibility, then a backup command post should be designated at a safe external location.

Greenpeace had the infrastructure necessary to mobilize in support of a crisis. Although the organization was run locally, its headquarters in Amsterdam exercised effective central control of critical issues. Greenpeace prohibited local chapters from disagreeing with centrally dictated policy. As a result, the organization was able to coordinate an effective international campaign.

Designate a Crisis Response Team

Crisis response team members need to be identified in advance of a crisis. In most cases, the CEO should be in charge. But because the CEO probably can't afford to devote around-the-clock attention to the issue, a deputy crisis team leader should be designated to run the team in his or her absence. The deputy must have enough authority to resolve issues and commandeer the needed resources. Therefore, legal, public relations, government relations, and a menu of technical experts should be identified in advance. Team members should be identified by function rather than by name, since over time individuals will change functional positions or leave the organization.

Greenpeace had the right people on its crisis management team. Ship captains and crew, the "rubber suit guys" who boarded the *Spar*, lawyers, and public relations people all worked in concert. The team had worked together before in similar situations and had well-developed communications and operations policies and procedures.

Set Up Communication Protocols

Clear triggers are needed to move the organization from "normal" to "war-fighting" mode and to activate specific response modules. There also have to be "all-clear" signals that shift the organization back to its normal operating mode. Communication plans should therefore be developed to ensure that the right people are notified about the crisis in a timely manner. These plans might also include background information and draft statements for release to the press early in the crisis to help shape public perceptions. Communication plans can prevent internal confusion and help ensure that a consistent and effective message is presented to the press and public.

One person, or a small group of people, should be designated as the public voice of the company, thus providing a clear channel between the CEO and external stakeholders. Allowing self-appointed spokespeople to represent the company can cause chaos and damage the company's credibility. The spokespersons should be part of the crisis management team and have full authority to speak for the company.

Greenpeace executive director Steve D'Esposito served as the organization's sole voice and directed the operation. Greenpeace also had a communications director, who was an experienced journalist, and a public relations staff of twenty-nine people. The group also had excellent technical communications capabilities. During the *Spar* operation, Greenpeace provided the only communication links from the oil platform to the international press, using a sophisticated "squisher" to transmit video feeds quickly and cheaply to the world. As one Shell executive noted, Greenpeace's "provision of pictures, facilities and information . . . [was] a Trojan horse for editorial and political spin."[7]

Develop Key Relationships

Effective relationships with the right external parties are often critical in crisis situations. Government agencies, emergency response groups, community organizations, unions, and press agencies can all play significant roles in resolving the situation. However, these relationships must be cultivated before the crisis hits. After all, you would not want to introduce yourself to your neighbors at 2 A.M. when your house is on fire.

Relationships with the press can be particularly important. Journalist Dimitri Mitropoulos suggests that a company be proactive in developing durable relationships with reporters by consistently providing them with access to inside information.[8] Reporters who are concerned about professional relationships and future access to inside information about a company will tend to be more sympathetic in their coverage of the crisis. Companies should also be prepared to "blow the lid" preemptively by releasing sensitive or potentially damaging information before any individual reporter gets a scoop on the story. A preemptive release to a broad group of journalists precludes exclusivity and increases the chances that the story will be relegated to the less visible inside pages. It also allows the company to have more control in the framing of the story.

Greenpeace spent many years cultivating effective relationships with government and press officials around the world. The grassroots protests organized by Greenpeace Germany involved both local and national political officials, in addition to churches and trade unions. The organization's relationships with print news agencies, television stations, and press offices in Greenpeace member countries allowed the organization to disseminate its video and photographic coverage of events quickly during the crisis.

Secure Backup Resources

Critical resource stocks should be accumulated to be tapped if necessary. Examples include backup power generation and gas supplies, modest reserves of food and water, and medical supplies. Agreements should also be negotiated with external agencies to provide specific resources, such as augmented private security, in time of crisis.

Conduct Regular Rehearsals

The best plans are worthless if they exist only on paper. Team members must develop relationships, and resources, communication channels, and crisis response procedures must be checked before a crisis hits. This calls for regular (biannual) exercises conducted by the crisis response team and regular testing of channels, inventorying of resources, and so forth. These tests should be unscheduled to test speed of response. Rehearsals are especially important when an organization is seldom called on to respond to real-world crises.

RESPONDING TO CRISIS SITUATIONS

If an organization is prepared and has exercised its crisis response capability, its chances of successfully managing the problem increase dramatically. Once the senior management identifies an issue as a potential crisis, the company can notify crisis response team members, alert employees, and open communication channels with external agencies. The crisis team can review procedures and use the communication capabilities of the command post to keep informed of, and manage, ongoing events.

Specific responses and actions depend on the situation. In general, however, the crisis team leader must balance the need to gather information against the requirement to act. In crisis situations, speed is important, and the team leader must be prepared to make decisions with less than complete information. A good decision made in a timely manner is almost always better than a perfect decision made late. Indecision can allow problems to cascade or cause confusion, disastrous in a crisis situation. Also, timely and proactive communication with the public about what is known and what is not known establishes credibility and preempts others from taking control of public perceptions.

Greenpeace was able to leverage its crisis management capabilities to stage a dramatic, attention-getting operation by occupying the unmanned *Spar*. Its superb communication and coordination capabilities equipped the organization to get its message to the public quickly and with emotional impact. By leveraging its reputation and framing the situation as a David and Goliath scenario in which a big oil company was "dumping its car into the village pond," Greenpeace rendered the technical merits of the issue irrelevant to the public. Greenpeace was able to control public perceptions by presenting the issue in emotional terms.

LEARNING FROM THE CRISIS

Each crisis provides an opportunity for organizational learning to occur and plans to be revised. But learning takes place only if the mechanisms are in place to make it happen. A postcrisis review should be conducted by the crisis response team after each significant event. The guiding questions should be: What went well, and what went poorly? What are the key lessons learned? What changes do we need to make to our organization, procedures, and support resources?

The crisis management team should review what happened, what caused the incident, and what internal and external factors contributed to the crisis. The team should also survey what the organization did well in responding to the crisis, what it did poorly, whether the organization is still vulnerable to the same type of situation, and what steps must be taken to reduce a risk of recurrence. As part of this postcrisis review, the team should interview managers, employees, and a full range of external stakeholders.

The results of the postcrisis audit must then be integrated into the organization's daily operations and crisis management practices.[9] It is often helpful to document the investigation's findings in a report so that lessons can be captured for future reference, disseminated throughout the organization, and communicated to external agencies (when appropriate). The team should make sure that managers are assigned responsibility to implement corrective actions and make organizational changes to prevent a similar crisis or improve response in the future. Corrective actions might include changes to practices and procedures, management changes, creation of new organizational capabilities, and initiation of new relationships with external parties. Finally, senior management should ensure that people who distinguished themselves during the crisis are identified and rewarded.

Shell's postcrisis lessons learned highlight the need to involve the public in the decision process and account for public perceptions based on emotion rather than fact. After abandoning the plan to sink the *Brent Spar,* Shell undertook a process, called "Way Forward," to solicit public input on developing technical plans. The result was the company's decision to remove and bury toxic elements and then use the structure as part of a quayside development in Melqarvik in Norway.

By making appropriate organizational changes and updating training and crisis management programs to institutionalize this hard-earned knowledge, Shell also reduced the risk of reliving a similar crisis.

Shell's Lessons Learned

- The views of "experts" are no longer accepted without challenge.
- Technical arrogance must be avoided. That engineering logic has been applied to a problem does not necessarily make an answer correct.
- Sound science and regulatory compliance are not in themselves sufficient to secure public support.
- It is crucial to inform the public about the issues involved in such decisions, correct misconceptions, resolve misunderstandings, and illustrate the difficulties of finding a balance among social, environmental, economic, and safety issues.
- Engineers and other technical experts must be able to communicate the complexities of an analysis, so that "nonexperts" can understand and meaningfully contribute before a decision is made.
- The importance of external perception should never be underestimated. The views of a wider public may be based more on perceptions than on facts.

- Public perception of what is "safe enough" may be quite different from the view of an expert trained in logical risk analysis.

- Avoid DAD (Decide-Announce-Defend) in favor of DDD (Dialogue-Decide-Deliver). Dialogue should start as early as possible in the decision making process.

The days when companies were judged solely in terms of economic performance and wealth creation have long since disappeared. Today, companies have far wider responsibilities to the environment, local communities, and society at large. These are not optional extras. Listening, dialogue, more open communications, greater social accountability—and integrating these processes into the ways that business is done—are all here to stay.

DIAGNOSING CRISIS RESPONSE PREPAREDNESS

The best way to negotiate a crisis is to avoid it, but even the most effective manager will find himself or herself in a crisis situation at some point in his or her career. The case of Shell and the *Brent Spar* illustrates how preparation and effective crisis management can mitigate damage and prevent an escalation that can ruin companies and careers.

The table on pages 231–232 presents a checklist for assessing the adequacy of your organization's crisis response plans.

Assessing Crisis Response Plans

Question	Assessment	Actions
Crisis Planning		
1. Do we have a representative set of planning scenarios?	not at all |———|———|———| absolutely adequate	
2. Do we have a flexible set of response modules?	not at all |———|———|———| absolutely adequate	
3. Do we have an established process for matching response modules to scenarios?	not at all |———|———|———| absolutely adequate	
4. Do we have preset signals for activating the crisis response organization and for reverting to normal operations?	not at all |———|———|———| absolutely adequate	

Assessing Crisis Response Plans (*continued*)

Question	Assessment			Actions
Crisis Organization				
5. Do we have a clear chain of command?	not at all	adequate	absolutely	
6. Do we have a command post and backup?	not at all	adequate	absolutely	
7. Do we have the right communication channels?	not at all	adequate	absolutely	
8. Have we put in place the right backup resources?	not at all	adequate	absolutely	
Organizational Learning				
9. Do we conduct regular rehearsals?	not at all	adequate	absolutely	
10. Do we do disciplined postcrisis reviews?	not at all	adequate	absolutely	

Conclusion: Building Breakthrough Negotiation Capabilities

By now, you are probably convinced that negotiating skills can be learned. Some people do seem to have more natural ability to negotiate than others. But it is a misconception that great negotiators' innate temperaments have endowed them with unique insight and skills. This romantic notion grossly undervalues the importance of systematic analysis and development of strategy, and it gives short shrift to the impact of learning by doing and formal training.

Regardless of inherent ability, everyone can learn to be a better negotiator. To ask, "How can we develop negotiating ability?" is in essence to ask about the nature and development of expertise. How does the expert mind differ from the novice mind? What mental capacities do skilled negotiators employ that are absent in their less accomplished colleagues? How might such capacities be enhanced?

DEVELOPING INDIVIDUAL EXPERTISE

Research suggests that experts manage complexity better than novices and that they do so because of superior abilities at pattern recognition, mental simulation, parallel management, and reflection-in-action.

Pattern recognition is the ability to see patterns, such as potential coalitional alignments, in complex and unstructured situations.

Like expert chess players, skilled negotiators filter out irrelevant clutter; they see configurations that represent threats and opportunities.

Mental simulation is the ability to envision promising courses of action and to project them forward in time imaginatively. This skill equips experienced negotiators to develop provisional action sequences, anticipate reactions and contingencies, and refine or discard plans as necessary.[1]

Parallel management is the ability to track the substance of a negotiation while simultaneously shaping the evolution of the process. In *Education for Judgment,* Roland Christensen calls this "dual competency" a central component of expertise of all kinds.[2]

Reflection-in-action is the ability to "go to the balcony," as negotiation theorist William Ury put it, during tense and difficult proceedings for perspective on what is happening and why, and to adjust strategies accordingly.[3]

Experienced negotiators also adopt a *continuous-improvement mind-set.* They don't merely collect and analyze information. They immerse themselves in information about their circumstances, searching for emerging threats and opportunities; they systematically identify and tap into good sources of information and build networks of relationships to support intelligence gathering. Perhaps most crucially, they reflect on their experiences in an effort to learn from them.

Skilled negotiators cultivate an *integrated awareness* that helps them extract useful knowledge from a combination of verbal and nonverbal information. They also recognize and control their own reactions to what their counterparts say and thus avoid creating unnecessary barriers to learning. They develop strategies for eliciting information at the table, such as through active listening. As one gifted negotiator put it:

You have to have the ability to look at the big picture—to set the strategy in accordance with concrete goals. From that goal to devise not only the strategy but also the tactics: how to achieve these goals. It's the ability to combine the big things with the small things. I think it's a rare quality. You have people who can deal very cleverly with the big things, with the forest, but they are getting lost while dealing with the trees. So you need people that can deal effectively with both.[4]

DEVELOPING EXPERTISE

How can you acquire all these capabilities? The best way is to experience a range of negotiations, real and simulated, and then to take the time to reflect actively on them and to absorb their lessons. Gary Klein, a leading authority on the development of expertise, observes:

> If you want people to size up situations quickly and accurately, you need to expand their experience base. One way is to arrange for a person to receive more difficult cases. . . . Another approach is to develop a training program, perhaps with exercises and realistic scenarios, so the person has a chance to size up numerous situations very quickly. A good simulation can sometimes provide more training value than direct experience. A good simulation lets you stop the action, back up and see what went on, and cram many trials so a person can develop a sense of typicality.[5]

Structured on-the-job training and formal development programs are the ideal combination. Formal programs are important because negotiations come in such a range of types and magnitudes that it can be difficult to generalize well from real-world work experience. Those who learn from experience alone are prone to developing characteristic styles that work well in some situations and not in others, without fully understanding why.

DEVELOPING ORGANIZATIONAL CAPABILITIES

Important business negotiations typically involve teams of people. Capturing learning synergies within a team of individuals with distinct skills (and preventing uncontrolled leakage of information to the other side) translates into increased effectiveness.

Furthermore, companies often have many negotiators who undertake very similar negotiations. Consider, for example, a real estate agency with many agents or a manufacturing company with many purchasing managers and salespeople. If these negotiators learn from their past negotiations, capture the resulting insights, and, crucially, share these insights among themselves, they will intensify the overall negotiating effectiveness of their organizations.

UNDERSTANDING ORGANIZATIONAL LEARNING

All too often, the expensive lessons that negotiators learn are not shared. There may be incentives for the best people *not* to share their knowledge; after all, expertise is a source of status. Some people are too busy to share what they have learned or awkward at teaching less experienced people. Important knowledge about how to negotiate may even be "forgotten" by an organization. When turnover of skilled people is high, for example, the risk of loss of institutional memory is very high.

Training individual negotiators is a necessary prerequisite for organizational learning, but it's not sufficient. You have to focus on management of organizational knowledge, not just individual competence. Knowledge sharing can be facilitated, and memory loss avoided, only through self-conscious management of the acquisition and dissemination of knowledge. Ask yourself about your own organization:

- How do new employees learn to negotiate?
- Are there incentives or disincentives for skilled people to share their knowledge?

- Are insights from past negotiations captured and shared among negotiators?
- How is knowledge preserved and forgetting discouraged?

BUILDING A LEARNING ORGANIZATION

If individual learning is to contribute to organizational learning, specific mechanisms must be set up to encourage collective knowledge sharing and reflection.[6] The key is flexible, time-efficient processes for sharing knowledge, usually emphasizing person-to-person transmission over written documents. Flexibility and time efficiency are important because the pace at which most negotiators operate can crowd out time for reflection and discussion. Busyness is often the enemy of effective organizational learning.

Among the most useful mechanisms for enhancing organizational learning are common languages, apprenticeships, templates, and postmortems.

Common languages are conceptual frameworks that an organization's negotiators all understand and use to communicate among themselves. Adoption of a common negotiating language (such as the lexicon used in this book) can dramatically streamline communication among groups of negotiators, and particularly between more skilled and less skilled people.

Apprenticeships are arrangements, formal or informal, between highly skilled negotiators ("masters") and less experienced people ("apprentices"). For an apprenticeship to work well, the apprentice must work closely with and observe the master over an extended time. Apprentices can perform a useful support role, such as various forms of analysis, to make this arrangement an attractive bargain for the skilled negotiators from whom they learn. This sort of arrangement is common at investment banks and private equity firms, where partners teach (and simultaneously evaluate and leverage) associates. The basic model can be applied in any organization if there are incentives for masters to teach and for apprentices to learn.

Templates are documents that codify the fruits of experience, such as common traps to avoid in a given kind of negotiation. Good venture capital companies, for example, develop standardized approaches to doing due diligence on potential investments. Often templates take the form of checklists with which an organization's negotiators ensure that certain bases are covered. Templates are a way of transforming tacit knowledge into general principles or rules that all of an organization's negotiators can follow. As such, they must be carefully distilled from collective experience and kept simple and actionable. Crucially, they must be kept "alive"; they cannot be compiled in a one-time effort and then followed slavishly in perpetuity. The organization needs to devote ongoing effort to identifying and codifying new lessons learned (and to unlearning old rules that have been superseded).

Postmortems are postnegotiation debriefings of the participants and others involved in similar negotiations. The point is to distill and share the lessons learned in specific kinds of negotiations. It is best to meet soon after a negotiation ends to discuss what happened and to translate what the team members learned into organizational learning. Here are some questions to ask during postmortems:

What to Ask After a Failed Negotiation

- Was not pursuing this opportunity a win or a loss for the company?
- If a loss, what could we have done differently?
- If a win, what did we do well that caused us to opt out of this situation?
- How could we have spotted the flaws earlier and spent less time on this opportunity?

What to Ask After a Successful Negotiation

- What did we do well?
- What problems did we overlook and when?

- How can we improve our ability to uncover such problems earlier?

- How does what we got compare with what we thought we were getting?

Common languages, apprenticeships, templates, and post-mortems are the backbone of a system for effective development of organizational negotiating capabilities. When undertaken by good people dedicated to their own personal improvement, the result is a learning organization.

I hope that this book will help you become a better negotiator. Your agenda from this point forward should be to get diverse negotiating experience under your belt and to reflect on and organize it in your mind. Doing so will foster intuition and heighten your situational awareness. These capacities will equip you to develop workable options under time pressure—the true hallmark of the breakthrough negotiator—and to build superior negotiating organizations.

Notes

INTRODUCTION

1. For an early effort to characterize the structure of negotiations, see H. Raiffa, *The Art and Science of Negotiation* (Cambridge, Mass.: Harvard University Press, 1982), ch. 1. For a more developed framework, see J. Sebenius, "Negotiation Analysis: A Characterization and Review," *Management Science* 38 (1992): 18–38.

2. Jim Sebenius made the important distinction between actions taken at and away from the bargaining table. See J. Sebenius, "Introduction to Negotiation Analysis: Structure, People, and Context," HBS Note 896–034 (Boston: Harvard Business School Publishing, 1996).

PART ONE

1. This model accounts for both the impact of structure on process and the impact of process on structure. An earlier version of this model is presented in M. Watkins, "Shaping the Structure of Negotiations," Program on Negotiation Monograph M98–1, Program on Negotiation at Harvard Law School (1998). Walton, McKersie, and Cutcher-Gershenfeld developed a related framework, analyzing negotiation in terms of forces shaping negotiators' choices and an interaction system consisting of strategies, processes, and

structures. See R. Walton, R. McKersie, and J. Cutcher-Gershenfeld, *Strategic Negotiations: A Theory of Change in Labor-Management Relations* (Boston: Harvard Business School Press, 1994). Sebenius analyzed negotiation in terms of structure, people, and context, as well as barriers and opportunities for creating and claiming value. See J. Sebenius, "Introduction to Negotiation Analysis: Structure, People, and Context," HBS Note 896–034 (Boston: Harvard Business School Publishing, 1996).

CHAPTER ONE

1. This augments a conceptual framework for negotiation analysis developed by Jim Sebenius. Key additions are the inclusion of rules of the game and linkages. See J. Sebenius, "Negotiation Analysis: A Characterization and Review," *Management Science* 38 (1992): 18–38.

2. The focus on barriers to agreement in negotiation was inspired by K. Arrow, R. Mnookin, L. Ross, A. Tversky, and R. Wilson (eds.), *Barriers to Conflict Resolution* (New York: Norton, 1995), an important cross-disciplinary examination of reasons that conflicts persist. Sebenius has analyzed negotiation in terms of structure, people, and context, as well as barriers and opportunities for creating and claiming value. See J. Sebenius, "Introduction to Negotiation Analysis: Structure, People, and Context," HBS Note 896–034 (Boston: Harvard Business School Publishing, 1996).

3. See D. Lax and J. Sebenius, "Thinking Coalitionally," in P. Young (ed.), *Negotiation Analysis* (Ann Arbor: University of Michigan Press, 1991).

4. Ibid.

5. This term is attributable to Lax and Sebenius, *The Manager as Negotiator* (New York: Free Press, 1986). In their more detailed discussion of unbundling in Chapter 5, they write, "Where different interests are bundled into a negotiation, a good strategy can be to unbundle and seek creative ways to dovetail them" (p. 94).

6. See J. Z. Rubin, D. G. Pruitt, and S. H. Kim, *Social Conflict: Escalation, Stalemate, and Settlement* (New York: McGraw-Hill, 1994).

7. Roger Fisher and William Ury made the crucial distinction between positions and interests. See R. Fisher, W. Ury, and B. Patton, *Getting to Yes: Negotiating Agreement Without Giving In*, 2nd ed. (New York: Penguin, 1991).

8. For a detailed discussion of differences as a potential source of joint gains, see J. Sebenius, *Negotiating the Law of the Sea* (Cambridge, Mass.: Harvard University Press, 1984), ch. 5, and Lax and Sebenius, *The Manager as Negotiator*, ch. 5.

9. F. C Iklé, *How Nations Negotiate* (Millwood, N.Y.: Kraus, 1964), p. 2.

10. For a deeper treatment of approaches to evaluating trade-offs and making better decisions, see J. Hammond, H. Raiffa, and R. Keeney, *Smart Choices* (Boston: Harvard Business School Press, 1999).

11. In *Getting to Yes*, Fisher, Ury, and Patton note that negotiators have interests in substance and relationships: "Every negotiator wants an agreement that satisfies his substantive interests. That is why one negotiates. Beyond that, a negotiator also has an interest in his relationship with the other side" (p. 19).

12. People tend to have a strong psychological need for consistency. For an interesting discussion, see R. B. Cialdini, *Influence: The Psychology of Persuasion* (New York: Morrow, 1984), ch. 3. See also P. Zimbardo and M. Leippe, *The Psychology of Attitude Change and Social Influence* (New York: McGraw-Hill, 1991).

13. For a discussion of side effects that can flow from negotiations, see Iklé, *How Nations Negotiate*, ch. 4.

14. W. Ury, *Getting Past No: Negotiating Your Way from Confrontations to Cooperation* (New York: Bantam Books, 1991).

15. Fisher, Ury, and Patton, *Getting to Yes*.

16. For a discussion of the relationships among BATNAs, bargaining ranges, and reservation prices, see Raiffa, *Art and Science of Negotiation*, ch. 4.

17. These ideas are developed in M. Watkins, "Building Momentum in Negotiations: Time-Related Costs and Action-Forcing Events," *Negotiation Journal* 14 (1998): 241–256.

18. For an in-depth discussion of this and other biases in decision making and their impact on negotiations, see M. Bazerman and M. Neale, *Negotiating Rationally* (New York: Free Press, 1992).

19. Walton and McKersie, *A Behavioral Theory of Labor Negotiations* (Ithaca, N.Y.: ILR Press, 1965), used the term *bargaining range*. Raiffa used *zone of agreement*. Lax and Sebenius call it the *zone of possible agreement*.

20. Walton and McKersie, *A Behavioral Theory of Labor Negotiations*, made the important distinction between distributive and integrative bargaining in Chapters 2, 3, 4, and 5. They also noted that negotiators may engage in a mix of distributive and integrative bargaining, which they termed *mixed-motive*. See Chapter 5. Lax and Sebenius, *The Manager as Negotiator*, reconceptualized the distinction between distributive and integrative bargaining. Rather than discrete types of bargaining, they view value claiming and value creating as processes that go on in parallel in most negotiations: "Negotiators should focus on the dynamic aspects of negotiation, the process of creating and claiming value" (p. 254). "Value creating and value claiming are linked parts of negotiation. Both processes are present. No matter how much creative problem-solving enlarges the pie, it still must be divided; value that has been created must be claimed" (p. 33).

21. See Lax and Sebenius, *The Manager as Negotiator*, ch. 5.

22. For a discussion of commitment tactics, see T. C. Schelling, *The Strategy of Conflict* (Cambridge, Mass.: Harvard University Press, 1960), ch. 2.

23. Raiffa, *Art and Science of Negotiation*, ch. 10, develops the idea of the efficient frontier in the context of two-party, many-issue negotiation. "The efficient frontier—sometimes called the Pareto Frontier after economist Vilfredo Pareto—is defined as the locus of achievable joint evaluations from which no joint gains are possible" (p. 139).

24. These ideas are developed in M. Watkins and S. Passow, "Analyzing Linked Systems of Negotiations," *Negotiation Journal* 12 (1996): 325–340.

25. See J. Sebenius, "Introduction to Negotiation Analysis: Structure, People, and Context," HBS Note 896–034 (Boston: Harvard Business School Publishing, 1996).

CHAPTER TWO

1. See D. Lax and J. Sebenius, "Thinking Coalitionally," in P. Young (ed.), *Negotiation Analysis* (Ann Arbor: University of Michigan Press, 1991).

2. O. Harries, "A Primer for Polemicists," *Commentary* 78 (September 1984): 58.

3. For a discussion of framing, see I. Goffman, *Frame Analysis: An Essay on the Organization of Experience* (Cambridge, Mass.: Harvard University Press, 1974); M. Bazerman, *Judgment in Managerial Decision Making,* 4th ed. (New York: Wiley, 1998); and G. T. Fairhurst and R. A. Sarr, *The Art of Framing: Managing the Language of Leadership* (San Francisco: Jossey-Bass, 1996).

4. C. Devereaux, "International Trade Meets Intellectual Property," unpublished case study, Harvard Business School, 2001.

5. See P. N. Johnson-Laid, *Mental Models* (Cambridge, Mass.: Harvard University Press, 1983).

6. One of William Ury's core principles of negotiation is, "Don't reject, reframe." See W. Ury, *Getting Past No: Negotiating Your Way from Confrontation to Cooperation* (New York: Bantam Books, 1991), p. 59.

7. In "Thinking Coalitionally," Lax and Sebenius developed the idea of process opportunism, a core part of which is control of information.

8. G. S. Jowett and V. O'Donnell, *Propaganda and Persuasion* (Thousand Oaks, Calif.: Sage, 1992), p. 32.

9. For a fascinating discussion of the relationship between issue sequencing and coalition formation, see W. H. Riker, *The Art of Political Manipulation* (New Haven, Conn.: Yale University Press, 1986).

10. See M. Watkins, "Building Momentum in Negotiations: Time-Related Costs and Action-Forcing Events," *Negotiation Journal* 14 (1998): 241–256.

11. Lax and Sebenius in "Thinking Coalitionally" developed sequencing in the context of coalition building. See also J. Sebenius, "Sequencing to Build Coalitions: With Whom Should I Talk First?" in R. Zeckhauser, R. Keeney, and J. Sebenius (eds.), *Wise Choices: Decisions, Games, and Negotiations* (Boston: Harvard Business School Press, 1996).

CHAPTER THREE

1. Zartman and Berman termed these stages the diagnostic phase, the formula phase, and the detail phase. See I. W. Zartman and M. Berman, *The Practical Negotiator* (New Haven, Conn.: Yale University Press, 1982).

2. For an accessible introduction to nonlinear systems theory, see J. Gleick, *Chaos: The Making of a New Science* (New York: Viking Press, 1987).

3. Cialdini termed this the *commitment effect*. See R. B. Cialdini, *Influence: The Psychology of Persuasion* (New York: Morrow, 1984), ch. 3.

4. For a fascinating discussion of tipping points, see M. Gladwell, *The Tipping Point: How Little Things Can Make a Big Difference* (New York: Little, Brown, 2000).

5. See P. N. Johnson-Laid, *Mental Models* (Cambridge, Mass.: Harvard University Press, 1983).

6. I. Goffman, *Frame Analysis: An Essay on the Organization of Experience* (Cambridge, Mass.: Harvard University Press, 1974).

7. See Robert J. Robinson, "Errors in Social Judgment: Implications for Negotiation and Conflict Resolution, Parts 1 and 2," Harvard Business School Notes 897103 and 897–104 (Boston: Harvard Business School Press, 1997), and M. Bazerman and M. Neale, *Negotiating Rationally* (New York: Free Press, 1992).

8. People tend to have a strong psychological need for consistency.

For an interesting discussion, see Cialdini, *Influence*, ch. 3. See also P. Zimbardo and M. Leippe, *The Psychology of Attitude Change and Social Influence* (New York: McGraw-Hill, 1991).

9. See Bazerman and Neale, *Negotiating Rationally*, for an in-depth discussion of anchoring and adjustment.

10. H. Raiffa, *The Art and Science of Negotiation* (Cambridge, Mass.: Harvard University Press, 1982), ch. 4.

11. J. Z. Rubin, D. G. Pruitt, and S. H. Kim, *Social Conflict: Escalation, Stalemate, and Settlement* (New York: McGraw-Hill, 1994).

12. For a seminal discussion of threats and warnings, see T. C. Schelling, *The Strategy of Conflict* (Cambridge, Mass.: Harvard University Press, 1960), ch. 2.

13. See M. Watkins, "Building Momentum in Negotiations: Time-Related Costs and Action-Forcing Events," *Negotiation Journal* 14 (1998): 241–256.

14. Lax and Sebenius define power as the ability to shape perceptions of bargaining range. See D. A. Lax and J. K. Sebenius, *The Manager as Negotiator* (New York: Free Press, 1986), ch. 9.

15. This concept is explicated in ibid., ch. 2.

CHAPTER FOUR

1. See W. Ury, *Getting Past No: Negotiating Your Way from Confrontation to Cooperation* (New York: Bantam Books, 1991), p. 11.

2. See H. Raiffa, *The Art and Science of Negotiation* (Cambridge, Mass.: Harvard University Press, 1982), ch. 4.

3. S. Rosegrant, "Getting to Dayton: Negotiating an End to the War in Bosnia," Case C125–96–1356.0 (Cambridge, Mass.: John F. Kennedy School of Government, Harvard University, 1996), p. 26.

4. D. D. Eisenhower, *Crusade in Europe* (New York: Doubleday, 1948), p. 256.

5. These ideas are drawn from S. Rosen and M. Watkins, "Rethinking 'Preparation' in Negotiation," Harvard Business School Work-

ing Paper 99–042 (Cambridge, Mass.: Harvard Business School, 1999).

6. Much work has been done, for example, on quantifying interests and assigning values to issues and resolutions, to arm negotiators with a clear understanding of their preferences and an ability to "score" the other party's proposals. See R. Keeney and H. Raiffa, "Structuring and Analyzing Values for Multiple Issue Negotiations," in P. Young (ed.), *Negotiation Analysis* (Ann Arbor: University of Michigan Press, 1991). While valuable, such preparation carries with it the risk of solidifying misperceptions about the other side.

7. Confidence that one already understands the other party's interests may also promote selective perception when the parties do begin to talk. Combined with selective perception, stereotypes and mistaken assumptions can become self-fulfilling prophecies and sabotage opportunities for agreement. See J. Z. Rubin, D. G. Pruitt, and S. H. Kim, *Social Conflict: Escalation, Stalemate and Settlement*, 2nd ed. (New York: McGraw-Hill, 1994).

CHAPTER FIVE

1. J. Kaplan, *Startup: A Silicon Valley Adventure* (Boston: Houghton Mifflin, 1995).

2. S. Matthews and M. Watkins, "Strategic Deal-making at Millennium Pharmaceuticals," HBS Case 800–032 (Boston: Harvard Business School Publishing, 2000).

3. Ibid., p. 10.

4. See D. Lax and J. Sebenius, "Thinking Coalitionally," in P. Young (ed.), *Negotiation Analysis* (Ann Arbor: University of Michigan Press, 1991); and J. Sebenius, "Sequencing to Build Coalitions: With Whom Should I Talk First?" in R. Zeckhauser, R. Keeney, and J. Sebenius (eds.), *Wise Choices: Decisions, Games, and Negotiations* (Boston: Harvard Business School Press, 1996).

5. Matthews and Watkins, "Strategic Deal-Making," p. 12.

6. For a seminal discussion of the strategic use of commitments, see T. C. Schelling, *The Strategy of Conflict* (Cambridge, Mass.: Harvard University Press, 1960), ch. 2.

7. The term *informational high ground* was coined by Robert Aiello, a managing director at Updata Capital, a New Jersey–based mergers and acquisitions firm.

8. Matthews and Watkins, "Strategic Deal-Making," p. 12.

9. Ibid.

10. Ibid.

11. Ibid.

12. Ibid.

13. Ibid., p. 13.

14. Ibid.

CHAPTER SIX

1. Alderfer distinguished between organizational groups and identity groups within organizations. In his terms, groups are defined by (1) boundaries, both physical and psychological, that determine who is and is not a group member; (2) power differences, or differences in the types of resources groups can obtain and use; (3) affective patterns, or polarization of feeling among and between members of groups; and (4) cognitive formations, including distinct in-group languages. Identity groups are groups that individuals join at birth. People belong to organizational groups as a result of distinct choices on the part of the person and the organization. Examples of the former include ethnic and family groups. Examples of the latter include task groups and functions. C. P. Alderfer, "An Intergroup Perspective on Group Dynamics," in J. W. Lorsch (ed.), *Handbook of Organizational Behavior* (Upper Saddle River, N.J.: Prentice Hall, 1987).

2. See D. Krackhardt and J. R. Hanson, "Informal Networks: The Company Behind the Chart," *Harvard Business Review*

(July-August 1993): 104–112. See also R. B. Cialdini, *Influence: The Psychology of Persuasion* (New York: Morrow, 1993), ch. 6, an excellent introduction to the psychology of interpersonal persuasion, exploring such processes as consistency and commitment.

3. In their studies of the 1940 presidential election, Lazarfeld and his associates made the early observation that people were influenced by both information and the people who passed along the information or to whom they went for clues about "right thinking." The result was a "multi-step flow" model of opinion formation. See P. Lazerfeld, L. Bereson, and H. Gaudet, *The People's Choice: How the Voter Makes Up His Mind in a Presidential Campaign* (New York: Duell, Sloan & Pearce, 1948). See also M. A. Milburn, *Persuasion and Politics: The Social Psychology of Public Opinion* (Pacific Grove, Calif.: Brooks/Cole, 1991), ch. 8.

4. O. Harries, "A Primer for Polemicists," *Commentary* 78 (1984): 57–60.

5. Kurt Lewin, a pioneer in the field of group dynamics, proposed a model of social change based on the idea of driving and restraining forces. One of Lewin's fundamental insights is that human collectives—including groups, organizations, and nations—are social systems that exist in a state of tension between forces pressing for change and forces resisting change: "[The behavior of a social system is] . . . the result of a multitude of forces. Some forces support each other, some oppose each other. Some are driving forces, others restraining forces. Like the velocity of a river, the actual conduct of a group depends upon the level . . . at which these conflicting forces reach an equilibrium." K. Lewin, *Field Theory in Social Science* (New York: HarperCollins, 1951), p. 173.

6. See M. H. Bazerman, A. E. Tenebrunsel, and K. Wade-Benzoni, "Negotiating with Yourself and Losing: Making Decisions with Competing Internal Preferences," *Academy of Management Review* 23 (1998): 225–241.

7. M. Mitchell, *Propaganda, Polls, and Public Opinion* (Upper Saddle River, N.J.: Prentice Hall, 1970), p. 111.

8. See D. Kahneman and A. Tversky, "Conflict Resolution: A Cognitive Perspective," in K. Arrow, R. Mnookin, M. L. Ross, A.

Tversky, and R. Wilson (eds.), *Barriers to Conflict Resolution* (New York: Norton, 1995). For a good summary of "nonrational" biases in decision making, see "Cognitive Limitations and Consumer Behavior," in R. H. Frank, *Microeconomics and Human Behavior* (New York: McGraw-Hill, 1994), ch. 8.

9. See "The Economics of Information and Choice Under Uncertainty," in R. H. Frank, *Microeconomics and Human Behavior* (New York: McGraw-Hill, 1994), ch. 6.

10. For a discussion of anchoring, see M. Bazerman and M. Neale, *Negotiating Rationally* (New York: Free Press, 1992), ch. 4.

11. See H. Raiffa, *The Art and Science of Negotiation* (Cambridge, Mass.: Harvard University Press, 1982), ch. 11.

12. For a classic statement of the mechanisms of social influence, see J. R. French and B. Raven, "The Bases of Social Power," in D. Cartwright and A. Zander (eds.), *Group Dynamics: Research and Theory* (New York: HarperCollins, 1960).

13. See P. G. Zimbardo and M. R. Leippe, *The Psychology of Attitude Change and Social Influence* (Boston: McGraw-Hill, 1991), ch. 2.

14. See Cialdini, *Influence*, ch. 3.

15. See ibid., ch. 2.

16 See Zimbardo and Leippe, *Psychology of Attitude Change*, ch. 3.

17. In "Thinking Coalitionally," Lax and Sebenius use the term *patterns of deference*.

18. Lax and Sebenius discuss sequencing in the context of coalition building. See also J. Sebenius, "Sequencing to Build Coalitions: With Whom Should I Talk First?" in R. Zeckhauser, R. Keeney, and J. Sebenius (eds.), *Wise Choices: Decisions, Games, and Negotiations* (Boston: Harvard Business School Press, 1996), p. 58.

19. Harries, "Primer for Polemicists," p. 58.

20. W. C. Kim and R. Mauborgne, "Fair Process: Managing in the Knowledge Economy," *Harvard Business Review* (July-August 1997): 65–76.

21. See C. Rogers and F. J. Roethlisberger, "Barriers and Gateways to

Communication," *Harvard Business Review* (July–August 1952): 105–112.

22. G. S. Jowett and V. O'Donnell, *Propaganda and Persuasion* (Thousand Oaks, Calif.: Sage, 1992), p. 32.

23. For an accessible summary of research on communication, see Zimbardo and Leippe, *Psychology of Attitude Change*, ch. 4.

24. Ibid.

25. In the literature on propaganda, this is known as source credibility. Jowett and O'Donnell note that "source credibility is one of the contributing factors that seems to influence change. People have a tendency to look up to authority figures for knowledge and direction. Expert opinion is effective in establishing the legitimacy of change and is tied to information control. Once a source is accepted on one issue, another issue may be established as well on the basis of prior acceptance of the source." Jowett and O'Donnell, *Propaganda and Persuasion*, p. 222.

26. Rhetoric, Book One, Chapter 2 from *The Complete Works of Aristotle*, vol. 2, ed. J. Barnes (Princeton, N.J.: Princeton University Press, 1984).

CHAPTER SEVEN

1. See J. Z. Rubin, D. G. Pruitt, and S. H. Kim, *Social Conflict: Escalation, Stalemate and Settlement*, 2nd ed. (New York: McGraw-Hill, 1994).

2. For a discussion of the importance of ripeness in conflict resolution, see S. Touval and I. W. Zartman, *International Mediation in Theory and Practice* (Boulder, Colo.: Westview Press, 1985).

3. This section and the next draw on ideas developed in Rubin, Pruitt, and Kim, *Social Conflict*, ch. 5–7.

4. Ibid., p. 77.

5. According to Rubin, Pruitt, and Kim, *Social Conflict*, p. 69, conflicts undergo transformations as they escalate. Although separate transformations occur on each side, they affect the conflict as a

whole because they are usually mirrored by the other side. As a result, the conflict is intensified in ways that are sometimes exceedingly difficult to undo.

6. A hurting stalemate can be defined as a situation in which the parties feel uncomfortable and events may be on the threshold either of worsening, perhaps through escalation of the conflict, or of getting better through resolution of the conflict. See P. T. Hopmann, *The Negotiation Process and the Resolution of International Conflicts* (Columbia: University of South Carolina Press, 1996), p. 222.

7. For a detailed discussion of these and other cognitive biases, see M. Bazerman and M. Neale, *Negotiating Rationally* (New York: Free Press, 1992).

8. Ibid., ch. 8.

9. See "Conflict Resolution: A Cognitive Perspective," in K. Arrow, R. Mnookin, M. L. Ross, A. Tversky, and R. Wilson (eds.), *Barriers to Conflict Resolution* (New York: Norton, 1995), ch. 3. For a good summary of "nonrational" biases in decision making, see R. H. Frank, *Microeconomics and Human Behavior* (New York: McGraw-Hill, 1994), ch. 8.

10. The principal-agent problem is discussed in Arrow and others (eds.), *Barriers to Conflict Resolution*, ch. 1. See also J. Pratt and R. Zeckhauser (eds.), *Principals and Agents: The Structure of Business* (Boston: Harvard Business School Press, 1985).

11. This conceptual framework was originally presented in M. Watkins and K. Lundberg, "Getting to the Table in Oslo: Driving Forces and Channel Factors," *Negotiation Journal* 14, 2 (April 1998): 115–136.

12. This framework was inspired by a model of social change developed by Kurt Lewin, a pioneer in the field of group dynamics, and by work on nonlinear systems dynamics. See K. Lewin, *Field Theory in Social Science* (New York: HarperCollins, 1951). One of Lewin's fundamental insights is that human collectives—including groups, organizations, and nations—are systems that always exist in a state of tension between forces pushing for change and

forces resisting change. See also L. Ross and R. E. Nisbett, *The Person and the Situation: Perspectives on Social Psychology* (New York: McGraw-Hill, 1991), pp. 13–14.

13. See M. Gladwell, *The Tipping Point: How Little Things Can Make a Big Difference* (New York: Little, Brown, 2000).

14. See Robert J. Robinson, "Errors in Social Judgment: Implications for Negotiation and Conflict Resolution, Part 2," Harvard Business School Note 897–104 (Boston: Harvard Business School Publishing, 1997).

15. Robert Robinson and his colleagues coined the phrase *naive realism* to designate an individual's unawareness of his own subjectivity in making predictions about himself and others. See R. J. Robinson, D. Keltner, A. Ward, and L. Ross, "Actual Versus Assumed Differences in Construal: 'Naive Realism' in Inter-group Perception and Conflict," *Journal of Personality and Social Psychology* 68 (1995): 404–417.

16. Robinson notes that partisans "exaggerate their own group's extremism, suggesting that they view themselves as 'lone moderates' within their conflict. The lone moderate pattern suggests that people tend to dissociate themselves from partisan groups, perceive ideological extremism with some disdain, and assume that they alone are models of rational, principled judgment." See Robinson, *Errors in Social Judgment*, p. 5.

17. Ross and Ward define *reactive devaluation* in the context of conflict resolution as "the fact that the very act of offering a particular proposal or concession may diminish its apparent value or attractiveness in the eyes of the recipient." See L. Ross and A. Ward, "Psychological Barriers to Dispute Resolution," *Advances in Experimental Social Psychology* 27 (1995): 270.

18. In *Groupthink: Psychological Studies of Policy Decisions and Fiascoes* (Boston: Houghton Mifflin, 1982), Irving Janus defines groupthink as "a quick and easy way to refer to a mode of thinking that people engage in when they are deeply involved in a cohesive ingroup, when the members' strivings for unanimity override their motivation to realistically appraise alternative courses of action.

Groupthink refers to a deterioration of mental efficiency, reality testing, and moral judgment that results from in-group pressures" (p. 9).

19. For example, it cost the U.S.-led coalition $61 billion to win the Gulf War. See S. Rosegrant, "The Gulf Crisis: Building a Coalition for War," case 1264.0 (Cambridge, Mass.: John F. Kennedy School of Government, 1995).

20. For a discussion, see J. R. Idaszak and P. Carnevale, "Third Party Power: Some Negative Effects of Positive Incentives," *Journal of Applied Social Psychology* 19 (May 1989): 449–466.

21. As Leonard Riskin notes, the choice of which way to go is not straightforward, because it involves unavoidable trade-offs. A narrow problem definition can increase the chances of resolution and reduce the time needed for the mediation. In addition, a narrow focus can avoid a danger inherent in broader approaches—that personal relations or other "extraneous issues" might exacerbate the conflict and make it more difficult to settle. On the other hand, the narrow approach can increase the chance of impasse because it allows little room for creative option generation or other means of addressing underlying interests which, if unsatisfied, could block agreement. Also, a narrow approach to mediation might preclude the parties from addressing other long-term mutual interests that could lead to long-lasting, mutually beneficial arrangements. See L. L. Riskin, "Understanding Mediators' Orientations, Strategies, and Techniques: A Grid for the Perplexed," *Harvard Negotiation Law Review* 1 (1996): 43.

22. Once again, as Riskin notes, this is a difficult decision: "The evaluative mediator, by providing assessments, predictions, or direction, removes some of the decision-making burden from the parties. . . . In some cases, this makes it easier for the parties to reach an agreement. Evaluations by the mediator can give a participant a better understanding of his 'Best Alternative to a Negotiated Agreement' (BATNA), a feeling of vindication or an enhanced ability to deal with his constituency. . . . Yet in some situations, an assessment, prediction or recommendation can make

it more difficult for the parties to reach agreement by impairing a party's faith in the mediator's neutrality or restricting a party's flexibility. . . . Moreover these evaluative techniques decrease the extent of the parties' participation, and thereby may lower the participants' satisfaction with both the process and the outcome." Riskin, "Understanding Mediators' Orientations," pp. 44–45.

23. See D. Lax and J. Sebenius, *The Manager as Negotiator* (New York: Free Press, 1986).

24. F. C. Iklé, *How Nations Negotiate* (Millwood, N.Y.: Kraus, 1964), pp. 134–135.

CHAPTER EIGHT

1. For a wide-ranging exploration of issues in representation, see R. H. Mnookin and L. E. Susskind (eds.), *Negotiating on Behalf of Others* (Thousand Oaks, Calif.: Sage, 1999).

2. For a discussion of the challenges of managing external and internal negotiations, see R. Putnam, "Diplomacy and Domestic Politics: The Logic of Two Level Games," *International Organizations* 42 (1988): 427–460. See also R. Walton and R. McKersie, *A Behavioral Theory of Labor Negotiations* (Ithaca, N.Y.: ILR Press, 1965).

3. This section draws on work done jointly with Joel Cutcher-Gershenfeld. See J. Cutcher-Gershenfeld and M. Watkins, "Toward a Theory of Representation in Negotiation," in Mnookin and Susskind (eds.), *Negotiating on Behalf of Others*.

4. See J. Rubin and F. Sander, "When Should We Use Agents? Direct Versus Representative Negotiations," *Negotiation Journal* 7 (1988): 395–401.

5. For a detailed exploration of agency problems, see J. W. Pratt and R. J. Zeckhauser (eds.), *Principals and Agents: The Structure of Business* (Cambridge, Mass.: Harvard Business School Press, 1985). See also D. A. Lax and J. K. Sebenius, *The Manager as Negotiator: Bargaining for Cooperation and Competitive Gain* (New York: Free Press, 1986), ch. 15.

6. For a thorough survey of the existing research on teams in negotiation, see L. Thompson, *The Mind and Heart of the Negotiator* (New York: Prentice-Hall, 1998), ch. 9.

7. This section draws on work done jointly with Robert Aiello. See R. Aiello and M. Watkins, "The Fine Art of Friendly Acquisition," *Harvard Business Review* (November-December 2000): 100–107.

8. Ibid.

CHAPTER NINE

1 "Sunk Costs: The Plan to Dump the Brent Spar (A)," HBS Case 9–800–028 (Boston: Harvard Business School Publishing, 1999).

2. Ibid., p. 6.

3. Ibid.

4. Ibid., p. 10.

5. Work on the ideas presented in this chapter was done jointly with Bruce Stephenson.

6. For a thorough introduction to scenario planning, see K. Van Der Heijden, *Scenarios: The Art of Strategic Conversation* (New York: Wiley, 1996).

7. Ibid., p. 8.

8. D. Mitropoulos, "The Reporter's Dilemma: News Gathering as Negotiation," *Negotiation Journal* 1 (July 1999): 229–243.

9. See I. I. Mitroff, *Managing Crises Before They Happen* (New York: AMACOM, 2001), ch. 3.

CONCLUSION

1. The role of pattern recognition and mental simulation in making expert judgment possible is developed in detail in G. Klein, *Sources of Power: How People Make Decisions* (Cambridge, Mass.: MIT Press, 1998).

2. See R. C. Christensen, "Premises and Practices of Discussion Teaching," in C. R. Christensen, D. Garvin, and A. Sweet (eds.), *Education for Judgment: The Artistry of Discussion Leadership* (Cambridge, Mass.: Harvard Business School Press, 1991).

3. The idea of reflection-in-action as a hallmark of expertise is developed in detail in D. Schön, *The Reflective Practitioner: How Professionals Think in Action* (New York: Basic Books, 1983).

4. Interview with Avi Gil, director general of the Israeli Ministry of Foreign Affairs, Apr. 14, 1998.

5. Klein, *Sources of Power,* p. 42.

6. For an in-depth and illuminating discussion of learning organizations, see D. A. Garvin, *Learning in Action* (Boston: Harvard Business School Press), 2000.

Suggested Reading

ON NEGOTIATION

Bazerman, M., and Neale, M. *Negotiating Rationally*. New York: Free Press, 1992.

Cialdini, R. B. *Influence: The Psychology of Persuasion*. New York: Morrow, 1984.

Fisher, R., Ury, W., and Patton, B. *Getting to Yes: Negotiating Agreement Without Giving In*. (2nd ed.) New York: Penguin, 1991.

Hammond J., Raiffa, H., and Keeney, R. *Smart Choices*. Boston: Harvard Business School Press, 1999.

Kolb, D. M., and Williams, J. *The Shadow Negotiation: How Women Can Master the Hidden Agendas That Determine Bargaining Success*. New York: Simon & Schuster, 2000.

Lax, D. A., and Sebenius, J. K. *The Manager as Negotiator*. New York: Free Press, 1986.

Lewicki, R. J., Saunders, D. M., and Minton, J. W. *Essentials of Negotiation*. Boston: Irwin-McGraw-Hill, 1997.

Mnookin, R. H., Peppet, S. R., and Tulumello, A. S. *Beyond Winning: Negotiating to Create Value in Deals and Disputes*. Cambridge, Mass.: Harvard University Press, 2000.

Raiffa, H. *The Art and Science of Negotiation*. Cambridge, Mass.: Harvard University Press, 1982.

Salacuse, J. W. *Making Global Deals: Negotiating in the International Marketplace*. Boston: Houghton Mifflin, 1991.

Schein, E. H. *Organizational Culture and Leadership*. (2nd ed.) San Francisco: Jossey-Bass, 1992.

Shell, G. R. *Bargaining for Advantage: Negotiation Strategies for Reasonable People*. New York: Viking Press, 1999.

Thompson, L. *The Mind and Heart of the Negotiator*. Upper Saddle River, N.J.: Prentice-Hall. 1998.

Ury, W. *Getting Past No: Negotiating Your Way from Confrontation to Cooperation*. New York: Bantam Books, 1991.

Walton, R., and McKersie, R. 1965. *A Behavioral Theory of Labor Negotiations*. Ithaca, N.Y.: ILR Press, 1965.

Walton, R., McKersie, R., and Cutcher-Gershenfeld, J. *Strategic Negotiations: A Theory of Change in Labor-Management Relations*. Boston: Harvard Business School Press, 1994.

Zartman, I. W., and Berman, M. *The Practical Negotiator*. New Haven, Conn.: Yale University Press, 1982.

Zimbardo, P., and Lieppe, M. *The Psychology of Attitude Change and Social Influence*. New York: McGraw-Hill, 1991.

ON DISPUTE RESOLUTION

Arrow, K., Mnookin, R., Ross, L., Tversky, A., and Wilson, R. *Barriers to Conflict Resolution*. New York: Norton, 1995.

Fisher, R., Kopelman, E., and Schneider, A. K. *Beyond Machiavelli: Tools for Coping with Conflict*. Cambridge, Mass.: Harvard University Press, 1994.

Moore, C. W. *The Mediation Process*. (2nd ed.) San Francisco: Jossey-Bass, 1996.

Robinson, R. J. "Errors in Social Judgment: Implications for Negotiation and Conflict Resolution. Part 1: Biased Assimilation of Information." Case 897–103. Boston: Harvard Business School Publishing, 1997.

Robinson, R. J. "Errors in Social Judgment: Implications for Negotiation and Conflict Resolution. Part 2: Partisan Perceptions." Case 897–104. Boston: Harvard Business School Publishing, 1997.

Rubin, J. Z., Pruitt, D. G., and Kim, S. H. *Social Conflict: Escalation, Stalemate and Settlement*. (2nd ed.) New York: McGraw-Hill, 1994.

Ury, W., *The Third Side: Why We Fight and How We Can Stop*. New York: Penguin, 2000.

ON CRISIS MANAGEMENT

Augustine, N. R. "Managing the Crisis You Tried to Prevent." *Harvard Business Review on Crisis Management*. Boston: Harvard Business School Press, 2000.

Fink, S. *Crisis Management: Planning for the Inevitable*. New York: American Management Association, 1986.

Kanter, R. M. *Note on Management of Crisis*. Boston: Harvard Business School Publishing, 1988.

Mitroff, I. I. *Managing Crises Before They Happen*. New York: AMACOM, 2001.

Mitropoulos, D. "The Reporter's Dilemma: News Gathering as Negotiation, " *Negotiation Journal* 1 (July 1999): 229–243.

Van Der Heijden, K. *Scenarios: The Art of Strategic Conversation*. New York: Wiley, 1996.

ON DEVELOPING EXPERTISE

Christensen, C. R., Garvin, D., and Sweet, A. (eds.). *Education for Judgment: The Artistry of Discussion Leadership*. Boston: Harvard Business School Press, 1991.

Garvin, D. A. *Learning in Action*. Boston: Harvard Business School Press, 2000.

Goffman, I. *Frame Analysis: An Essay on the Organization of Experience*. Cambridge, Mass.: Harvard University Press, 1974.

Klein, G. *Sources of Power: How People Make Decisions*. Cambridge, Mass.: MIT Press, 1998.

Schön, D. *The Reflective Practitioner: How Professionals Think in Action*. New York: Basic Books, 1983.

Conceptual Glossary

Action-forcing events Clear breakpoints at which some or all of the participants must make hard choices or incur substantial costs. These breakpoints may result from outside forces or the actions of the negotiators.

Anchoring Choosing an opening position that indicates a narrow zone of possible agreement to the other side. Studies have shown that the other side will adjust its perception of what is possible to coincide with this initial position.

Arbitrator An objective third party, agreed to by the disputants, with the power to impose terms of agreement in a dispute. An arbitrator has no personal stake in the outcome and no bias toward either party.

Bandwagon effect The sense of momentum that builds as more people commit to go in a particular direction and "get on the bandwagon." As more support accumulates, the BATNAs of remaining holdouts get altered; they can't stop something from happening and may prefer to be part of the winning side and not end up isolated.

Bargaining range A hypothetical range of potential agreements in a given negotiation that would make all of the negotiators better off than their respective BATNAs. An agreement thus represents a solution to the joint problem of finding terms that all prefer to their best alternatives.

BATNA (best alternative to a negotiated agreement) The best option available if an agreement is not negotiated. The better the alternative is, the higher the threshold of value that must be met in order to enter into an agreement.

Blocking coalition An alliance of parties who may agree on nothing but their opposition to a specific outcome. Such parties band together to prevent the unwanted outcome and preserve the status quo.

Bootstrapping Negotiating conditional commitments with two or more parties in order to gain agreement to move a project, deal, or initiative forward. *See* Conditional commitments.

Commitment tactics Steps taken for the purpose of persuading the other side to commit, including ultimatums and deadlines, threats, staged agreements, and contingent agreements.

Conditional commitments Commitments to enter into agreements conditional on some set of future events occurring, for example the willingness of other parties also to agree. *See* Bootstrapping.

Claiming value The goal of the adversarial win-lose approach to negotiation characterized by a fixed pie that the winner will capture most of.

Competitive linkage The relationship between two simultaneous negotiations in which agreement in one precludes agreements in the other.

Creating value The basis of a creative approach to negotiation in which the parties jointly try to enlarge the pie through inventive trade-offs.

Distributive negotiation A negotiation in which the parties' interests are completely in conflict: there is a fixed pie of potential value to be divided, and anything one side gains, the other loses.

Driving forces Escalatory actions that push a conflict toward all-out violence or conciliatory actions that push a conflict toward a state of peaceful coexistence.

Efficient frontier The range of hypothetical agreements that maximizes the joint value the parties can create by making trades. Agreements are efficient only if neither side can be made better off without making the other worse off.

End-game effects The tendency for negotiators to give primacy to value claiming if they anticipate that there will not be future interactions and if the amount of value to be claimed is significant.

Escalation An often-abrupt increase in the intensity of conflict between contending parties.

Exploding offer An offer that expires at a specific time. Exploding offers are a form of action-forcing event, designed to compel the recipients to accept before they have time to develop alternatives. *See* Action-forcing events.

Framing The use of argument, analogy, and metaphor to promote a favorable definition of "the problem" to be solved and "the options" open to consideration. Negotiators often joust to establish the dominant frame in order to create and claim value.

Frame game Competition among negotiators to establish the dominant framing of the problem and the options.

Informational asymmetries Imbalances in contending negotiators' access to information (about each other's interests, bottom lines, and intentions). Informational asymmetries represent significant advantage for one side and generate perceived vulnerability and defensive reactions on the other.

Interests The parties' desires and goals (as distinguished from the positions they take).

Integrative negotiation A negotiation in which the parties have shared interests or possess complementary resources but initially don't know it. If they exchange information and discover their shared interests, the process shifts to joint problem solving and can produce a win-win outcome. Preoccupation with positions rather than interests, or refusal to share information about interests, can prevent joint gains from being realized.

Intervenors Outside parties who become involved in a negotiation. Intervenors include mediators, arbitrators, and negotiators with partisan interests. *See* Co-mediation.

Joint gains Results of mutually beneficial trades in which the parties exchange things that they value differently.

Learning-shaping dilemma The difficulty posed by the fact that efforts to learn about the other side's BATNA and walk-away can be confounded by counterparts' efforts to shape one's perceptions, and vice versa.

Linkage: Reciprocal linkage The relationship between two simultaneous negotiations in which agreement in either requires agreement in both.

Loss aversion The tendency to be more sensitive to potential losses than to equivalent potential gains.

Mediator An objective third party with no personal stake in the outcome whose role is to help the parties reach agreement. A mediator has no authority to impose or enforce agreement.

Mental models People's established beliefs about cause-effect relationships and the lessons of history. Mental models represent the crucial connection between objective reality and subjective perceptions. Negotiators view the situations they face through the lens of their preexisting frames and form beliefs accordingly about what is at stake (issues and interests) and how their counterparts will behave.

Midpoint rule The tendency of a final agreement to occupy the middle of the zone of possible agreement.

Moves at the table Actions taken during a face-to-face negotiation that have a direct impact on the other party, such as offers, ultimatums, threats, and concessions.

Moves away from the table Actions taken during a negotiation that do not involve face-to-face interaction but can affect the outcome, such as involving other parties and building coalitions, gathering information that could affect a bargaining position, and invoking force.

Negotiator A participant in a negotiation who has a partisan interest in the outcome.

Negotiator's dilemma A fundamental tension between cooperating to create joint gains (and thus enlarge the pie) and competing to secure maximum gains for one's own side.

Outcome The resolution of a negotiation. Outcomes include agreements, breakdowns, and deferrals.

Overcommitment Irrational continued commitment to a failing course of action.

Partisan perceptions Perceptions on the part of the contending parties, transformed by the experience of conflict, that tend to make the conflict self-sustaining. The combatants accumulate psychological residues—emotional associations, expectations, and assumptions—that irreversibly alter their attitudes toward each other.

Pattern of concessions Usually, large early concessions followed by progressively smaller concessions, signaling increasing resistance.

Perceptual distortions Profoundly biased perceptions and interpretations of information about each other on the part of contending parties in a sustained conflict.

Position The stated objectives of a party to negotiation, which may or may not reflect the party's true goals (interests).

Principal-agent problem The inevitability of differences of interest between representatives (agents) and the decision makers they represent (principals). This conflict leads principals to try to create incentive systems to align interests and to monitor agents, both of which represent agency costs.

Ratification tactic Assertions that key decision makers who are not directly involved in the negotiations are demanding more than their representatives. This is a commonly used approach to claiming value. *See* Claiming value.

Reactive devaluation Active discounting of gestures by the other side that are intended to be conciliatory.

Restraining forces Resistance to escalation or to efforts to make peace.

Sequencing The order in which issues or parties are dealt with in a negotiation, which can affect the outcome and build momentum toward agreement.

Sequencing plan A plan to interact with negotiators in a specific order or deal with the issues on the agenda in a particular order, or both.

Sequential linkage The relationship between two negotiations in which (1) the outcome of a past negotiation affects a current negotiation, or (2) the outcome of a current negotiation affects the negotiators' scope of action in a future negotiation.

Strategy A plan that integrates goals and action sequences into a cohesive whole.

Structure The terrain on which the negotiator operates, whose key features are parties, issues, type of negotiation, information, action-forcing events, and linkages.

Trade-offs The relative value of gains and losses on different issues. In multi-issue negotiations, negotiators may have different trade-offs, which create the opportunity for mutually beneficial trades.

Unbundling The process of subdividing complex issues into their component parts in order to identify possible trades or reach agreement on individual issues.

Vicious cycle A type of feedback loop in which uncertainty and vulnerability lead the negotiator to behave defensively, evoking a similar response.

Virtuous cycle A type of feedback loop in which effective learning bolsters confidence and fosters judicious information-sharing, promoting reciprocal responses.

Walk-away The minimum value negotiators need to get to enter into an agreement. Walk-aways are established by translating the BATNA (the best alternative course of action in case no agreement is reached) into an equivalent minimum value in the negotiation.

Winning coalition An alliance that represents a critical mass of support for an agreement. In a multiparty situation, an agreement can be achieved only if a critical mass on both sides supports agreement.

About the Author

Michael Watkins is an associate professor of business administration at Harvard Business School, where he teaches negotiation and corporate diplomacy. He is an associate and frequent participant in the Program on Negotiation at Harvard Law School, and has also taught at Harvard's Kennedy School of Government. He is the coauthor of the recent *Breakthrough International Negotiation: How Great Negotiators Transformed the World's Toughest Post-Cold War Conflicts* and of *Right from the Start: Taking Charge in a New Leadership Role* and *Winning the Influence Game: What Every Business Leader Should Know About Government.*

Index

A

Accountants, as external advisers, 204, 206

Acquisition negotiations: in Bolton–Airline Pilots' Union case study, 72–101; closing the deal phase in, 210; due diligence in, 203–204, 207, 208; external advisors in, 204–205; in FHE-Argus case study, 189–213; final agreement phase in, 208–209, 211; initial agreement phase in, 207–208, 211; integration of team leadership and representation in, 210–213; internal consultations in, 210–211; leading, 189–213; leading teams for, 205, 207–210; matching people to phases in, 79–80, 205, 207–210; partner selection phase in, 205, 207, 211; stages of, 79–80, 205, 207–210. *See also* Bolton–Airline Pilots' Union case study; FHE-Argus case study; Merger negotiations

Acquisition prevention, 128

Action-forcing events: defined, 263; impact of, on BATNA, 30; shaping perceptions with, 93, 100, 151; shaping structure with, 54, 66–67, 108; summits as, 184; third-party imposition of, 175

Active listening, 91, 153, 234

Adams, Stuart. *See* Bolton–Airline Pilots' Union case study

Agenda setting, 13–18; process management and, 98; self-assessment questions for, 60; to shape perceptions of alternatives, 150–151; as structure-shaping tool, 54, 56–60, 107; timing of, 58–59. *See also* Interests; Issues

Agents: principal-agent issues of, 165, 192–193; roles and dilemmas of, 192–197, 212. *See also* Leading negotiations; Representing others

Agreements, final, in acquisition negotiation, 208–209, 211

Agreements, multiphase, 184–185

Agreements, potential: in acquisition negotiations, 207–208, 211; bargaining range and, 32–39; barriers connected with, 44, 49; diagnosing, 8, 32–39, 44, 49, 76, 104; in distributive negotiations, 32–34; in integrative negotiations, 34–37; opportunities connected with, 44, 49; power of good information and, 37; questions for diagnosing, 38–39; securing insecure, 19, 23–24, 52, 110; sequencing and, 68; shared uncertainties and, 38

Airline pilots labor negotiation. *See* Bolton–Airline Pilots' Union case study

Airline Pilots' Union (APU). *See* Bolton–Airline Pilots' Union case study

All-clear signals, 224